ABOUT THE AUTHORS

Dan Taylor was a twenty-year veteran of the financial services industry, an attorney, and president of his own North Carolina-based advisory firm, Wealth Capital Group. A native of West Virginia, Taylor graduated with honors from West Virginia University College of Law in 1983, after serving in the U.S. Air Force and completing Officer Candidate School. Following law school, he entered the financial services industry, where he was instrumental in designing and implementing the executive financial planning department at what is now the headquarters of Bank of America. Taylor became affiliated with the nationally known and highly acclaimed Strategic Coach program, where he served as a mentor and coach to more than three thousand business entrepreneurs in more than sixty different industries throughout the United States, Canada, Europe and Australia. After heroically and fiercely battling a stage four glioblastoma brain tumor, Taylor passed away in his home on December 24, 2009.

Christine Sheffield is president of The Parent Care Solution, LLC. She graduated Summa Cum Laude from Winthrop University with a degree in Psychology and Marketing. She teamed up with Dan Taylor to create The Parent Care Solution in 2004, a process that helps people have critical, but very difficult conversations around eldercare and create plans for aging parents. She now lives in Charleston, South Carolina with her chocolate lab named Zack.

Dr. Kevin Skipper has been a financial consultant for over 20 years. Utilizing the media, he seeks to help others understand the financial strategies by explaining the concepts in simple language. Dr. Skipper has hosted his financial radio show, The Discipline Financial Show, for over 17 years. As the President of Discipline Financial Management, LLC (www.disciplinefinancial.com), he and his advisors meet with clients to help with their retirement, investment, and financial planning. Securities offered through LPL Financial, Member of FINRA/SIPC.

THE PARENT CARE CONVERSATION

11.5 STRATEGIES FOR TRANSFORMING THE EMOTIONAL AND FINANCIAL FUTURE OF YOUR AGING PARENTS

Daniel Taylor
Christine Sheffield
Dr. Kevin Skipper, ChFC

authorHOUSE®

AuthorHouse™
1663 Liberty Drive
Bloomington, IN 47403
www.authorhouse.com
Phone: 1 (800) 839-8640

Published by AuthorHouse 08/29/2015

ISBN: 978-1-5049-2637-9 (sc)
ISBN: 978-1-5049-2636-2 (hc)
ISBN: 978-1-5049-2635-5 (e)

Library of Congress Control Number: 2015912403

Print information available on the last page.

CONTENTS

Part Three: Implementing Parent Care Decisions

INTRODUCTION

No Family Left Behind

A Living Nightmare

Let us tell you about Joshua, a fifty-eight-year-old corporate executive who lives in Bethesda, Maryland, with his fifty-seven-year-old wife Ann. They have a daughter who is a senior in a private school and a son who is attending the University of Maryland. Both Joshua and Ann also have parents who are in various stages of elder care.

Ann's folks, both of them in their seventies, live in a West Virginia retirement village they "sort of like". She visits them every other week, making the round-trip in just about four hours – in time for her to be home when her daughter gets out of school. She does this during the week so she can help Joshua out with his aging parents on the weekends.

Joshua's seventy-eight-year-old dad lived in the addition they built onto their home in Bethesda, where he moved after Joshua's mom, also in her seventies and suffering from Alzheimer's disease, went into a nursing home. The nursing home is about forty-five minutes away. Ann drives Joshua's dad there to visit at least twice during the week and once on the weekends. Sometimes Joshua will accompany her if he isn't away on company business.

As a senior vice president, Joshua is responsible for $50 million a year in revenue and forty-five salespeople who work in his division. He leaves for work at six thirty in the morning and often arrives home after seven in the evening. Part of each Saturday morning is spent catching up on e-mail and planning the next week's activities. At least once a month he and Ann are involved in a weekend company function, hosting salespeople, suppliers, and vendors or entertaining key accounts to maintain business relationships.

Joshua also spends an increasing amount of time each day talking to his father on the phone and consoling him. He fears that his father is slipping into depression but feels powerless to do anything about it; given his limited free time during the week, he simply cannot afford to spend more than just a few minutes a day checking in on his dad, and suffers guilt about it. Joshua and Ann's daughter loves her grandfather, but she is a busy senior with lots of activities and the demands of endless amounts of homework required to get the grades she needs to be accepted at the colleges she is considering. When she is home, her grandfather always wants to chat, ask her about her day, and reminisce. She has taken to staying at her friend's house after school just to have some privacy. She secretly wishes her grandfather would go to "the home" with her grandmother so that they could all have their lives back again, and is guilty about her feelings. Meanwhile, most days Ann doesn't know whether she's coming or going. Caught, between her parents and Joshua's, in an endless cycle of care giving, trying to be a mom, and keeping up the corporate spouse duties that Joshua's position requires, she has absolutely no time for relaxation, reflection, or respite.

Adding to the emotional stress is financial pressure, since both sets of parents are virtually broke, having exhausted much of their assets to pay for their current care regimen. Joshua and Ann help out with a monthly subsidy of $2,700 and supply their folks with extra clothing and gifts during the year as well. That's the tangible cost. The intangible costs to Joshua and Ann of driving time, reduced energy, increased stress, sleepless nights, and related health problems are almost impossible to calculate.

Joshua has been dipping into his 401(k) at work to help out with the situation and keeping this a secret from his wife. The raise he was hoping for didn't come through, and he doesn't want Ann to be worried about money. He has set up an equity line of credit on their house as a backup and has the monthly statements sent to his office so Ann will not be alarmed by seeing them. He also has not told her that this is a do-or-die year for his division. If the division doesn't make its numbers, he and everyone else will be looking for another job. That scares the hell out of him. He can't even imagine how he will find one at his age, just seven years away from retirement. He's told the kids to take out loans for college, and he will pay them off after they graduate, but deep inside he knows he's reaching.

Just at the time of their lives when they thought they would be able to slow down and relax a bit, Joshua and Ann find themselves working harder than ever, watching their savings dwindle, and feeling their life go emotionally, physically, and financially out of their control.

All Too Common

Nightmare scenarios like this are not rare these days. In fact, they are all too common. They have become the norm rather than the exception and are only growing more widespread as America's graying population explodes in size.

Reports *USA Today:* "Studies show that [adult children] providing the highest level of care [for aging parents] – 40 hours a week and more – are stressed, develop health problems and often don't have ways to cope. In fact, 46 percent of those providing the highest level of care rate their physical strain 4 or 5 on a 5-point scale; 63 percent rate emotional stress 4 or 5; and 34 percent rate their financial burden as 4 or 5.

How are you sleeping at night? *Fine.* How many times do you get up during the night? *Not many.* How many times were you up last night? *Oh, twelve.* It's just another sleepless night for the Alzheimer caregiver.

Providing care for someone with Alzheimer's disease takes a tremendous toll on the physical and emotional health of the primary caregiver, yet many caregivers often don't recognize the warning signs, or deny its effects on their health. Many caregivers tend to set their own needs aside while caring for the person with Alzheimer's disease and hope that if they don't think about it, the stress might just go away.

Nevertheless, long-term care for our parents remains a huge but neglected issue, especially on the home front. Most parents and their kids avoid talking about it. They put off having this important discussion or ignore it altogether, thinking they'll get by, but then suddenly something happens – a catastrophic even or prolonged illness – and everybody must scramble to figure things out under the worst possible conditions, at the worst possible time.

So how many questions need answering: What's the best thing to do? How to do it? Where to turn? How much will it cost? Where will the money come from? And more questions keep piling up, each of them underscored by the financial realities at stake. Worse even than the financial crisis this can lead to is the relationship crisis that often follows in its wake between parents and children, siblings, and other family members, causing wounds that may never heal.

In Loving memory of one of the most incredible, loving and intelligent men, Dan Taylor. May his "Legacy of Love" continue with this book in hopes that it will help others with this very difficult task in the area of elder care.

Purpose of the Update Parent Care Conversation

The update of this book is to honor the Legacy of Dan Taylor who passed away December 24, 2009. Dan's partner and companion for 16 years, Christine Sheffield and his business partner and cherished friend, Kevin Skipper were affected greatly by the life, example, teachings and wisdom of Dan Taylor. Dan wrote about and thought about Parent Care with passion like no other. Over the past 9 years, Christine and Kevin have been able to live in the real world of Parent Care because of their experiences with Dan and later with their own parents. The update of the book is designed to expand upon what Dan had created and offer some insights into areas of concern that Dan may not have covered in the original book. We hope that our additions will help you even more in the task and journey of parent care.

Dan Taylor's Story

No parent wants to be a burden on his or her children, but very often that is exactly the result of ignoring the parent care issue. Rather than protecting them, parents unwittingly make their children and grandchildren the recipients of tremendous financial and emotional burdens.

Dan Taylor learned this from his own experience with his dad.

On a spring Sunday, in April 2000, Dan received a strange phone call concerning his father. On the other end of the phone was a friend of his family who relayed to him that his father was in protective custody of the police in Danville, Virginia, a small town about a hundred miles north of his home in Winston-Salem, North Carolina. The police had stopped him for driving erratically at four thirty in the morning. By their account, he was disoriented and confused, and from all reports had been driving through the night.

When Dan finally arrived a day later, Dan's dad seemed a bit nonchalant about the entire matter – as if he had forgotten to shut the kitchen door or perhaps left a light on in the car. Little did Dan know that the reason for this casualness was that in his mind nothing had happened worth remembering – in fact, he didn't even recall the incident. The only thing he thought strange was that it was Tuesday now, and his son almost never came to see him on Tuesday.

On Thursday, Dan and his father drove together to Baptist Hospital in Winston-Salem for an appointment with a gerontologist. Dan was grateful that day for the physician's assessment. Although, if Dan had known what the next five years were going to bring, he may have been less amazed and more concerned.

During the nearly four-hour assessment, Dan's father was given a battery of mental, neuropsychological, physical, and emotional evaluations designed to pinpoint the cause of his rather bizarre behavior.

After what seemed an endless afternoon in the waiting room, the young doctor came out and asked if Dan could speak with him. He introduced himself with all the calmness that physicians, clergy, and prison wardens exhibit when the news they have is not the news you want to hear, nor could ever imagine.

It seems Dan's father was suffering from late-stage dementia (he had been progressively forgetful for almost five years) and was, in fact, in the early stages of Alzheimer's disease. The doctor explained what had happened with the driving incident. His dad had simply turned left instead of right, or perhaps forgot where he was going, and simply kept driving as if that is what he had intended to do in the first place.

The doctor continued for the next fifteen minutes or so, explaining all the signs and symptoms of Alzheimer's, the progression of the disease, and the realistic outcome the family could expect. In retrospect, Dan listened with the sort of numbness that a ballplayer might feel listening to his coach send him back to the huddle with a play when two minutes before he had been clotheslined by someone twice his size.

In his closing words, he said, "Your father is fine, but he cannot live alone or drive alone again." In Dan's numbed naivety he asked, "From what point?" The young doctor, with all the patience of one who deals with the mentally ill on a daily basis replied, "Why, from right now."

That afternoon, on the Thursday before Palm Sunday in the year 2000, the intergenerational transfer of power, wealth, and influence in the Taylor family of Winston-Salem, North Carolina, took place. Dan's father became his child, and Dan became his parent.

The next five days were a blur of action, reaction, shock, anger, denial, disbelief, depression, rage, elation, sadness, pain, and fatigue. Looking back, Dan was not sure how he made it through those five days without permanently damaging everything he held dear.

Dan phoned his companion of nine years, Christine, to tell her that he was bringing his dad home for a few days until he could sort things out, and that she should let her fourteen-year-old daughter, Ashley, know that he was coming, as well as their two dogs, two cats, and whoever else happened to be in our home at the time.

Dan's home in Charlotte was a 4,200 square-foot, three-story stucco house with a swimming pool, lots of stairs, original art, and nothing at all to make a seventy-four-year-old retired railroad foreman feel comfortable. At the time, Dan had no idea that the interior design deficiencies would be the least of his and Christine's concern.

When Dan and his father arrived, Dan helped his father downstairs to the combination library, home theater, doggy domicile, and entrance to the pool that is otherwise known as the basement of their house. Most of that Thursday was spent making small talk, fixing assorted meals, and, when his dad couldn't see Dan, he was sneaking into Christine's office to cry about the entire situation. Dan lost count of the visits he made to that office over the weekend.

That night Dan had to bathe, dress, shave, and generally get his father ready for bed. Any modesty, on either of their parts, was quickly dispensed with, since they both intuitively knew what he had to do. He had to let Dan do what he could no longer do or remember to do for himself. Dan slept with the proverbial one eye open as he listened for him to get up, miss the bathroom, and trip down the stairs to be impaled on a blown-glass flower in the hallway. When morning finally came, Dan began what was to become the ritual for the next few days: newspaper small talk, coffee, two eggs and bacon, and assisting with his bowel movement. It was the beginning of a day of news, talk shows, and repetitive stares.

Sometime about 1 p.m. on Good Friday, it occurred to Dan that he had to be in Florida the next Wednesday on business, and that he truly, honest to goodness, had no plan B for his father's care. It further occurred to Dan, that unless he found a solution to this dilemma he would have more than parent care issues to deal with when he returned.

With all the confidence that comes with ignorance, Dan began phoning nursing homes, geriatric centers, retirement homes (Dan thought they were all the same) to inquire whether there might be some room at the inn for his father. Since Dan had never been faced with this before, he assumed you just drove up, weekend bag in hand, with proof of insurability, a pure heart, and a small down payment, and that his

Dad would be greeted, treated and checked right in, much like a Four Seasons visit.

The next six hours were more like a visit to Dante's circle of special-care hell. Not only did Dan not know what questions to ask, he didn't know the language, the culture, or the raison d'être ("reason for being") of assisted living centers. He likened it to his first trip to France, when he wanted to visit the Eiffel Tower, and the French either refused or didn't know how to speak English, and the only words he knew were *please*, and *croissant*. A lawyer by training, financial advisor by occupation, and genetically wired to be an entrepreneur, Dan had always prided himself on his ability to outthink, out-innovate, and outperform any set of obstacles, challenges, or difficulties placed in his path. By the end of the afternoon, he had gotten some of the language, understood a little of what he needed to know and do, and made an appointment with a center in Charlotte and another in Winston-Salem. They said that if he worked diligently, he could have his dad safe and sound in his new facility by Monday.

While those visits are stories for another chapter, what was to follow after the facility decision made it seem like deciding if he wanted fries with his order.

After a restless Easter Sunday filled with a hurriedly assembled Easter basket, faux joviality, and the myopic conversation that occurs between father and son when there are no more superficial subjects to discuss. Monday and transport time arrived.

Whether Dan's father knew he was going to a new place to live or not, he didn't know. What Dan did know, and acutely remembered, is that *he* knew, and was completely aware that his life and his father's would never be the same.

As Dan walked his father out to the car, he felt his emotions in the back of his throat. Dan helped him in, fastened him in his seat belt, and mumbled some excuse about having to go back in to get something. As Dan opened the door and shut it quickly, Christine came into the foyer and asked, "What's wrong?" The pent-up emotions of the past five days came out in a torrent of tears and gut-wrenching sobs. He cried out that he could not do this and fell on his knees in a flood of tears, rage, and frustration over what had happened. He cried for a few minutes longer, took another few moments to get himself together, and walked back out to the car to begin the two-hour ride to the Village Care facility in King, North Carolina.

During the next two hours, Dan's father told him the same story six times, and Dan listened for the sixth time with the same level of attention as he had the first. It was Dan's sixth time hearing it, but each time it was his dad's first time telling it. Dan remembered thinking that this must be what living in a mental institution is like. They arrived and began the in-processing that is specific to every facility of this kind in the United States. Dan's father was not sure why he was there; all he knew was that he wanted to go home and to have Dan take him.

Dan lied that day to his father – the only lie he had ever told him. Dan said that he was there for a checkup and that he would go home a bit later. By the time later got there, he had not only forgotten the lie but where he was and where home might be. As Dan settled him into his room, he realized he had forgotten to bring a couple of things from his home that might make him more comfortable. Things like pictures, his favorite shirt, and his table radio. While the doctors were checking him out, Dan asked him if there was anything else special that he would like.

He said, "I want my two caps."

Surprised at the specificity of the response, Dan asked him which two caps out of his collection he wanted. He said that he wanted his Shriners cap. Dan's father was a lifelong Mason in a family of Masons, and I'm sure that cap created some security for him. Dan asked him what other cap he wanted him to bring. He said, "I want the Navy SEAL cap. Dan's dad, who had been in the Navy but never a SEAL, had somehow gotten a copy with the SEAL logo on it. Curious, Dan asked, "Why do you want the Navy SEAL cap?"

He replied, "Because the SEALs never leave anyone behind – and I know you won't leave me behind."

This is a book about not leaving anyone behind. More importantly, it's a book about how to have the conversations, make the plans, and extend the relationship with the most important people you have ever been in a relationship with: your parents. It is a book about how to think, communicate, and take action before the inevitable time when your parents are no longer able to be responsible for themselves. It is a book about how to begin a conversation that will deepen over time.

Dan's experience with his dad, and the mistakes he made, also showed him that he wasn't alone. This is a *big* problem. As Dan wrote these words, millions of others had already gone or were currently going through some version of their own "parent care crisis." And these instances will only increase: the parent care crisis will affect many millions more in the coming years, as we live longer and longer lives than previous generations. There needs to be a major dialog between adult children and their aging parents about how best to prepare for and how best to be able to spend, these extra years, in terms of quality of care and quality of life. And the dialog needs to occur *now*. There also needs to be conversations between those adults and their own children, now, while they're young and capable of making decisions and creating plans.

Christine Sheffield's Story:

The Parent Care Solution, A Legacy of Love

The series of events leading up to the death of the love of my life, Dan Taylor, will be etched in my memory for the rest of my life. When they say that life can change in an instant I wasn't truly aware of what that meant until I lost Dan. I'd never lost anyone close to me except for my grandparents and their passing was more of a relief than a tragedy. They were ready to die and we were ready to let them go. Life on this earth for them was much more painful than our selfish fear of losing them. Losing Dan however was absolutely contrary to the proverbial laws of nature. It also changed me personally and professionally in extraordinary ways...one of the many things I am grateful to Dan for.

Dan and I met on a blind date, set up by a close mutual friend who is to this day still trying to hit me up for a "pimping" fee. Dan used to tell people that the minute he saw me cross the room his knees went weak. How could you not adore someone who spoke of you in that manner? I, on the other hand, fell in love the minute I heard him speak. He was a brilliant man, full of wonderful stories, an unending array of fascinating observations and absolutely hysterical analogies which later were coined "Danisms". He created a huge cast of characters that he'd imitate which would leave your sides painful from laughter.

We spent the next 16 years living and working together, traveling all over the United States and internationally doing speeches, conducting workshops and working with clients. We created The Parent Care Solution together after the horrible experience we had caring for his father with Alzheimer's. We had three dogs and two cats and raised my daughter Ashley together which he described as "the best thing he ever accomplished in his life". Dan was an incredible guy, he ran marathons and he was an unwavering advocate for people without a voice. His two passions were pets and the elderly. You see, as people age others tend to treat them as if they aren't there. They talk AT them and ABOUT them but never TO them.

On November 12, 2008, Dan was in Atlanta conducting a workshop. He was in the buffet line at breakfast and his legs started to shake so he grabbed the wall and then fell to the floor. Everyone ran up to him to see if he was okay and after a few moments he came to and looked around at everyone with a questioning look. "I'm fine", he said, "I have a workshop to finish." Dan did finish the workshop but seized up several more times during the day.

When he returned home the next day he complained of a terrible headache. He'd been having considerable back pain so he assumed it was the consequence of that so he drove himself up to the nearby Urgent Care facility and got a migraine shot. This seemed to help until the next day when I awoke to find him with a cold cloth on his forehead in anguish...the head ache had returned and was even worse than the day before. We ran up to the Urgent Care together this time and he asked the Physician's Assistant for another shot but she pulled me aside and said, "You need to take him to his primary care doctor or to the Emergency Room. I believe this could possibly be something much more than a migraine." Dan being the typical stubborn man that he was refused to go, but I insisted and we headed to the Emergency Room much to his chagrin. They did a CAT scan and as we waited for the results, I remember him being tremendously irritated that it was taking so long. He hadn't wanted to go there in the first place and now it was ruining his free day. Finally the doctor returned with the test results and the next few moments changed my life forever. He said, "I have some good news and I have some bad news. The good news is it is not your back as you had thought, the bad news is you have a lemon size tumor in your right frontal lobe and we will have to remove it immediately or you will be dead in less than three months." I sat there in shock for a few seconds and when I finally made sense of what he had just said and the ramifications became clear, I started to cry uncontrollably and continued to do so while the doctor described to Dan the sequence of events that were about to unfold. They were planning to transport him directly to the main hospital where a room was waiting for him, a team of neurosurgeons would come by to discuss his options and another series of tests would need to be conducted. When I finally gained composure Dan said to me very calmly but firmly "you need to go home and pick up a few things for me and take care of the dogs. You can meet me up there when you finish. I'll be fine." I could see that a cloud now covered his laughing eyes. I remember thinking...no, you won't be fine...and I'll never be the same but I brushed that thought away and that's when I began to live my life in 'robot mode'...nothing seemed real anymore. I felt like someone else was living my life for me...and I sat and watched them without any feelings whatsoever.

I drove home to check on the dogs and my family. My elderly mother and father were visiting as well as my younger brother. It was my mother's birthday and we had a party planned for her with cake and ice cream and presents waiting to be opened. The moment I walked in the door, my father asked me what had taken us so long and why had Dan not come home with me. I lied to him and told him we didn't know anything yet and that Dan was still going through a series of tests but that he had asked me to check on the dogs. I lied because I didn't want to upset him. He'd just had a stroke the year before and I thought the stress would be too much for him. I asked my brother to follow me into the basement so we could speak privately making an excuse to my father that I needed to show him something. I remember seeing the shock on my brother's face when I told him what really was happening. I tried to calmly give him some instructions for the dogs and asked that he not tell mom and dad and that I would contact him later when I knew more but in between sentences my voice would catch and tears streamed down my face. He hugged me and said he'd do whatever I needed him to do and I ran upstairs to pack a bag for Dan and myself.

I drove back to the hospital in a complete state of shock trying desperately not to run off the road or get a speeding ticket. I believe the only thing that kept me safe was the fact that I was determined to get back to Dan in one piece so I could make sure he was properly taken care of. Upon arrival I ran frantically through the hospital searching for his room. When I finally found him he was sitting on a gurney in his new room waiting patiently for me to arrive. He put on his hospital gown climbed into bed and we waited for what seemed like an eternity for the neurosurgeons. When they finally arrived they explained in detail the surgical procedure and all the risks that were associated. It was terrifying. I sat there completely numb trying to keep my composure. Dan on the other hand was in 'Navy SEAL' mode and went on to ask a series of probing questions. When the doctors left we were inundated with one form after the other. We had to fill out lovely things like Do Not Resuscitate forms, next of kin, and organ donor forms...each one felt as if a knife was being inserted into my already broken heart.

Our strength was tested again when we called our daughter Ashley that evening to give her the news. Thank goodness her boyfriend was with her when she took our call. When I explained to her Dan's prognosis I could literally feel her pain over the phone line. She was silent for a moment until the severity and reality of what I'd just told her was able to process then she started to cry and we cried together for a few minutes. I told her to make reservations and no matter how much it cost to get home as soon as possible, we needed each other and nothing else was more important than Dan right now.

I slept in the hospital room that night...if you could call that sleep...all night I vigilantly listened for his breathing, to the constant hum of his monitor and the inevitable ear shattering beeping sound which alerted the nurses whenever his medications were low.

His surgery was scheduled for Tuesday because the young neurosurgeon wanted his A-team working with him for the procedure and that was the earliest date they were available. We spent the next few days in utter shock, trying desperately to pretend like life was still normal and that everything was going to be fine. We were inundated in the hospital with a steady stream of friends and family kindly offering their support and becoming a murky blur in my mind. I remember taking breaks to step out of the room and cry. I didn't want to let Dan see how much this had destroyed me. He had his happy face on for me as well, but periodically I'd catch a glimpse of the fear deep within his eyes and my heart would ache.

Tuesday morning arrived and Dan's room was abuzz with nurses and more forms and more well-wishers. They wheeled him down to prepare him for surgery and Ashley and I followed not wanting to leave his side. They made us wait in a room until he was ready and let us see him just before reeling him into the operating room. My heart sank, my lip quivered, my strength was gone. The reality sunk in that it was very possible that I'd never see him again. Dan was his usual witty, strong and positive self. He even told Ashley to look at the good side...that if anything happened, she'd get to have his brand new Range Rover Sport. Ashley, with all the strength I had no idea she was capable of, told him that would never happen because he was going to be needing it! Then came the worst part...the long wait.

I was absolutely blessed with an unbelievable daughter and a group of fabulous friends who waited with me, reassuring me, giving me hugs and allowing me to cry. What seemed like forever but in reality was only several hours later, the nurse asked me to follow her into a private room. I took Ashley and a couple of close friends with me...thank goodness because when the young neurosurgeon entered the room moments later the news was devastating. Again, more good news, more bad news. The surgery went very well and Dan was going to have a complete recovery....BUT the horrifying bad news was that the tumor was a stage four glioblastoma multiforme. The deadliest tumor you can get. I was in complete denial, not hearing most of what was said past the fact that he was going to recover it was only later that I realized how horrible his prognosis was. Glioblastoma multiforme is an aggressive brain tumor that has no cure. Very few patients live for more than a year. None of them live for much longer past a year. I didn't register any of this information into my consciousness all I could think about at the moment was that I would be able to hear his glorious voice again, feel his wonderful bear hugs and kiss his bald head!

Dan did recover and afterwards confirmed to me on countless occasions that he was the most courageous man that I've ever met. He valiantly lived through aggressive radiation treatments, unbearable nausea, weekly visits to the Oncologist where he was stuck with needles so many times that eventually his veins collapsed and they had to put in a port. A port has to be implanted by a surgeon and can be located either in your arm or your chest, and is connected by a soft, slim catheter tube that goes through your vein all the way to your heart. It was extremely painful and tremendously uncomfortable but he NEVER complained and he worked every day only taking breaks when he was exceedingly sick or exhausted. He even flew to Atlanta, Chicago and Toronto to work for The Strategic Coach a coaching program for entrepreneurs created by Dan Sullivan. In November of 2009 he designed a process called My Victory Solution with his friend Jon Loducca. He created it to help others deal with life's unexpected challenges with a sense of confidence and to bring simplicity, balance, and focus back into their lives. He worked, created and brought tremendous joy and inspiration to hundreds of his clients and friends all during his illness. His standing joke was that if death was coming after him he better bring an all-day pass and a box lunch because it was going to be a big job.

Throughout all of this, we both worked and in private cried but never with each other except for once when I broke down crying and desperately begged him not to leave me. Sometimes the pressure of everything would get the best of me and I'd have a selfish moment like that. Even worse was the fact that unfortunately, Dan and I never created the very plan that he and I had been helping people create for 7 years. We thought we were too young and had plenty of time; we procrastinated like we've heard so many people had done. The planners didn't plan. We only had $3,000 cash in the bank when Dan was diagnosed, we had no idea whether he would ever work again we were pretty sure he wouldn't live for much longer. Compounding this was the fact that Dan was the "face" of our company, The Parent Care Solution. Even though we had built it together and worked in it together for the past 7 years he was the face on the book and the spokesperson for the company. The thought of running out of money was incapacitating. We spent the next 13 months filled with fear, anxiety and emotional turmoil. We were incapable of thinking clearly about our future or anything else for that matter. We made many horrible financial decisions because of that fear and when Dan passed, on December 24, 2009, the pain was overwhelming and the loneliness was crippling and I was unprepared mentally or emotionally to handle the avalanche of messes that followed. I felt like I was being pecked at by vultures who wouldn't give me a moment to breathe and wouldn't give up their attack. Add to that stress there were physical issues from the aftermath of my 13 months of "high alert" caregiving.

Caregiving has all the features of a chronic stress experience: It creates physical and psychological strain over extended periods of time, is accompanied by high levels of unpredictability and uncontrollability, has the capacity to create secondary stress in work and family relationships, and frequently requires high levels of vigilance which affects physical and psychological health. Depression is one of the common negative effects of caregiving and I was launched into the depths of the most debilitating depression I'd ever experienced.

If this weren't bad enough, I was in the middle of my own parent care crisis which I will tell you more about throughout the book. My mother was in mid stage Alzheimer's Disease, my 85 year old father was caring for her and Dan and I were always the ones who helped them financially and strategically with their planning. My daughter Ashley had returned to the University of Texas to finish her studies but after Dan passed she returned home to Charlotte to live with me. I was sandwiched in and in no shape emotionally, physically or financially to handle it. It was a ticking time bomb that could detonate at any moment. Fortunately I was able to stay afloat until my head cleared and I could reason well enough to start tackling each challenge in a "triage" manner. I knew that I was alone now and had to pull myself together because there was no one else to rely on; a very lonely and frightening new feeling because Dan was always my rock.

I handled every situation as best I could and after about a year I saw light at the end of the tunnel. I never knew how strong I was until that year. I had no idea I was capable of handling so much adversity but I attribute most of this strength to the work we had done in creating The Parent Care Solution, the unending lessons I had learned from Dan who was an attorney and financial advisor as well as the work we had done with our Parent Care clients. I had the tools to handle the messes but unfortunately I didn't have the mental or emotional strength to do it well. When I look back, what I really needed was a trusted advisor who could help me. Someone I could turn to for advice as well as someone who could take the wheel and allow me to grieve.

In February after the one year anniversary of Dan's death, I was sorting through some paperwork and found a copy of a flyer Dan had created with his friend Jon Loducca of The Wisdom Link. It was for the process My Victory Solution. As I read it I saw the website www.MyVictorySolution.com and wondered if it was still active. I opened my laptop and typed in the address and there it was before my eyes, a picture of Dan and a link to a video. I clicked on the link and unbelievably sat in shock as I watched Dan being interviewed by Jon as he described the new process he had just finished. The date was November 2009...only one month before he passed on December 24, 2009. It tore my heart to shreds and as I listened crying softly, he said something that shook me to my core. Jon had asked him what he had learned from his experience with cancer and Dan said that he wanted to be remembered and that he wanted to matter; he said he wanted to know that at the end of his life he had meant well and it was good he was here and not only that he meant well but that he managed to do some things well. These words resonated through me with such force that I felt as if a very heavy weight had been lifted from my chest and my head cleared from the constant fog it was in for so long. I realized that I needed to get myself up and continue my work with our company not only for myself and the clients I could help, but for Dan and the legacy I needed to be sure he left behind. I also realized that now I was even more prepared for this task than I had been when I started it 7 years before. Now I had lived the result of not planning, of not having the conversations earlier in my life, of thinking I had plenty of time to prepare. What I realized is that these plans are not only for those who they're prepared for, more importantly they are for those that you leave behind. They are imperative for your loved ones because when they lose you, they will be in tremendous pain and incapable of making rational decisions even though they believe they are thinking rationally. What I really wanted to do in that last year with Dan, was to just be with him, and love him. How ironic that when Dan created the logo for our company, it was The Parent Care Solution, A Legacy of Love. Thank you, Dan, for leaving me your legacy.

Christine Sheffield's Parent Care Story:

I grew up on the wonderful shores of Lake Michigan where the summers are sunny and warm and the beaches are sandy and beautiful. Unfortunately in the winter the weather is brutal and long and the skies are cloudy and dreary. Soon after my daughter, Ashley was born, I moved to Charlotte, NC where the winters are much shorter and milder. Each year my parents would venture down to see their granddaughter and spend progressively more time with me during the winter months. Because of this, I spent a significant amount of one-on-one time with both my parents. Due to my experience with Dan's father and his progression and ultimate demise from Alzheimer's and our newly evolving business helping families who were dealing with similar issues, I was well attuned to the symptoms of this disease and I began to notice similar symptoms in my own mother. My father initially tried frantically to hide them either he was embarrassed or fearful or felt he was being helpful but eventually they became painfully obvious.

Dan and I had discussed many times what was becoming frightfully evident to both of us and realized we had better quickly continue with The Parent Care Conversations that we had initiated the year before. We had just finished the book tour and were heavily involved in our new business doing training, coaching and counseling clients so we were tremendously busy but we forced ourselves to take the time to sit with them and have the conversations that we had done for many other families many times before. Ironically I found that it was very different doing this for my own parents. I found myself doing exactly what I tried to prevent other children from doing with their parents. I had to consciously focus on adhering to our process very carefully to keep the conversations on track and to ensure we focused on my parents' wishes and not superimpose our own. This was a very emotional experience for me because this time these were MY parents and not someone else's. It was amazing to me, but also very validating, that by using the process we had created and using the C.A.R.E. acronym it made it a lot less difficult which is exactly what we had been telling families for the past several years.

I come from a family of twelve children, 10 boys and 2 girls, and we are scattered all over the United States so getting all of us together at one time was nearly impossible. I tried to discuss this with as many of my siblings as possible and quickly realized this was a very different process than what I was used to...they didn't want to listen to me. I realized the family dynamics were getting in the way because in their eyes I was still the "baby sister", or the "older sister", not the seasoned professional and this was a very difficult topic for them to discuss not having experienced anything like it before and being caught off guard. I was hit with a lot of resistance and procrastination. Everyone's lives were busy and this didn't seem to them to be an issue of very high importance yet. Unfortunately for them, they had not seen what I had seen with my father-in-law and many of our clients who procrastinated about having these conversations and making plans and were unwittingly caught in a tsunami-type experience when the "unfortunate event" occurred.

I had to take the reigns and move forward without them. Not something I preferred to do, but something I felt was necessary. One of the challenges we had discovered during our conversations was the issue with their home. They lived in an old three-story farmhouse with a very large double lot. Their bedrooms and only full bath was on the second floor and the laundry was in the basement. The stairs were old and very difficult for an elderly person to manage. The neighborhood was also an issue. It had deteriorated to the point where my mother didn't feel safe in her own home. The experience that she had always wanted was to be in a small brick ranch home with everything on one floor. I can still remember hearing my mother express this wish many times in the past and I knew that soon because of the progression of her disease, she would need to be moved quickly so as she progressed she would be in a familiar environment as she started to lose her ability to remember.

Because of my tremendous time constraints (we were just starting up a new business as well as running our existing practice plus I had a daughter, three dogs and two cats) and geographically challenging issues, (I lived in Charlotte, they lived in Michigan over 550 miles away) I hired my cousin, Brenda Regan who was a realtor, to help me proceed and relied heavily on her expertise to help me identify several homes that fit their specific wants and needs which she emailed to me and my father for our approval. I then flew up for a weekend and looked at as many homes as we could possibly fit within the few days I was there. We identified a home that almost perfectly fit their criteria and from my home in Charlotte, NC, I negotiated, purchased and financed their new home. Thirty days later I flew back to help move them from their home of 30 years to their new, safe, and conveniently located home. Several of my siblings were not pleased with the decision and it became painfully clear that I would not receive the "sister of the year" award that year. I had to let this pass since I felt confident that the decision was made by my parents with their needs in mind and not by me and my needs or my siblings'.

As the years past, we continued to monitor my mother's progress and my parents continued to visit annually during the winter months until Dan's fateful diagnosis and ultimate death. This was a game changer. I became a caregiver once again, but this time it was for my spouse, not an experience I had ever anticipated or was prepared to do. I remember thinking that this must be what it's like to hit bottom in the emotional cycle of my life. It was overwhelming emotionally, it was demanding both physically and mentally and it was the hardest thing I ever had to do in my life. Quitting was not an option. Resting was a luxury. And denial was the norm.

When the fog of grief had lifted and I was able to continue with my life and the care of my parents, I realized it was time to have another session with them about their future. My mother was at the point where she remembered us, but she wasn't capable of caring for herself. I knew that soon there would come a day when we would need to put her in a facility or provide 24 hour care. I flew to Michigan to visit care facilities with several of my siblings, a very stressful and emotional experience... again I felt the old familiar family dynamic issues looming over me.

My mother lived in her beloved small, brick ranch for the next 8 years with my 89 year old father, who cared for her every day. Because of the conversations I had had with my parents, I knew that that is what my dad wanted to do and where my mom wanted to be until she could no longer do so. As time progressed, my mother didn't know who my dad was or where she was but she knew she was safe and in a place she loved. I relieved some of my dad's stress by hiring a caregiver several times a week so he could rest but for the most part he was there, cooking, cleaning, and caring for my mother every day. In March we were forced to put her in a care facility. She died six months later. I know that now Dan is up there in heaven taking care of her making sure she is greeted and treated like a queen. My dad is still living in his small brick ranch grieving the woman he had lost many years ago. He was a loving, valiant and steadfast caregiver and I know that when his time comes there will be a very special place in heaven for him as well and I know that Dan will have the road paved and waiting for him when he's ready.

Meeting Dan Taylor

As a young man, I learned that you should find people who are in life where you want to be and listen to them. I have been a proponent of mentors and coaching for many years. As I considered Dan Sullivan's strategic coaching program, I was told that Dan Taylor was the best of the best and that I should make sure I got him as a coach. I first met Dan Taylor in the coaching class in the spring of 2006. Going into the class I had always seen myself as a pretty good reader and enthusiastic about life. When I met Dan, I realized I would have to read much more to learn what he knows. He read books constantly and being in his class was always informative. I was with him in the Strategic Coach program from 2006 to 2008.

Early in the program we connected on the element of Parent Care. My dad had been diagnosed with Alzheimer's and I got a copy of Dan's book and he began to help me navigate parent care decisions with my father. I then had him as a guest on my radio show in 2007. Dan and I had great chemistry on the radio. Dan once told me, "Kevin, I have done hundreds of radio interviews; being on with you was the best." I took that as a huge compliment like a grasshopper from his master. From there the seeds were sown for The Parent Care Show and The Parent Care Minutes that are still on air today. Dan and I would do the Parent Care Report each week and Dan would do the Parent Care Inspiration. The show was aired in Columbia, South Carolina and we were discussing expanding the show when he was diagnosed with cancer. Dan amazed me with his courage, tenacity, and drive up until the very end. Now Chris and I want to take the work Dan did in this book to make it even better as we pay tribute to Dan Taylor.

Kevin Skipper's Father Parent Care Story

My father was born in 1936 on a small farm between Conway and Aynor in South Carolina. After a farming dispute with his father, he joined the US Air Force. He was a military Veteran serving in the Air Force from 1956 to 1976. After retiring from the US Air Force, he worked for 20 years for the US Postal Service in Orlando, Florida.

As the years went by after retirement, I noticed, as many children notice, that dad was getting older. I could see the small signs as they progressed. The graying of the hair, the slight shake in the hands, the repetition when talking, the slower pace of walking, the shuffling of the feet and other signs that let me know that dad was indeed getting older.

One Sunday morning about 7:30 a.m. in June 2005, I got a call I will never forget. My mother called me from her garage so that dad could not hear the conversation, saying, "Your dad and I went to the doctor this week and the doctor says he has Dementia, which will likely move towards Alzheimer's disease." It seemed so unreal; like I was having a nightmare. My dad has Alzheimer's-- that only happens to other people, surely not my dad. I hung up the phone and cried the tears that many people have cried when they get similar news.

I then began the research phase to understand what this meant. How does it progress? How can I help? What are the medications? These are the same feelings that many of you or your children will feel on the day you receive the diagnosis.

I also realized that if I was going to have some special times with my dad, I needed to get to Florida more often to be with him while he still remembered who I was. In 2006, I made five or six trips to Florida to spend time with dad as I watched him worsen with each trip.

The most memorable trip I made was in February 2006 when I took dad to Kennedy Space Center at Cape Canaveral, Florida. We had a great and special day. Dad was shuffling his feet so I suggested that we get a wheel chair. He said, "I don't need a wheel chair." I said, "Oh it is not for you, it is for me…if we get a wheel chair we will get front row seats." He said, "Oh okay." It was that day that I changed my dad's diaper for the first time and he was aware of what I was doing and apologized for putting me through this. I said, "Dad…real men can change their father's diaper."

It was on that day as I headed back to Orlando that I saw one of the most memorable sunsets of my life. At least a half a dozen times on the way back my dad said, "This was a great day, son…this was a great day." He also gave me that day one of the biggest blessings of my life when he said, "Son, can I tell you something? I am very proud of you and I want you to know that I believe that you are a Man's Man!" That was the last day with my dad that he had any similarity of the dad I grew up with.

The next visits began to show the awful impact of Alzheimer's and how it changes the people you love into a person you don't know. Other trips included less mobility, the stage of irritability, the belligerent attitudes, and more loss of memory. There was the day dad got lost when he normally is very good with directions. There was the day they told him he could not drive anymore. And many other signs that Alzheimer's was taking his mind away.

In November of 2006 I paid dad a visit in Florida and he wanted to go home. He thought that I had gone to Florida to bring him to his home of childhood which is Conway, South Carolina. He was upset when I told him that I could not bring him to South Carolina. Mom then determined that she would bring him to South Carolina over Thanksgiving 2006 for what was likely his final trip home. I met them in Conway and took my dad to his parents' graveside, to his high school in Aynor and down the street where he had lived the first 19 years of his life. I asked him, "Do you remember?" and each time the answer came back, "I don't remember that…" We knew that the days of any recollection were over.

My final memory with my dad was on June 8, 2007. I had gone to Florida to visit and I managed to get him into the car and we went to see the space shuttle launch. I am not sure how much he knew about being there. On June 9, 2007 I asked him, "What is my name…what is my name?" And with that blank stare…there was no response. I knew that some very difficult parent care decisions were about to be upon our family.

The family began the research process of looking for home health care, home companion care, nursing home care, and hospice. I had the experience that many do with their parent several states away, making phone calls to find the right help and not knowing what I was really looking for. We thought that the next chapter of care was going to be very long. However, things turned for the worse sooner than expected.

On July 18, 2007, my father passed away and I was asked to officiate the funeral service. It one of the most meaningful things and the most emotional things I have ever had to do in my life.

I know that this story is or will be a similar story to what millions of you will be going through. Current numbers estimate that 15,000 baby boomers (those born between 1946 and 1964) each day are turning age 60 and there are over 87 million baby boomers. Currently, my wife's parents are still living and I know that we have many more parent care decisions to make.

Whether you are the parent or the child, you probably will have a number of parent care decisions ahead. We at Parent Care Consultants, LLC will work with parents and/or their children to assist them with consulting services to discuss the legal, financial, emotional, and logistical decisions that need to be made regarding parent care. I invite you to look at the various areas of the website to see how our unique processes and The Parent Care Solutions can be instrumental in helping you make the best decisions with parent care. Once you have reviewed our site, give us a call to set a meeting to develop your parent care plan.

Kevin Skipper's Mother's Parent Care Story

One of the things I learned from my training from Dan Taylor was to look for the signs that a parent needs attention and parent care. Sometimes these signs are hard to detect over the telephone. When I went home for Christmas to see mom in Conway, South Carolina, in December of 2009, I saw clear signs that it was time for mom not to live alone. Her personal hygiene had declined, the house was not being well kept, the dog had lost weight from not being fed, and mom was not eating properly. I saw signs of depression and more and more isolation and less social activity.

Over the next few weeks I began to build my "coalition of love." Meaning I talked with mom's sisters, neighbors, church friends and pastors and began to tell them, "I don't think mom needs to continue to live alone...what are your observations?" They all agreed with the conclusions that I had made that it was time.

So about the second week of January 2010 I went to mom and told her that I would give her three choices to choose from and they were not negotiable:

1. I could bring help into her house on a daily basis to take care of her.
2. She could move to an independent living facility in Myrtle Beach.
3. She could move to an independent living facility in Columbia.

There was some lack of cooperation, but she decided on the Columbia option. It was then that I realized that the child shall become the parent.

Independent Living

At the independent living level of care, I thought that mom would jump right in and be the life of the party. I thought that the interaction with others and the social stimulation would help her blossom like a rose. It did not quite happen. Mom did gain about 14 pounds and we did get her on anti-depression medicine and made some improvements.

However, mom would spend more time in her room alone and would not engage in many of the social activities that she had available to her. In September 2010, there were many signs of memory loss and decline. She would be confused about the day of the week; she would put her clothes on inside out and her shoes on the wrong feet. She would want to eat ice cream and chocolate kisses and not a lot of nutritious food. It was then that the doctor put her on Aricept which upset her stomach, so he put her on Namenda. As winter came that year there were more signs that mom's mental "winter" had arrived. When should I make the next move from independent living to assisted living?

I used technology to help me make the decision. I had security cameras installed in mom's apartment so I could see her in real time and what she was doing. Through the internet and my smart phone I could look in to see how mom was doing. It was then that I saw mom up at midnight getting ready for breakfast. I saw her walking in the night at times leaving the room and I would have to call the facility to guide her back to her room. It was then that I saw her restless at night and then sleeping in the morning from 10 a.m. to 12 noon. After a few weeks of observation, it was apparent it was time to move from independent to assisted level of care.

Assisted Living

The next chapter for mom was an assisted living facility in Columbia. As I checked her in, I learned the difference between base pricing and the "extras." The base price was $3,400 and when they helped give her medicine, bathe, and dress her then the price would increase to $4,200 per month.

At the assisted living level, mom showed much confusion and rapid decline. As I was moving her into her room, she saw a mirror on the back of her room door. She saw someone standing there; she did not know it was her. She would go to the door and open it as if to let them into her room. When she opened it, she got frustrated that no one was there. She repeated this several times. This episode would be followed by her thinking that she saw people out her window and making up things that were not reality. This coincided with her decline in eating and it was only a matter of a month or so that she had to be moved to the dementia unit of the facility. In one area she was the weakest of the stronger seniors, in the other area she was the strongest of some very weak seniors. It tore my heart out to go to this unit and see how "out of it" these seniors were. This care moved the bill to $4,500 per month and I knew we were stretching mom's budget to the limit.

The End Game

I made a few calls to friends I knew over in Conway, South Carolina. I reasoned that there had to be a place in the state that is cheaper with the same level and quality of care. Through making several calls, I found the only "not for profit" facility in the state, which was in Conway, South Carolina. They are an assisted living facility that was started by a group of Christians that wanted to provide quality care at the lowest possible price. I was able to lower mom's bill to $3,000 per month with a great quality of care.

At this chapter of parent care, mom showed even more confusion, bewilderment, and first stage of belligerence. She would get angry, bite, push, scratch, and say things that were very ugly. After a few months, it finally got so bad that I had to move her to a geriatric psychological care facility. It was there that mom ceased eating and we could not find the right combination of medications for here to live in an assisted living facility. Finally, the dementia, with her lack of eating and will to live, took over and mom went to be with the Lord on December 13, 2011.

On that last day, I had been with her day and night for about six days. Her living will had stopped hydration and nutrition. Several times, it seemed that she was gone and then she would recover. On that last night I had gone to the facility she had been in to load up her furniture onto a U-Haul. I came back to the room around 9 p.m. and totally exhausted, I went to the side of mom's bed and said, "Mom…I am so tired…I can't keep going.…What are we going to do?" I told her I was going to play some of her favorite music. So, I took my smart phone and went to YouTube and played "What a Day That Will Be", "Victory in Jesus", "Only Trust Him", "There is Peace like a River", and "Because He Lives". After more than an hour of gospel songs…mom's breathing got shallow and at 11:30 p.m. she went to be with the Lord. I could not have planned a more glorious exit for mom.

The *Real* Problem

I recently read an article that admonished baby boomers for not talking to their parents about long-term care. It suggested that perhaps the subject could be brought up at dinner. I can just imagine that conversation. "Would you please pass the butter? Oh, by the way, Mom, have you chosen a nursing home yet?" The absurdity of that suggestion, however, does not show why parents and children alike delay, or ignore, confronting the issue and its myriad aspects until it is often too late.

Most discussions about parent care start with decision making, i.e., what insurance policy you should buy, which nursing home you should pick, and so on. This puts the cart before the horse and leads to a plan formed in a vacuum. How are aging parents and their families to *know* which nursing home to pick – or even what to look for – without having first discussed the *why* of such a momentous decision, encompassing the many financial, emotional, and health-related issues connected with it?

Most of us, however, don't know how or where to begin this discussion because up until now there has been no model for it. The reason is that our financial and legal institutions, and the parent care industry at large, focus instead on the *support structure* (i.e., how to *write* a will) of parent care rather than on what to consider (and to anticipate) and the decision making involved in *creating* that support structure (i.e., deciding what you want the will to achieve).

This book at last puts the horse before the cart. It starts by recognizing the *real problem:* the awkwardness, the strain, the overall feeling of unease and discomfort that children and their folks have about confronting the parent care issue in the first place. It offers families a model for creating such a support structure from the ground up; one that will result in strategic rather than chaotic planning, keyed to their *specific situation* so that you can face the issue together and partake in the critical exchange necessary to ensure that the best plan is designed.

A Series of Conversations

This model consists of a series of vital conversations between children and parents on the most important long-term care topics, ranging from what to do with the parents' home and property to money and health concerns.

Focusing on the "big picture," each conversation is framed to get families to envision what they want to happen down the road as a result of the care decisions they make now, so that they make the right choices needed to get them there.

What you learn from each conversation will inform the decision-making process, enabling you and your parents to plan more effectively by doing so together *as a team*, and to feel *good* about your decisions by ensuring that the best plan is designed.

This series of conversations brings organization to what is inevitable confusing, complex, and chaotic and builds communication, clarity, collaboration, and confidence.

The conversations will help you:

- Talk to your parents about their long-term care, as they age, and make plans as a family without the awkwardness and discomfort the subject usually creates.
- Arrive at an accumulated agreement with resolution and consensus.
- Understand all aspects of the parent care issue, from what kind of care your parents want (and you want for them) and who

will provide it, to often neglected legacy concerns such as how to avoid letting the issue of parent care define how you will remember your loved ones and how they wish to be remembered.

· Be aware of the key timelines that will affect your decisions, the critical documents you need to prepare, the important checklists you need to make and follow, and all the other resources you need for you and your folks to design a customized parent care plan and to keep it current so that nothing is forgotten in making that plan a reality.

A *Complete* Solution

The collaborative nature and conversational architecture of these discussions allow you to accomplish them in a single sitting or in a series of family meetings. Whichever way you choose, the challenges they address – on everything from quality of care to what to do with property and other assets – can be unbundled and dealt with separately so that the best possible parent care plan can be created.

By showing you how to emphasize design over default in creating your plan, you will at last have found a *complete solution* to the parent care issue, a solution flexible enough to work for anyone, in any circumstance, at any time.

A solution that ensures no family confronting the parent care crisis is left behind.

PART ONE
OPENING THE DOOR

Aging parents do not know how to discuss their economic, medical, psychological, emotional, and lifestyle requirements with their adult children, and their children are not confident about broaching any of these subjects. This is causing an expanding number of family-stressful maladies including neglect, estrangements, bankruptcy, poverty, guilt, resentment, and depression.

- Dan Sullivan, The Strategic Coach, Inc.

"Children should be seen and not heard..."
Written by an Augustinian clergyman called [John] Mirk's Festial, circa 1450:

"Use it up, wear it out, make it do or do without."

1

Excuses, Excuses

Procrastination is the art of keeping up with yesterday.

- Don Marquis, humorist

Situation Normal, All Fouled Up

Tim Johnson's mom and dad were typical Depression-era parents. Tim's dad was a manager at a local pipe-fitting plant for nearly forty years. Having started out as a laborer, through his own drive and initiative, he eventually became plant manager of the family-owned concern. Tim's dad retired nearly seven years ago, with a comfortable pension and the promise of a comfortable, if not extravagant, retirement.

Tim's mom retired a year before Tim's dad, after a thirty-five-year career as a registered nurse at a local hospital. Together they are able to cover all their bills and even have some money left over for trips, gifts for the grandkids, and their church tithe. Nevertheless, like many who grew up in the great depression, they have never felt economically secure. As a result, money has always been a taboo subject within the family.

Over the past several years, Tim approached his parents obliquely on numerous occasions about whether they had their affairs in order and whether there was anything they needed to do to make sure that things continued to go as they wanted them to in the future. Tim's dad reassured him each time that all the documents needed were "locked down tight" in a safe place. When Tim pressed his father for copies of those documents, however, his dad would always reply, "They're in storage. I'll get 'em for you next week." But "next week" would never come.

Tim was unable to press his mom about this because she left the family finances and legal affairs up to her husband. In fact, the only checks she'd write since getting married were for the groceries and the electricity bill. Though concerned about whether his dad really did have everything in order, Tim didn't want to confront him and potentially create a scene. Instead, he chose to trust that his dad knew what he was doing. Then the unexpected happened.

Tim's mom and dad were involved in a car accident on their way to church. Tim's dad was severely injured and lapsed into a coma from which he has not yet emerged. The doctors are not sure if he will come out of it but consider it likely that if he does, he will be paralyzed from the waist down due to his injuries. Tim's mom suffered a head injury that has limited her speech, voice, and cognitive abilities. She remains in critical care in the intensive care unit of the same hospital where she worked for thirty-five years.

Upon hearing of the accident from a neighbor, Tim immediately called the hospital only to be told that unless he had a health care power of attorney on behalf of his father and mother, no one would be able to speak with him directly.

Tim frantically began searching his parent' home for the documents his dad had told him were all in order. He finally found a box marked "important papers." Inside were his parents' respective wills and a living will, a general power of attorney, and a health care power of attorney – everything his dad had assured him was "locked down tight." Except that they weren't as "locked down" as his dad thought: *none of the documents were signed!*

There was a four-year-old letter from the family lawyer instructing Tim's parents to sign the documents, but no follow-up correspondence. When Tim called the lawyer's office, he was told the man had retired and that his records, if there were any, had been placed in storage.

Thinking the local bank might be able to help, Tim went there, but the branch manager, while sympathetic to Tim's plight, was prohibited by bank policy from discussing a client's affairs with anyone without *signed* authorization.

Tim's next course of action was to seek out an elder care law attorney who specialized in such matters to see if he could break the impasse. After thumbing through the phone book, he finally located one who, for a retainer of $5,000, said he would begin proceedings with the court to have Tim appointed as guardian. The lawyer told Tim that it could take as long as ten days to get before a judge, even for an emergency hearing, and cautioned him that even though Tim was the Johnsons' son, when they did get a hearing it would not be an automatic decision on the part of the court to appoint him guardian. Tim had no choice but to adopt a wait-and-see attitude.

In the interim, the hospital was treating his parents under what is called a "prudent professional" standard of care, meaning the hospital's lawyers have advised the doctors not to do anything that "could come back to haunt the hospital later." Tim could continue to visit his parents, of course, but until the court order was issued declaring him guardian, he was not able to obtain any essential information from the attending nurses, aides, or staff physician. He could only look on helplessly as his father and mother received the "do no harm" standard of care.

While this story may seem extreme, even almost contrived, every word of it is true. Worse still, cases like it occur throughout the United States, Canada, and most of the industrialized world every day. The moral of the story is that parents who think they are shielding their children from worry and stress by not discussing the realities of their situation with them are only setting their children up for worry and stress when the you-know-what hit the fan. And the children they want to shield only compound the problem for themselves and their parents by going along, or making possibly false assumptions so as not to rock the boat.

Nine Common Excuses for Doing Nothing

In this chapter I'll share with you the nine most common excuses people just like Tim and his parents make for avoiding or not following through on the parent care issue. Often, people are not even aware of making these excuses. Being aware of them, however, is the first step toward getting beyond them and opening the door for a frank and useful conversation.

See if any of the excuses resonate by reminding you of your family situation.

Excuse 1: *"My parents have money, property, and papers scattered all over the place. Even they aren't sure where everything is. There's no way to deal with a situation like that."*

This is called the "all must be perfect" syndrome. Unless your parents are accountants or engineers, the odds of finding their important records stored away neatly in boxes for you, arranged chronologically and fully indexed according to subject matter, are pretty slim. Most parents are like Tim's – and worse. Their record-keeping methods resemble the chaos of the fall of Saigon. The creation, in recent years, of software tools for improving money-management strategies and keeping better financial records has only ensured one thing: your hunt now will be for digital *as well as* hard copies of important family documents. I'll give you an example.

Ken and Beth Spratt have kept their financial affairs separate throughout most of their married life. Ken has his own checking account, Beth has hers, but they now have a joint account they use for common household bills. Over the years, they have both kept pretty good records but in different ways. Ken has his on the computer (he changes his password each month), with hard copies kept in a mini-storage unit to which he has the only key. Beth takes care of her checkbook as well as the joint checking account records, but over time she grew weary of the filing and started putting these records in boxes with the aim of "getting to them" some rainy day.

Ken and Beth executed wills, powers of attorney, and living wills ten years ago; they keep them at a local bank in a safety deposit box to which they have a key that, they maintain, they can put their hands on in a moment's notice. And even if the key went missing, Ben has a friend at the bank he *just knows* would give their children access to the box if necessary.

The excuse that's really at work here is called "life." The manner in which many people go about organizing and updating their financial affairs and records often resembles that familiar vacation spot called Someday Isle. The net result for the child, who must parachute in and find everything when an emergency arises, or organize assets for distribution following the death of a parent, can sometimes be like a scavenger hunt. In order to find the last house payment made, it may become necessary to sift through months of statements covering a host of expenses, ranging from gas bills and car payments to American Legion dues and Colonial Penn's guaranteed issue term life premiums. And typically, this must all be accomplished at a moment of maximum personal stress. So, what is a child to do if he or she has parents like Ken and Beth?

The worst thing to do is to follow in their footsteps and do nothing. The emotional toll and financial consequences can be disastrous (for more on this, see chapters 5 and 8, "The Property Conversation" and "The Legacy Conversation"). Here are some general tips for getting your folks off the dime with regard to organizing their important papers and making sure they are easy to locate:

- If you are skilled at organizing and it comes easy to you, offer to put your folks' papers in order as a present, instead of giving your mom that third set of designer dish towels or your dad that cardigan sweater he won't wear. It's a present that will help not only them but you too.
- On the other hand, if, like your parents (and most humans), you get a Dubious Achievement Award for organizing, then hire a professional organizer to do it for your folks and make that your gift. In fact, maybe you can get a package deal for yourself. It will pay off in the end. See chapter 5 "The Property Conversation," for help finding one in your area.
- Put your own affairs in order, and tell your parents how good doing this made you feel about finally knowing everything's been taken care of and where it is – hint, hint.

- Explain to your folks that by not keeping their affairs up-to-date and easily accessible so that you can help them when the time comes, they are creating a potentially dangerous situation where no one will be able to help anybody.
- If all else fails, pull out all the stops. Tell them that without access to their records, particularly their checkbook, you might not even be able to bury them; you might have to put them in storage instead! They'll think you're kidding…at first.

Excuse 2: *"My parents say they've already worked things out with their attorney and don't need to do it again,"*

This excuse is a variation on the one you made about bathing or brushing your teeth when you were five years old: you did it once really well, so there's no need to do it again. Here's a real-world example of the consequences of this type of thinking.

For thirty years, Pat and Sandy Caseman have used the same attorney for everything, from having their wills drawn up when they were first married to handling the real estate closings on their various residences and vacation homes. The problem is that they haven't reviewed and updated their estate planning and property ownership documents since. What would occur if either Pat or Sandy were to die or become incapacitated? Some assets are owned by Pat, some by Sandy; some properties are owned jointly and some in partnership with other couples. Titles to their automobiles are held by various corporate entities and ownership of some of those entities has changed, a common occurrence that is not reflected in their estate documents. Why? Because they just tell their lawyer, "Make sure this goes in our file, OK?" It may go in, or it may not. Either way, it's not enough.

What's behind this scenario is an assumption many of us make: that once something has been done, it may never again have to be revisited and redone – or if it does, that there is plenty of time to do so. We also assume it's the attorney's job, not ours, to stay on top of our affairs and that he or she will "take care of things automatically." But the most dangerous assumption we make is that the attorney will handle everything we expect of him or her *correctly.*

My experience with estate attorneys particularly, is that they are long on explanation, adequate with execution, and almost nonexistent when it comes to follow-up that is not initiated by the client. Most will notify clients of major changes to tax law (typically via the firm's newsletter or an e-mail or fax communication), but often that's as far as it goes. It is usually left to the client to set the wheels in motion for taking action and scheduling an appointment.

Estate attorneys are notorious for not doing work automatically; they do not want to rock the boat by sending unexpected bills to clients, who often balk at receiving such bills no matter how much they want their attorneys to "take care of things automatically." As a result, many elder clients, though alerted to the need to update their affairs, may go years without seeing their attorney and wind up doing nothing. With some documents such as general powers of attorney, health care directives, living wills, and so on, if the documents are not continually reviewed and updated to reflect the parents' current state of affairs, the impact on the family may be catastrophic.

What can you do to get beyond this excuse? Ask to see a copy of the most recent estate documents your parents have executed. This will tell you how recent those documents really are. Even though you may not be a lawyer, you can check for the following:

1. Are all of the document signed, dated, and if necessary, notarized?
2. Are you named in the documents in any way (such as executor) that will require you to understand what your rights and responsibilities are?
3. Do you share powers and responsibilities with other siblings or parties?

Since it is ultimately you who will be accountable, it is you who should assume immediate responsibility for verifying the existence and accuracy of the legal and estate documents your parents purport to have completed. If your folks drag their feet in producing them, say you will resign all the responsibilities you've been given in those documents should something happen. That is usually enough to make the documents appear for your examination.

Excuse 3: *"My parents are very private about their financial situation. It was a taboo subject when I was growing up. I can't get them to open up now."*

Oakley and Margaret Harland have retired comfortably but far from luxuriously, having raised three children on a railroad worker's salary and a substitute teacher's stipend. They often went without or had to borrow money from friends to make ends meet. None of the children had any idea of the sacrifices their parents made to give them a good life, and that's the way their folks wanted it. Now as the couple is getting older and seeing what little savings they managed to put aside dwindling, they are *embarrassed* to share the rue state of their financial affairs with their children, whose help they will indeed need not very far down the road. They are afraid their kids will think badly of them.

Here's what's going on. All parents want their kids to think they have done well in life financially. No parents that I know want to lay the burden of their fiscal problems on their kids. If the news is bad, they want to shield this information from their kids. Even if the news is good, they typically don't talk about it. Part of this is due to the irony that even though we in America are consumed by the almighty buck, we are extremely reluctant with those closest to us. We don't want them to know how much or how little of the almighty buck we have. People will gab on and on about their vacations, their children, their ailments, job insecurities, and religious beliefs, to family and even strangers, but will not, it seems, except under penalty of death, reveal having $2,700 in a savings account somewhere.

In this book, I penetrate that wall by treating money (see chapter 4 "The Money Conversation") strictly as a tool. I don't make judgments about whether the tool your parents have is good, bad, big, or little. I focus instead on using what there is to build on. Thus the conversation shifts away from money as a taboo subject, indicative of power, prestige, and status (or lack thereof), to thinking of money as something like a screwdriver, a chisel, a saw, or some other building tool.

Excuse 4: *"My parents and I have never been close, have never been able to talk about anything, and rarely see each other. It's too late to start a relationship now."*

Taylor Johnson and his wife Elizabeth have had very successful careers as executives working in Fortune 500 companies. He retired as president of a large industrial glass-making concern and she as a successful director of human resources for an international consulting firm. They have lived and traveled first class most of their lives, occasionally spending time abroad with their children, who attended various boarding and prep schools. A nanny or other member of the Johnson household staff typically looked after the children when they were growing up. As a result, the children have a cordial but not exactly intimate relationship with their parents. They respect their folks, admire them, even love them, but don't really connect with them. And now that their folks are aging, the children are reluctant and insecure about engaging them in an intimate conversation about the challenges ahead. As much as the children would like to raise the care issue, they really don't know how – in a way, it seems more normal to hand off the responsibility to their parents' staff, just as the staff took care of their needs when they were growing up.

It has been my experience that children at either end of the economic spectrum, rich or poor, wish to have had a "better past" as far as their relationship with their parents is concerned. But the cold, hard fact is: The past is past; there is no going back. It's the present that counts.

As long as you and your parents are breathing, there is an opportunity to communicate and build, not a "better past," but a "better future" with each other – or at the very least to improve upon your relationship. Maybe the damage is done and communication is no longer possible. You won't know until you try. Chapter 7 ("The Professional Care conversation") will show you how to reduce your feelings of insecurity and reluctance about broaching the care issue with your parents if you feel estranged from them. It gives you a structure for opening the door to having a genuine discussion based not on past experience but on future expectations.

Excuse 5: *"I don't have any siblings and can't do this by myself."*

Ashley Townsend is a thirty-five-year-old only child, born when her mother was forty and her father forty-five. Her parents had successful careers, as a college professor and dentist, respectively, and decided they wanted a child to round out their life experience.

Ashley was thus showered with attention, material goods, and the kind of protection typical of children with affluent parents. As a result, she is well-educated, well-mannered, financially self-sufficient, and, for the most part incapable of grasping the idea that there is anyone else on this planet but her. In fact, one of her fundamental beliefs is that when she closes her eyes, it is the world that can't see her. The concept of being the care giver to her parents is as foreign to her now as the thought of driving a used car when she was in high school.

Being an only child is a mixed blessing. Growing up, you receive all the attention, money, and opportunity without having to share them with any pesky siblings. But during the last part of your parents' lives, you have all the obligations, responsibilities, and duties of caring for them, without any siblings to help pick up the slack.

Instead of making an excuse about why you can't do this by yourself, turn it into a question: "If *I* don't do this for my parents, who will?" This opens the door to considering options. You never know, there may even be a person you hadn't thought of, outside the family, who could lend you a helping hand once in a while or at least provide moral support.

Recognize this: at some point in your parents' situation, *decisions will have to be made.* If not, messes will have to be cleaned up due to the decision that weren't made. Get over the idea that the parent care situation would be easier to deal with and free of internal and external conflict "if only there was someone else." It's not that kind of situation and not that kind of planet.

Excuse 6: *"My family is very close-knit. Everyone will want to be involved or, at a minimum, informed about what's going on. You know what they say about 'too many cooks': things will just get out of control."*

Juan and Anita Alvarez are retired guidance counselors in their seventies, living in a small Southern California town. The Alvarezes have six children (three girls, three boys), all married with children, successful, and as close as siblings can be; they vacation together.

Juan and Anita are beginning to show their age, however, and are experiencing some of the symptoms of people who have worked hard all their lives to raise a family, often neglecting their own health in the process. For example, Juan is beginning to exhibit signs of dementia, and Anita has had two hip-replacement surgeries within the last several years. The children have hired a housekeeper and a yardman to help their folks out, but they worry that this may not be enough, that it's just not safe anymore for their parents to live alone, even with help. But the prospect of so many voices involved in making decisions about their care (all six siblings, their spouses, plus Juan and Anita) makes the entire family jumpy about potential conflict that could drive them apart.

The fact is this: the Alvarez family probably has a greater chance of jointly creating and managing a parent care solution without undue conflict and harm to their relationships than do many smaller families with fewer siblings. This is because the Alvarezes have everything working for them: (1) they are a close-knit family; (2) there is ongoing, positive interaction among and between siblings and spouses; and (3) as evidenced by their jointly hiring a housekeeper and yardman for their parents, they already show a harmonious, collaborative commitment to their parents' well-being.

The challenge for them is to come up with a decision-making structure in which everyone has a vote, but no one can create gridlock. For example, they could establish a family management trust, in which three of the siblings form the executive committee and all six are board members. That way, everyone gets to voice an opinion and vote, but in the end it is up to the three members of the executive committee to make the final decisions based on a minimum two to one majority (for more on this, see chapter 7, "The Professional Care Conversation").

Think positively. If yours is a family with lots of siblings, focus not on how many voices there are to create potential conflict and chaos but on how wonderful it is that there are *so many* of you who can and want to help!

Excuse 7: *"I have my own life and my own responsibilities to take care of, and just can't do this."*

Elizabeth Chadwick is a forty-two-year-old mother of three, ages twelve, nine, and seven. Her husband, Arthur, is national sales manager for a large pharmaceutical firm and travels four days out of five during the week. On at least three weekends a month, the Chadwicks entertain physicians who prescribe, and who are the major distributors of, the firm's products. Between helping with homework, soccer practice, dance lessons, T-ball, and entertaining clients, Elizabeth is sure that at least 120 percent of her time is accounted for.

Adding to this, her parents are exhibiting signs of failing health and dementia, and are rapidly approaching the point where they will no longer be able to manage for themselves on a day-to-day basis. Currently, a home health care agency is providing minor assistance, but her parents depend on Elizabeth psychologically and physically for emotional support and transportation. As a result, there are moments when Elizabeth feels like she is at the absolute end of her rope.

Well, her rope is only going to get a lot shorter and her life more intense as her parents make the complete transition from living independently with some assistance to being totally dependent in an assisted-living situation. Welcome, Elizabeth, to the brave new world where many of us will spend as long a time taking care of our parents as they did raising us.

The two care situations, however, are 180 degrees apart. As children, we move gradually from dependence to interdependence. But as parents, we move from independence to interdependence to complete dependence on our children.

Elizabeth has only begun to experience the dynamics of this shift. Up to now, she has just been a member of the audience in that play called "Her Parents Life." Rapidly, she is now moving toward becoming a full-blown member of the cast. She is about to come face-to-face with a dramatic change in the demand on her time and energy and on her perspective as she moves from an increasingly less passive role in her parents' care to an increasingly more active one.

Her default position could be to excuse herself as being way too busy, way too tired, or way too involved with other responsibilities to be able to handle this too. To that excuse, my response is: Who doesn't feel overloaded from time to time? This isn't about *you! It's about your parents!* How about stepping up to the plate and taking a leadership role in bringing a sense of confidence to the situation? How about being the person your parents invested *their* time, *their* energy, *their* money, and *their* love raising you to become? How about using the situation not as an opportunity to indulge in self-pity, but for growing and developing additional reserves of character, strength, and integrity?

Excuse 8: *"I can't deal with the hurt and pain of talking to my parents about the end of their lives."*

Seeing the parent care situation as the end of the line for your parents is making a judgment that life is simply over for us as we deeply age. *Life isn't over. It is just different.* A centenarian has a future, even if it's just measured in mealtimes. As that baseball-playing philosopher Yogi Berra tells us, "It ain't over 'til it's over."

We tend to think that because our aging folks can no longer hop to the convenience store, mow the lawn, or sing in the choir, life for them has simply become one long, passive wait at the station for that next train to forever. But how about focusing instead on what is possible, not what's impossible. OK, so your seventy-year-old dad no longer has the pipes to sing in the choir. He can still talk, can't he? He can still communicate and interact with you and other people. No, it may not be possible any longer for him to satisfy his appetite for faraway places by traveling to them. But he can still read about the places that interest him even if he can't physically go there. Similarly, while it may no longer be possible for your seventy-year-old mom to attend to her garden outside, she can still tend to her flowers indoors. As long as you consider the idea of a tomorrow, you can plan to make the most of the reality of it.

Robert Aldridge, for example, has watched his aging father's life go from including a broad range of activities and a large circle of friends to a narrower range of activities and a smaller circle of friends. Part of this challenge is due to his father's worsening emphysema, and the natural attrition that occurs among any aging group of acquaintances. Rather than accept these changes as signposts of his dad's end, however, Robert has seized the opportunity to help his father (and thus himself) through the transition. He both encourages and has even participated in getting his father to create a community of new friends and acquaintances within the assisted-living center where his father now lives.

Once an avid gardener and feeder of the neighborhood squirrels, his father has now taken to tending a miniature green-house (supplied by his son) in his room. Through this activity he has become quite popular as the so-called gardener in residence at the center, where he goes from room to room with his watering cart and pruning tools, helping others attend to their plants, finding opportunities in the process to make friends and expand his interests. Instead of feeding the squirrels, he now watches them from the center's solarium or through binoculars from his room. Is everything the same as before the elderly man? No. Is it better? Who knows? It is different and interesting? Most assuredly it is; different from and more interesting than just doing nothing but waiting for that next train to forever to arrive.

If you think a scenario like this is not possible for *your* parents and thereby excuse yourself, you will be right. The key to overcoming this and every other excuse for inaction on the parent care issue is not to focus on what we think is true but on what can be *made* to become true.

Excuse 9: *"I have never been good with money. I wouldn't want to be responsible for any advice or decision making in that area on my parents' behalf."*

Andrea and John Simpson have been married for twenty-five years and have two children in college. The Simpsons enjoy life to the fullest, using their money to travel, keep a nice home, and provide for their children. As a result, they live pretty much paycheck to paycheck, never going too deeply into debt but never saving too much either, except for contributions to their respective company retirement plans. Neither of them feels especially adept at it, or even comfortable, managing their own money, let alone someone else's.

Recently, Andrea's dad was diagnosed with late-stage dementia and early-stage Alzheimer's. He has asked her to take over the day-to-day paying of bills and management of his assets (almost $400,000) because he feels he is becoming less and less confident in his own ability to do those things. Andrea is panic-stricken at the prospect of this. She is fearful of screwing up and making a costly mistake that will bring the wrath of her younger brother and half-sister down on her in the form of a lawsuit after her dad is gone.

Here's the straight dope. There is no reason for Andrea to take a pass because she feels uneasy about her lack of money-management skills. In fact, the realization that she isn't good at handling money is an important first step to competently handling her dad's affairs as he wishes. She just has to take the next step; i.e., to find someone who has those skills and to hire that person to help her. There are almost limitless options out there in the form of do-it-yourself software and other resources and safeguards to aid money-management-challenged people today. Many members of the financial planning and insurance industries and the legal and accounting professions are fast developing capabilities in this area just so they can provide such services to people like Andrea (see chapter 4, "The Money Conversation").

No More Excuses

Excuses are justifications for not taking control of a situation, for opting to do nothing instead of something so as to avoid assuming responsibility and accountability. In this case, however, since the subject is parent care, no matter how many excuses you make, responsibility and accountability will one day be thrust upon you anyway. You might as well act now.

To keep on making excuses is simply to prepare the way for suddenly finding yourself in the middle of a situation you *must* handle *now*, and for which, through your avoidance, you are totally unprepared. Also, by not planning early, your options become very limited and the expenses increase exponentially.

So, as the Boy Scouts' motto says: "Be prepared." It's in your own best interest, not to mention the right thing to do, to stop playing head game with yourself and making excuses for inaction – and to start taking control of your parents' protections as they age, just as they did for you when you were growing up.

2

THE CAR E "HEAR AND NOW" LISTENING SYSTEM

Learning is a result of listening, which in turn leads to even better listening and attentiveness to the other person.

- Alice Miller, psychoanalyst

Can You Hear Me Now?

William Salvone is a successful seventy-year-old businessman, now retired from the machine-manufacturing industry. A self-made man, he is someone who, in his own words, "has no time for idiots or people who know them." He attributes his success to an ability to see a solution, get what's needed to put that solution in place, and then move on to the next project. He is long on intelligence, short on patience, and all his life has practiced a communication style that falls somewhere between that of a NATO commander and a junior high school principal – a style his son, Robert, grew up experiencing on a daily basis. As a result, Robert early on developed a habit of pretending to listen to his dad's one-way conversations while in reality his attention was a million miles away. All he had to do to convince his dad that he was hanging on the man's every word was slap a smile on his face and now and then interject a "really", a "tell me more," an "I didn't know that," or a "you're kidding." It is a practice that Robert has carried with him even into adulthood.

The problem now is that even as father and son experience the fact of the father's aging, the same old patterns of communication continue.

And the father has now caught on to the fact that often his son is only half-listening to him. The same goes for other members of the family, who only half-listen to him as well. At a time of life when communication with others is so critical, he anguishes over being tuned out so much of the time (even if he did bring it on himself), seeing this as an acknowledgement by the people around him that he has nothing important to say. And so he clams up. William and his son now find themselves, as the Dave Mason song goes, "sitting here together, miles apart as time goes slipping by."

Either as parents or as children, all of us can identify with this story in some way. That's because as kids we grow up being told what to do by our folks. Certainly by our teenage years, we respond to this much of the time by turning a deaf (or semi-deaf) ear to what they say to us. Then we repeat this process with our own kids, only now we're the ones doing the telling, and they're the ones doing the half-listening.

Hearing someone without actually listening to them isn't practiced only by parents and their kids, however. Siblings and friends, husbands and wives, employers and employees engage in it too. We're *all* guilty of it at some time or another. In fact, today, hearing but not listening is almost the norm, exacerbated by the cacophony of visual and auditory "noise" that surrounds us, competing for our attention and consuming every centimeter of available space and ever decibel of available bandwidth.

Between aging parents and their grown children especially, there is a crying need for a system capable of breaking down this communication roadblock – a way for them to be able to open the door and converse with one another about important issues such as parent care in a way that actively promotes responsive listening.

Now there is.

"Hear and Now" Listening with CARE

Think about the listening experience this way: Remember the last time you saw a really good movie – you know, the kind that grabs you from the opening credits, pulling you into its world and its characters, making you part of the experience? Imagining how different that experience would be if a different movie with a different story and different characters were suddenly superimposed over it. That is what happens when you half-listen.

When people converse with you, they are inviting you in to see and experience the movie going on inside their heads. By not being fully present and engaged – an active listener – you miss important chunks and significant details of that movie because you are superimposing your own movie over theirs. Do this often enough, particularly with older people, and they will simply shut down, like William did in the previous story. You need to create an environment where this won't happen, an environment that encourages your parents to open up to you about their concerns and fears about the future (where previously they might not otherwise have been inclined to do so), and for you to really *hear* them, without missing a beat.

The system we have developed to achieve this grew out of the experience we had with our own dad's care, which was explained in the introduction to this book. It is a system structured around the acronym CARE, which stands for the following: challenges, alternatives, resources, and experience. (CARE makes them easy to remember.) This system will help you elicit telling responses from your parents on key issues relating to their future care – even those about which they may not have been forthcoming up to now – so that you get what you need to be able to work together to achieve a mutually satisfying parent care solution.

Let's look at the individual components of the CARE "hear and now" listening system:

- **Challenges.** It is typical of older people to point out dozens of reasons why something won't or can't work rather that how to make it work. That's why the CARE system begins here. We recognized the fact that as we grow older we tend to see change of almost any sort – but especially changes in ourselves physically, mentally, or in our lifestyle – as an insurmountable obstacle, a series of doors slamming shut rather than opening. We don't even want to think about these changes, much less talk about them. The objective here is to refocus your parents' thinking about their future in terms of what they *want* to happen when that future comes and not just what they fear will go awry. The idea is, if you can get them to articulate their feelings and fears about the future and to anticipate the inevitable changes as a series of challenges rather than insurmountable obstacles to be dreaded, then maybe they will begin to find ways of meeting those challenges and achieving what they want for their future instead of feeling that defeat is inevitable.

- **Alternatives.** There *are* options available to meet the challenges your parents face. By getting your parents to focus on what they *can* do rather than on all the reasons why they can't do something, you will help them to feed off the positive energy they gain from this, and their minds will naturally kick into idea-sorting/problem-solving mode. The more alternatives to each challenge they consider, the more confidence they will develop that they can successfully take on these challenges, giving them the self-assurance to move forward.

- **Resources.** In the movie *Castaway* starring Tom Hanks, he plays a FedEx employee who crash-lands in the ocean and suddenly finds himself stranded on an island with almost nothing to rely on for survival but his wits. He learns to fish and make shelter, to withstand severe rainstorms and extreme sun, and even fashions a companion to talk to from a soccer ball that made it to shore with him. The resources component of CARE does much the same thing; it enables your parents to see that, like Tom Hanks in the movie, they are in possession of and have access to more resources than they ever imagined (of their own and from elsewhere) for addressing the challenges they face.

- **Experience.** Based on the challenges they have anticipated, the alternatives they know they have, and the resources they now know are available to them, the last step in the CARE process is for your parents to lay out a series of realistic outcomes they can reasonably expect if they start taking action now. In other words, here is where you get your parents to visualize the *experience* they want to have as the result of meeting each challenge head-on. Armed with this knowledge, you can plan together as a family to bring that experience to fruition.

The Parent Care Conversations

The CARE "hear and now" listening system is all about asking the *right* questions now in order to avoid confusion and conflict later on from chaotic decision making. In part 2, you will learn how to apply this system in framing your questions for the 11.5 key conversations you must have with your parents in order to work toward an effective solution. These 11.5 parent care conversations are structured around the 11.5 fundamental areas parents need to be concerned about in contemplating their future care – and that you need information on in order to empower your parents to play a meaningful role in the design of their own long-term care solution, and not just be bystanders.

The Odds of Miscommunicating

The potential for miscommunication between people is staggering, especially when we consider that of the estimated 800,000 words in the English language, we use only about eight hundred of them consistently. And there are, on average, between fifteen and seventeen meanings in the dictionary, and in our vernacular, for each of those words. This means that even conservatively speaking, we have a one in seventeen chance of being misunderstood. Further complicating matters, approximately 55 percent of what we communicate is transmitted nonverbally, via gestures, facial expressions, a lifted eyebrow, a look in the eyes; 38 percent is communicated by the tone, rhythm, and pacing of how we speak; and only 7 percent is communicated through words. This is why being fully present and engaged ("hear and now" listening) is central to getting your parents to open up to you (and thereby to themselves) on the issue of future care – and for you to *really* take in what they are telling you – so that strategic planning becomes possible.

The 11.5 conversations and their objectives

1. **The Big Picture Conversation.** It all starts with your parents having a vision of their future and you knowing what that vision

is. If your parents have shared very little or nothing with you about how they see their future and the issue of their future care, then there isn't much to discuss, is there? This conversation is all about getting your parents to reveal how they see the rest of their lives unfolding so that their fears and concerns, hopes and dreams are broadly exposed for all of you to address.

2. **The Money Conversation.** This is a biggie. The objective here is to obtain an overall grasp of your parents' current financial situation, their future financial needs, and the financial structure they will need to create in order to maximize the growth and income opportunities of their financial resources.

3. **The Property Conversation.** This discussion focuses on looking at (and perhaps inventorying) what your parents have collected over the years in terms of property and possessions, and determining how they would like that property to be managed and/or distributed, both in the years they have left and after they're gone.

4. **The House Conversation.** This can be an extremely emotional issue. The objective is to get a fix on how your parents feel about their ability to keep living where they are now. For example, is their home already, or do they see it becoming, a physical or financial burden? If so, what is their preferred next step? Staying but with help or selling and moving? And if the latter, to where: a newer, smaller home, a retirement community, an assisted-living facility or perhaps a special care facility?

5. **The Professional Care Conversation.** This discussion follows directly on the house conversation if the decision to move to an assisted-living facility, nursing home, or other institutional setting is immediate or in the cards. It focuses on the type of care our parents will need (thus determining the setting) and the type of attention (visitation and other considerations) your parents would like (and can reasonably expect) from you depending upon where they relocate, so that your relationship does not become strained and distant but even closer.

6. **The Attention Conversation.** This Conversation focuses on the best way to communicate with your senior parent and the use of technology to give them attention. Those in their fifties who are trying to care for their parents in their seventies and eighties are living busy lives. They often don't live next door. They can leverage their contacts with their parent by the use of technology and by teaching their parents about technology.

7. **The Identity Theft and Personal Safety Conversation.** Protecting Your Parents against Money scams. Our parents cannot imagine that someone would do them harm. Much less, take their personal information and use it to do them harm. They come from the generation where your word is your bond and when you say it you mean it. With these beliefs our parent can easily become victims of identity theft and other scams.

8. **The Legacy Conversation.** This conversation gets your parents thinking about their lives, their achievements, the journey they have made through life so far, and considering how they want to be remembered by family, friends, and the organizations to which they either belonged or donated. The legacy conversation is where they start laying the groundwork for creating and preserving that legacy through declaration of assets, making gifts and other bequests, and numerous other methods.

Other considerations in Your Parent Care Conversations
(Self-Conversations and Insights)

9. **Parent Care Matters with Unwilling Parents.** These conversations are used when parents don't want to talk. What are your parents' legal rights and what are the children's legal rights? Many children are ready to have the parent care conversations, however their parents are unwilling to talk and unwilling to cooperate. This can be because of denial or the refusal to let the adult child move into the role of being in control. A child must tread lightly when dealing with parents who will not cooperate.

10. **Parent Care Matters When The 'Equal' Is No Longer 'Fair'.** I don't know why it is but the task of parent care often falls on the shoulders of one of the adult children. Many of the other children are comfortable to sit back and be spectators. When this happens one child can quit work or cut back hours and make other sacrifices for the sake of parent care. When these unequal actions begin to occur....how can the family make adjustments to make things 'fair'?

11. **The Final Preparation Conversation.** What to do when dad is gone. The final task of parent care is the funeral and memorial services. Do you know your parents' desires? Advanced planning for this occasion can help relieve families from the added stress of planning after the loss of a loved one.

Some Parent Care Axioms to Live By:

You have heard the expression...been there, done that, got a T-Shirt. Sometimes I'd love to hand out Parent Care T-Shirts to those who are going the distance.

You are worthy of a Parent Care Warrior T-Shirt if you can say the following:

- I've changed my parent's diaper.
- I've been cursed at by a senior Alzheimer's or dementia parent for things I didn't do.
- I've driven over 100 miles for parent care over 30 days this year.
- I've moved my mom or dad over 4 times this year for different levels of parent care.
- I had to balance my parents' checkbook and pay the bills for them.
- I've held mom or dad's hand as they breathed their last breath.
- I've planned a parent's funeral
- I've taken care of my parents while my siblings sat on their rears.
- I've stayed up all night at my parent's side counting their last breaths.

You might be a Parent Care Punk if:

- You let your siblings do everything and you do nothing or little in the task of parent care.
- You do none of the parent care work, but expect an equal inheritance. How fair is that?
- You drop by for an hour once a month when they need much more help than that.
- All you do is complain about the ones who are actively involved in the parent care.
- You verbally or physically abuse a senior.
- You scam a senior.
- You don't respect the seniors that your parents are, or are not.

The Parent Care 11 Commandments

1. I will seek to honor my father and mother through the test of parent care.
2. I will seek knowledge so that I better understand the choices, decisions, and strategies of parent care.
3. I know the task of parent care may require tough love, and I am prepared to use it if needed.
4. I know that the task of parent care, if not kept in perspective, can destroy health, wealth, and relationships. I vow not to let that happen.
5. I know some parents are not financially secure and have not saved enough. I will help as much as I can, but cannot lose my financial security because of their lack of planning.
6. I will strive to encourage as many people as possible in parent care, but at the end of the day it may fall to me.
7. I know that parents with dementia or Alzheimer's can say or do ugly things to their children. I will do the task based on duty with a guarded heart, knowing it is the disease, and not the parent I once knew.
8. I know that my spouse may be going through parent care…I will do all I can to support them in the difficult task.
9. I know that at times "the parent becomes the child"….when the time is right I will lead with such tenacity that my parents will be proud.

10. I know the bible says…. "honor your father and mother and so shall your days on the earth be long…" I will seek to honor them all the days of my life…
11. I know the 11th commandment, take care of your parents the way you want your children to take care of you.

While the subject of parent care may be new to you and the statements above not clearly understood, our hope is that by the time you complete the book, you will have greater insight, wisdom, and knowledge into the task of parent care.

By confronting the daunting, seemingly unmanageable issue of long-term care planning in this unique conversational style, you and your parents will be able to:

·   Cut the issue down to size, transforming fear into focused thinking and strategic planning.
·   Perceive what you initially thought were weaknesses in the situation as strengths instead.
·   Turn potential obstacles into opportunities for innovation.
·   Fashion breakthroughs out of setbacks that may occur along the way.
·   Deal with every challenge, consider every alternative, and maximize every resource at hand to design the long-term care experience your parents *want* to have.

In short, in place of silence and dread, chaos and confusion over the parent care issue, you and your folks will be able to substitute absolute unremitting, and total confidence in your ability to handle that issue successfully.

Initiating the Parent Care Conversations

Talking to the elderly about aging is a lot like talking to the poor about poverty; no matter how delicately we approach the subject, we run the risk of scaring, offending, outright alienating them merely by bringing it up. Therefore, initiating the parent care conversations is not simply a matter of choosing a time and place (though each are important), then launching in, but of careful preparation. Here are some suggestions for how to prepare:

- **Work on your mind-set first.** At all costs, you want to avoid coming across in an intrusive or invasive manner. This manner only communicates the following message, one that is a real turn-off: "Listen, Mom and Dad, I have thought everything through about your future care on your behalf, have come up with all the answers, and only need you to affirm my conclusions." This approach is guaranteed to alienate anybody; take it up with your parents and they are sure to put you off for more urgent subjects of interest like weeding the backyard or wetlands planning. Put yourself in their shoes. The whole idea is to partner with your parents, to help them strategize about their own future care. It is not to be a vendor or pitchman for a particular product or approach. That's what the legal and financial services industries are all about. The structure of each parent care conversation is designed to help you become that partner, but before engaging your parents in discussion, you must first open yourself to seeing all the facets of that discussion from their perspective, not yours, so that the plans you collectively make will be a reflection of their thoughts, their ideas, their feelings, and their goals, not some boilerplate solution that says, "here's what you need to do to be OK."

- **Easy does it.** The parent care conversations are designed to open you and your parents up to achieving deeper and deeper levels of intimacy in order to arrive at a clear, mutual understanding of your respective feelings about the issue of future care. To penetrate these levels, it is best to ease in at first by talking to your parents in abstract terms about elder care – as if the time to get down to brass tacks and actually start making plans to confront the issue were yet years away, not here knocking at the door. This approach is less intimidating for all concerned and really helps open up communication. The Big Picture Conversation facilitates this because it not only takes the abstract approach, but it does so in the broadest terms, which is why it is the first conversation in line.

- **Pick a time and place that best suits the conversation.** The kitchen or dining room table, at night or on a weekend, is a great place to have the money conversation. It's an informal setting used for family gatherings, and there's plenty of room to spread out financial records and other papers so everyone can see and discuss them. Or, you might select the patio or porch one lazy afternoon as the perfect place (and time) to have the legacy conversation. Choose whatever works to create the most relaxed, reflective atmosphere possible.

- What if my parents won't talk? What if they won't cooperate? We discuss this in more detail on page 203.

The Heart of the Matter

The Wilson family of Fayetteville, North Carolina, is a good example of how the CARE system, when applied to these 11.5 conversations, really gets to the heart of the matter — the deep-down concerns parents have as they age and the impact their aging has on their children as the family moves through this life transition together.

Leonard Wilson has been a tobacco farmer all his life. He comes from a family of tobacco farmers going all the way back to before North Carolina became a state. Now seventy-four, Leonard's memory isn't what it used to be. It takes him a little longer to get going in the morning on the walks he takes with his wife, Betty, also in her seventies. He is at a place where there are many unspoken things he has long wanted to say to his family — about the future of the farm and his relationships with his children — that he fears it may be too late to say, even if he knew how. Tension has developed between him and his oldest son, Ben, over the old man having sold off parcels of acreage to developers over the years at less than maximum value rather than holding out for a higher price, which Ben had always urged. But as his father told him: "holding out for a while as you get older feels a lot scarier than holding out for a while at forty-five. A bird in the hand is important."

The root of the tension between Ben and his father lies not so much in their ongoing differences of opinion on financial matters, however, but in the fact that the two of them are so much alike. Both are strong-willed and full of opinions (all of them right), possessed of all the answers (mostly to questions never asked), and free with their advice (to which neither of them listens). In short, they can't communicate.

Even though his father was skeptical when Ben approached him about the CARE system and the 11.5 parent care conversations, the old man agreed to listen, and then to participate. The result, he and his son would later say, was a transforming experience for each of them and for the entire family as well.

During the conversations with Ben and his other children (Allison and Charles), Leonard talked about the small fortune he had amassed over the years by shopping frugally and saving well. Not only had every mortgage he'd ever taken out on the farm been paid off years ago, but unbeknownst to his children, he had their college funds completely established by the time they graduated high school. Thus, the reasons why his father had sold off acreage at lower prices for ready cash at last became clear to Ben.

The children were amused to find out that their father had pretended to be broke and made them take out college loans — only to pay off those loans himself when they graduated — because he wanted to make sure they were as committed to finishing their education as he was to providing for it.

Further, Leonard and his wife revealed how long they saw themselves staying at the farm until it became unsafe for them to do so. That day, they admitted, was coming soon, and when it came, they would like to go to the Shriner's Village, an assisted-living facility nearby. This way they would still be close by for family visits and holidays while at the same time being in a secure facility geared to the needs and challenges of older folks like them.

On the subject of family visits, they revealed how often they would like their kids to come and visit — at least once a month — and that they would use e-mail to communicate with their children and grandchildren on a regular basis.

They talked about what to do with all the "stuff" they had accumulated over the years, not just the things they wanted distributed after they were gone, like clothes and shoes, and years of accumulated *National Geographic* magazines (Leonard's so-called rainy day books), but things they wanted to give away while they were still living; Leonard's two

Labrador dogs, for example. They didn't do much but sleep and eat, but he loved them anyway, and he wanted to be sure that when he and his wife got to the point where they couldn't take care of the dogs anymore, whoever took the dogs would keep the pair together. Ben — with whom Leonard had always had the most communication problems — said he completely understood his dad's attitude and in a surprise gesture added that he would take the two dogs himself, since he and his wife had been looking at dogs for some time.

The family then began designing a plan for inventorying everything so that the children would know what their parents wanted to stay in the family and what they wanted given away. In this way, there would be no gray areas that might lead to upset feelings later on, and everybody got the chance to put in their two cents.

The final conversation got Leonard and Betty to reflecting upon their lives. In many ways, this was for them the most important of the six conversations because it encouraged them to open up about how they saw themselves as people, describe how they had grown up, how they had met each other, and to tell about their life's journey and what matters to them. From this, the idea was launched to set down their story and the history of the family farm in writing as a "memory book." Then their daughter Allison, who holds a degree in film from the University of North Carolina, ran with the idea and suggested videotaping her parents as they shared their thoughts and feelings and strolled down memory lane. This could be a *living* memory book for grandkids and future generations to experience. Though a bit uncomfortable at first about going on camera, Leonard and Betty soon warmed to the idea, and in the end Allison wound up recording more than ten hours of legacy conversations with her father and mother. She eventually edited the footage down to a forty-five-minute documentary that she gave to her folks and to each of her siblings on videocassette as Christmas gifts. She also saved all the outtakes so that none of this permanent record of her parents' legacy conversation would be lost.

Maybe Not the Be- and End-All, but Wow!

The upshot of conducting these 11.5 conversations using the CARE system was that after years of difficulty communicating with each other, of family tension due to misunderstandings, and (on Leonard's part especially), of not feeling appreciated or listened to, the Wilson family had finally absorbed a lot of information about themselves, about each other, and about family dynamics, and about how much they really mattered to one another. Most important, they knew where to go in terms of laying out an effective strategy for Leonard and Betty's long-term care (see Part 3) and in continuing to strengthen their relationships with each other as well.

Will this mean an end to all family disagreements? No, of course not. Between family members — especially strong-willed people such as Leonard Wilson and his son Ben — there will always be disagreements. But in the Wilsons' case, there is now a strong bond of communication to mitigate such quarrels. How powerful is that!

So, let's not delay any longer. Let's proceed to the first important conversation, the big-picture conversation, and learn how to help you help your parents uncover the challenges, alternatives, and resources that exist in their particular situation, and to focus on the big picture regarding the experience they want for their long term future care.

Practice with your parents: Learn from your experience with your parents and remember the frustration, stress and anxiety you are feeling now. Be sure you don't do the same thing to your own children. Parent care plans need to be created as early as possible so you have many more choices and your stress level and that of your children is low.

PART TWO
THE PARENT CARE CONVERSATIONS

There are two barriers that often prevent communication between the young and their elders. The first is middle-aged forgetfulness of the fact that they themselves are no longer young. The second is youthful ignorance of the fact that the middle-aged are still alive.

- Jessamyn West, novelist

3

THE BIG-PICTURE
CONVERSATION

The best way to predict the future is to invent it.

- Dr. Alan Kay, Hewlett Packard Labs

A Process Problem

In addition to the emotional obstacles holding us back from dialoguing with our parents or with our children about the parent care issue that I have already discussed in previous chapters, there is another culprit at work — arguably the biggest culprit of all. It is the fact that we throw ourselves off balance by putting the cart before the horse. Let me explain.

Most elder adults really *do* want to talk to their spouses and children about their future care and all the issues related to it, but they don't know how. Neither, in most cases, do spouses or kids know how to begin such a dialog. This is because the major industries and service professions involved in parent care focus almost exclusively on a product-oriented approach to opening the discussion and addressing the problem. That approach can be, and all too often is, a nonstarter.

Typically, the legal, financial services, insurance industry, or CPA approach to parent care begins (and ends) with pitching a product that purportedly will solve part, or all, of the parent care problem. For example, a lawyer will tell you the solution is to make out a will, or perhaps, set up a trust, or employ some other legal tool that will protect your parents' assets, enrich their beneficiaries (that's you), and create an extension of their legal rights through general or health care powers of attorney.

Reality Check

Parental Myth: "I have it all figured out and know *exactly* what I want to do. I've talked to my professional advisors and have everything in order. I'm *certain* of it!"

Fact: Don't believe your folks have their future care all figured out and have started putting things in order unless you see it all figured out and in order — on paper. Take it with a grain of salt that they have consulted their professional advisors (assuming they have them) about anything. Most likely, they have not. And while they may express certainty about how to proceed, realize this: they are probably just as certain about that as they were about how to raise you. In other words, they are pretty much making it up as they go along.

The financial services industry approach is not dissimilar. Here, the discussion focuses on growth and income over pure growth, weighted against your parents' risk profile and sensitivity to market volatility, with the emphasis on preservation of capital for preserving purchasing power, and so on. The insurance industry approach is only minimally less confusing and off-putting. Here the discussed solution typically revolves around long-term care costs, available assets, Social Security contributions, pension benefits, and the minimization of potential estate taxes with an artfully structured individual or second-to-die life insurance policy. Just choose the tool you want, let it work its magic, and when events dictate, be ready to reap the windfall.

Last but not least, there is the CPA approach, which is to focus on the various state and federal regulations that affect the purchase of investment and insurance industry products, and the tax ramifications of those decisions. This will spark a scintillating conversation about the use of qualified versus nonqualified monies, Social Security taxation potential, IRA withdrawal tax traps, and whether or not there will be a sunrise after the sunset of current estate tax legislation. Good grief, no wonder our parents put off having this discussion. It's enough to make their heads spin.

Reality Check

Parental Myth: "There's no need to plan. The government will take care of us."

Fact: While government assistance (Social Security, Medicare, and Medicaid) does indeed offer an avenue of support for older Americans, it is fast becoming a less certain avenue. Who knows where these programs will be in a few years in terms of solvency and benefits? Government assistance should be relied on as a last resort, not as a primary means of care and support.

Don't misunderstand me. I'm not saying that these solutions are inappropriate for dealing with the parent care issue, just that they are inappropriate as openers to any discussion of the issue. Parent care is first and foremost a process issue, not a product one. In other words, it is first and foremost about the conversation itself. The challenges our parents face, the alternatives they have, the resources they possess, and the experience they want to have as they age: that determines the "how." Without this in-depth conversation, the "how" will be just another force-fed quick fix and a transitory one too.

Deep Support

In her book *The Support Economy*,* Harvard Business School professor Shoshana Zuboff argues that what today's consumers (especially today's older consumers, the baby boomers and their parents) yearn for is not more product presentation but a set of relationships — a system of *deep support* — that will allow them to reach their personal goals of psychological self-determination. Her point is this: Today's consumers

---

* With James Maxmin. New York: Viking Press, 2002.

are swamped by choice, whether it's the sixty-three different models of SUV they can buy, the nine thousand separate mutual funds they can invest in, or the twenty-three different kinds of deep-dish pizza they can order. Choice is not the issue. The issue is that I want what I want when I want it, in the way I want it, at the price I want it — *now*. In other words, the issue is about maximizing the *consumer experience* in relation to goals and desires as opposed to maximizing the *consumption of products* and therefore being affected by that consumption in unpredictable and unintended ways.

The conversations in this book lay the groundwork for maximizing the consumer experience of deep support in the area of parent care. In fact, they are the *beginning* of that experience. Once you have determined the type of deep support desired and the type of deep support that can be provided (the structure) to create the experience, the selection of the various professional, financial, or investment products to support that structure and maximize that experience is no longer the driving decision but almost a fait accompli.

With that in mind, let's help your parents draw a big picture of where they want to be a few years from now in terms of maximizing the experience of their future care.

TIP! Choose a Facilitator

The parent care conversations cover many critical areas. Without someone to keep the discussion organized and moving forward, it can get bogged down or turn into a free-for-all. Choosing a facilitator within the family should be approached the same way as borrowing money from a family member — with care. The facilitator should be someone everyone trusts, who is not only able to articulate his or her own positions clearly but is a superb listener capable of understanding and restating the positions of others just as clearly. He or she should be someone with a history of working well and building consensus with family members, who engages conflict with a feather duster and not a crowbar. Granted, it may be that no one in the family is able to fill this bill 100 percent, but in order for the parent care conversations to work smoothly and effectively, a preponderance of these characteristics should be apparent in whomever you choose.

Christine trains Parent Care Specialists throughout the country who can help with the Parent Care conversations. If you feel that you cannot have these conversations on your own, contact Christine for her assistance or that of a Parent Care Specialist at www.parentcaresolution.com.

The Big-Picture Conversation

The series of parent care conversations starts with what I call The Big Picture Conversation because it will give you an insight into the kind of future your parents would like to experience and therefore create. Their responses here will tell you two important things:

1. That they have thought about their future as it relates to this topic.
2. That they trust you enough to talk to you about it. If your parents have not, will not, or cannot bring themselves to think about their long-term care from a conceptual standpoint, you have a huge challenge ahead of you. If they cannot or will not

trust you enough to discuss the view they have, then you have an impossible task. *You cannot participate in or be held responsible for your parents' care unless you are a part of the conversation about that care.*

With that in mind, let's apply the CARE "hear and now" listening system to the big-picture conversation and see what results. Remember, the fundamental premise of CARE is that if people have a formula for organizing their thoughts around a subject, they will feel more comfortable about venturing forth and discussing the subject. CARE provides that formula for you and your parents.

1. **Challenges**

"Mom and Dad, let's look down the road at the issue of your long-term care and discuss what you think are some of the biggest challenges you will face."

The idea here is to uncover whatever is preying on their minds about their future. Typically, what will emerge from the responses you get is an expression of overall panic, from many different angles, at the prospect of losing control over their future.

From the responses you get to this question, a big picture will emerge of the concerns and outright fears your parents have about their future and the issue of care in particular. Only when these challenges are spelled out will your parents begin to see the various options that exist to address them.

My experience is that there are at least ten big-picture challenges most parents say they face; maybe yours will add to this list:

- "How do we talk about this with our children without making them feel responsible for us?"
- "How can we get the children to work together on this instead of fighting with each other like when they were kids?"
- "How do we downsize and organize all our belongings without feeling as though we're giving up everything?"
- "The subject is too complicated. How can we prepare properly if we don't understand?"

- "How do we simplify our financial and legal affairs so that, if the time comes, our kids can step in and make decisions for us?"
- "How do we stay independent for as long as possible without being a danger to ourselves or others?"
- "How do we make sure we don't end up all alone and forgotten?"
- "How do we face the fact that we may not have enough money to do everything required of us to plan ahead successfully?"
- "How will we avoid alienating the rest of our children if we entrust just one of them to carry out our wishes?"
- "Can't we just die here so our kids will just have to have us buried?"

Reality Check

Parental Myth: "We'll just be burdening our children more if we share things with them."

Fact: Parents actually burden their kids more by tuning them out on this subject or stonewalling them. This is one area where kids are very happy not having surprises thrust upon them. And once the parents are gone, it's too late for them to ease the burden by helping the kids sort things out.

TIP! It's Not About You

Remember, the parent care conversations are about your parents' thoughts and feelings, not yours. If asked for your opinion or suggestions, politely decline. Say you will be happy to share your opinion or make suggestions but only after they have shared theirs with you. This helps to reinforce the trust they must feel that you are truly focused *on them.*

---

2. Alternatives

"Mom and Dad, let's discuss some of the options that you think might be available to you in dealing with the challenges we just discussed."

The goal here is to help your parents shift their focus away from what they fear they will lose by making a decision about their future care to what they stand to gain from making that decision if they maximize their options. It may take some digging to discover these options, but together you can do it. That's the whole idea of this conversation (and all others in the book): to discover the alternatives that exist, *together*.

For example, some might be:

- "We can break each decision down into manageable steps and plan one step at a time so we feel less overwhelmed."
- "We can start laying the groundwork by doing some investigating without having to lay out any cash."
- "We can use this book to help us discover what issues we have regarding our future care."

TIP! Beware Procrastination

Procrastination transforms potentially resolvable situations into eternal dilemmas incapable of resolution. Teenagers are masters of this game: whatever solution you propose is simply impossible or unworkable for a thousand different reasons. Behind this procrastinating lurks the fear of making a decision in the first place or of not making the one that is "totally right"; i.e., finding the perfect solution, which of course can't be found because it doesn't exist. Like teenagers, your parents really have just two big-picture alternatives to consider: (1) they can make a decision that, while perhaps imperfect, does take into account their wishes and what's important to them, or (2) they can default to a decision created in crisis mode with little or no regard to their wishes and what's important to them.

- "We can see if there is such a thing as a professional mediator in this field to help us work things through."
- "We can ask friends who have already gone through this problem about what they did; maybe we can learn from them."

3. **Resources**

"Mom and Dad, let's think of some resources that you are familiar with already that we could use to help maximize your options and minimize these challenges."

Once your parents know the alternatives that exist to meet the challenges they face, they will be better able to put a name to the resources available to help with each alternative. In this and the five parent care conversations to come, your parents will discover more resources available than they would have ever thought existed. For example:

- "Get some basic information from our lawyer (CPA, banker, insurance agent, investment advisor) to help us map out a plan. Then hire them later to execute our desires for us."
- "Bounce ideas off each other as husband and wife, just as we've done throughout our married life."
- "Look at our children as adults who can and want to help us instead of continuing to look at them as kids whom we must shield."
- "Turn to our priest (pastor, rabbi) to help us think through some of these issues."
- "Start checking with our realtor to see what houses in this area, and others we might like, are going for now."
- "Visit some retirement communities and other types of care facilities to help us better understand the decisions we may be faced with."
- "Get a realistic view of where we stand financially."

Now that you have helped your parents to examine their challenges and consider their alternatives and resources, it is time to get them to imagine the experience they would like to create for themselves out of the decisions they will make.

4. **Experience**

"Mom and Dad, think about the long-term care experience you would ideally like to create for yourselves and tell me what that experience would look like."

Perhaps more than any other question, your parents may need some prompting here to get going. This, after all, is a difficult question to answer even if one has been considering the prospect of one's future care for some time; it calls upon parents to contemplate having made decisions about their future care they have not yet made and to imagine the good they want to come out of them, so they will feel confident about moving toward making those decisions. However, by having vented freely about the "dark side" of growing older early on in the process, your parents will begin to see, and to articulate, the upside of the experience they can create for themselves.

For example:

- "We're able to breathe again because our heads are not in the sand."
- "We've thought everything through and resolved things and are free of dread."
- "We've brought our children into our confidence and aren't stressed about having to ask them to help us."
- "Thinking through where we might have to live eventually, and why, has actually enabled us to find ways to be able to stay where we are longer."
- "We've come to a good understanding with our children so that our expectations of each other are realistic."
- "We were able to stretch our finances because we started looking at ways to rearrange and improve them early enough."

From typical responses to the experience question such as these, your parents will be able to develop a list of positives that will help spur them to take action. I call these positives "experience accelerators," and some of them related to the big picture might be:

- "Making decisions now in anticipation of future events will help us to build confidence about the future."
- "Just being able to hire someone to come in and help inventory and distribute some of our personal property removes all that complexity that clutter adds to our lives."

44

· "Making sure our legal affairs are in order now will give us the flexibility and adaptability to make changes later on as we need to."

· "Designating someone to help assist with health care decisions removes all the uncertainty that comes from not having anyone in charge."

· "Taking control of our finances will let us realistically determine what we have and what we need so that we won't be stressed out by the unknown."

· "Making decisions instead of avoiding them will restore balance in our personal and business affairs in such a way that we will be able to confront the issue of care in a less forbidding context."

· "Just thinking through the various pieces involved in making long-term care decisions will help us to focus better on what's really important *to us*."

These accelerators, when set down on paper in black-and-white, will help to put your parents in a positive frame of mind with regard to making decisions about their future — whether the actual move on those decisions will be made a month from now or a year from now.

Granted, some of the sample responses I've provided may give the impression of flowing a little too easily. They may even appear a bit too simple and straightforward given the complex nature of the questions themselves. But I can assure you that while many parents may have the care issue on their minds, they will very likely not have come up with many solutions to that issue, let alone simple and straightforward ones. By asking them the big-picture questions, you get the ball rolling. You give them structure for envisioning what's most important to them in the years they have left and how to achieve it.

> ## Keep in Mind!
>
> You may adapt the CARE questions to your own conversational style if it will make you feel more comfortable. Stay consistent, however, from conversation to conversation, and in order to elicit the information you need, be sure to maintain the essence of the questions as presented here.

Off and Running

Robert Meyer, seventy-two, and his wife Elizabeth, seventy-one, have each been retired for about ten years. They live in Boise, Idaho, where Robert had a very successful career as an executive at Bendix Corporation. They have two grown children, Kate and Zachary, both happily married with families of their own. Living in Denver and Salt Lake City, respectively, the children are close enough to make frequent trips home for the holidays and to pop in for the occasional visit with the grandkids as well.

The Meyers' son Zachary, having recently attended a Parent Care Conversation seminar, suggested to his parents that they meet with their life insurance agent to talk about their future plans and the issue of long-term care. Zachary participated in the meeting as well. Initially, Robert thought the agent was just going to make a pitch for long-term care insurance or picking up more life insurance coverage. But the agent had attended the seminar also and was well versed in the CARE system. Instead of launching into a product pitch, the insurance agent surprised Robert and Elizabeth by asking them to share their feelings about the challenges they saw ahead of them surrounding the issue of their future care.

Robert and Elizabeth had never thought about long-term care as something they could actually *anticipate* and thus *plan for*. They had always felt, "We'll just deal with it all when the time comes." As they thought about this, they realized there were a number of things that concerned them. For example: What do we do with the house? Should we move to a retirement community? What kinds of things should we look for in choosing one? What kinds of care will we need? What in the world will we do with all our stuff?

Zachary had absorbed his parents' responses to the agent's question, then asking them to share with him and the agent some of the options they could think of that might be available to help them deal with these issues. Neither Robert nor Elizabeth had thought about their future in terms of options. They had simply figured the path was preordained, with little room for innovation. But their son's question got them to thinking broadly. Maybe they could build a smaller, stand-alone house. Or, even more exciting, perhaps they could buy into a "retire cruise," a new time-share concept for retirees wherein you purchase a half-interest in a condominium for use half the year. But this condominium is onboard a ship, making it sort of a floating townhouse.

Next, the insurance agent jumped in again and asked them for some of the resources they thought they might be able to tap to help maximize their options. Through the years of saving and investing, the Meyers had put themselves in the position of not having to worry about money. They weren't wealthy, but they were very well-off. That was one resource they had on their side — a big one.

The fact that their physical health was so good was another huge resource they could tap. It meant they didn't need assisted living or special care considerations, at least not yet.

Their relationship with their children was yet another huge resource. Both kids said they would welcome it if their parents moved closer for even more frequent holiday get togethers and "pop ins" with the grandkids.

Robert and Elizabeth Meyers' social skills and adaptability were another big asset. They had always found it easy to settle in and make new friends wherever they went.

Finally, Zachary asked his folks to paint for the insurance agent a picture of the future they would like to have as a result of the care decisions they would make. It was this question, the hardest for them to answer, that pushed Robert and Elizabeth to get in touch with their vision about what getting older really meant to them. It made them consider what they wanted to experience more, rather than less of, as the years wore on and what they could realistically hope to achieve to make those years fulfilling.

They said they wanted to feel unafraid of the consequences of their decisions. They wanted to experience self-sufficiency and independence for as long as realistically possible. And they wanted to stay connected to each other and to their family as they aged — in other words, to grow old, as they described it, "naturally."

When the meeting finished, Robert and Elizabeth realized they had never contemplated the issue of their future care before in such a comfortable yet pointed manner. They had always dreaded the subject. But the meeting had gotten them to imagine how they wanted their lives to look in the near future, and to share that vision with their son and the insurance agent so that they could help them bring that picture to life. Previously, the insurance agent had always talked to them only about product and policy decisions. This time was different. This time the discussion was just about them. That didn't mean the agent didn't have any insurance product or policy ideas up his sleeve. But now when the pitch came, there would be a context for it that hadn't existed before, and the product and policy suggestions would be in full alignment with the Meyers' long-term care goals and desires.

What Robert and Elizabeth Meyers saw from having the big-picture conversation was that they could actually shape the future they wanted for themselves as they grew older instead of defaulting to a series of circumstances that were "just meant to be." It would take some hard thinking and imagination on their part to design that future, but they were now ready to start.

Having begun to find the sense of confidence they needed to begin planning for and making decisions about their future care, Robert and Elizabeth were eager to launch into the other parent care conversations with their son. Zachary called his sister Kate, and with that call, the entire Meyers clan was off and running—talking openly, communicating fully, and planning together, strategically.

4

THE MONEY CONVERSATION

"Blissfully" Unaware

Herb and Martha Pennington retired nearly ten years ago from the university where they had worked for most of their lives. Herb, a professor of biology, is a private man who, while open and affectionate with his wife and children, has always been very secretive on the subject of money. His father had died in bankruptcy, and perhaps as a result of that experience, Herb became very frugal, determined to never let himself fall into that trap.

As a young professor, Herb struggled to support his mother, his wife Martha, and their two children, and yet he managed to put away a little each pay period to begin building a small portfolio of rental properties near the university. He kept them in his name alone because he didn't want his wife to be responsible should anything happen to him before the mortgages were paid off. He now had ten such properties, all mostly paid off, and the rental income from them was meant to help subsidize his and Martha's retirement income.

Martha, a former professor in the theater department, had inherited a small amount ($100,000) from her late mother, which she had given to Herb to take care of since he seemed to be so good at finances. The couple also had some life insurance through the university as well as a long-term care policy purchased elsewhere. With their home owned free and clear, the rental income, and two pensions coming in, Herb felt that he and his wife were in a good position to enjoy the fruits of their lifetime of work.

Reality Check

Parental Myth: "We have enough money in our investments to be able to live forever just off the interest."

Fact: Here's a quick way to see if that's true. Take the total amount of money your parents have in their investment portfolio and multiply it by 3 percent. If that 3 percent meets their current living expenses, they may be right. If it doesn't, and their portfolio isn't earning at least 3 percent a year in interest, then they are in big trouble.

Another formula that some advisors use is to multiply your financial earnings times eight and that is the amount you need to retire with a comfortable lifestyle.

Recently, however, Herb was diagnosed with first-stage Alzheimer's and late-stage dementia. His son, an accountant, had for some time prior to the diagnosis attempted to talk with Herb about his finances, just to get a handle on where things were in the event something like this happened. But no matter how delicately Herb's son tried to broach the subject, the man begged off or changed the topic. Now, with his father's diagnosis of early Alzheimer's, the son was sure that if he didn't do something immediately, his parents (and possibly he as well) would be in serious financial jeopardy. The family physician had confided in him that Herb could probably expect to be able to live at home another year or so but due to the progression of the disease would likely have to go into an assisted-living situation directly after that because of the twenty-four-hour nature of the care that would be required.

Approximately a year after the initial diagnosis, Herb suffered a stroke that left him unable to communicate or to walk without assistance. With great pain and reluctance, but unable to care for him by herself any longer, his wife moved Herb to Cedar Village, an assisted-living center nearby, where she could at least visit him regularly. Cedar Village is a *complete* assisted-living center, which meant that it offered the possibility of transitioning Herb to a special care unit within the same facility if his situation required it.

The monthly cost of Cedar Village was $5,300, not including the medicine Herb required daily, which added another $450 to the monthly tab. The Genworth Summary of 2013 Cost of Care Survey findings has the following:

Summary of 2014 Findings

Over the past 11 years, Genworth has been able to recognize and identify trends across the long term care services landscape. Overall, while the cost of care among all care providers has steadily increased, the cost of facility-based providers has grown at a much greater rate than that for home care. As the American population ages and requires these services, it is vital to be aware of the associated costs in order to build a better long term care plan. Consumers have more choices than ever before.

Long term care can be provided in a variety of settings. A licensed health care practitioner such as a physician, registered nurse or social worker will determine a plan of care that could include the following:

HOME

Homemaker Services This service makes it possible for people to live in their own homes, or to return to their homes, by helping complete household tasks that they cannot manage alone. Homemaker services provide "hands-off" care such as cooking, cleaning or running errands.

NATIONAL MEDIAN HOURLY RATE	INCREASE OVER 2013	FIVE-YEAR ANNUAL GROWTH[1]
$19	4.11%	1.20%

Home Health Aide Services Personal and home health aides help those who live in their own homes instead of residential care facilities or nursing homes. Home health aides may offer services to people who need more extensive care than their family or friends are able – or have the time or resources – to provide. It is "hands-on" personal care, but not medical care. This is the rate charged by a non-Medicare certified, licensed agency.

NATIONAL MEDIAN HOURLY RATE	INCREASE OVER 2013	FIVE-YEAR ANNUAL GROWTH[1]
$20	1.59%	1.32%

COMMUNITY

Adult Day Health Care (ADC) This service provides social and related support services in a community-based, protective setting during any part of the day, but less than 24-hour care. ADC centers can offer a much-needed break to caregivers. There are a variety of models that intend to offer socialization, supervision and structured activities designed for individual needs. Some programs also provide personal care, transportation, medication management, social services, meals, personal assistance and therapeutic activities.

NATIONAL MEDIAN DAILY RATE	INCREASE OVER 2013	FIVE-YEAR ANNUAL GROWTH[1]
$65	0%	3.40%

Assisted Living Facility (ALF) These facilities are living arrangements that provide personal care and health services for people who may need assistance with Activities of Daily Living (ADLs). The level of care provided is not as extensive as that which may be provided in a nursing home. Assisted living is not an alternative to a nursing home, but an intermediate level of long term care.

NATIONAL MEDIAN MONTHLY RATE	INCREASE OVER 2013	FIVE-YEAR ANNUAL GROWTH[1]
$3,500	1.45%	4.29%

FACILITY

Nursing Home Care These facilities provide a higher level of supervision and care than Assisted Living Facilities. They offer residents personal care assistance, room and board, supervision, medication, therapies and rehabilitation, and skilled nursing care 24 hours a day.

Semi-Private Room		
NATIONAL MEDIAN DAILY RATE	INCREASE OVER 2013	FIVE-YEAR ANNUAL GROWTH[1]
$212	2.62%	3.91%

Private Room		
NATIONAL MEDIAN DAILY RATE	INCREASE OVER 2013	FIVE-YEAR ANNUAL GROWTH[1]
$240	4.35%	4.19%

[1] Percentage increase represents the compound annual growth rate for surveys conducted from 2009 to 2014.

It was now that Herb's son discovered that his father's retirement income plus Social Security came to $3,200 a month, almost $1,800 short. He further discovered that the long-term care policy his father had purchased to supplement any shortage only paid benefits for six months, at the rate of $50 per day, *if Herb was in an acute nursing facility.* Assisted living did not qualify as acute nursing.

Herb's son then looked to the rental properties to see if he could divert some of the monies to help subsidize his dad's care. The ten properties were bringing in a total of $2,400 a month. A believer that a bird in the hand is worth two in the bush, his father had not raised the rent in many, many years. In addition to the properties being under rented, the son discovered that they required a huge amount of maintenance, much of which had long been deferred; paint jobs, gutters, roofs, and carpeting that needed replacing, and so on. When he estimated the amount all this would cost, the total equaled 25 percent of the value of the properties. Understandably, the tenants were none too happy about the conditions they were living in and had banded together to withhold their rent as a protest. One tenant had even sued Herb over this, but because he was suffering from late-stage dementia, Herb had simply filed the letter away and forgotten about it.

When Herb's son combined the amount of money it would take to bring the properties up to a salable condition plus the tax bite incurred in selling them, the amount came to almost 40 percent of the properties' value. It was a complete between-a-rock-and-a-hard-place, rob-Peter-to-pay-Paul scenario.

Too fragile and upset over her husband's illness to remain in the family home, Martha decided to sell it and purchase a smaller, more manageable place. Her son estimated that she would realize $250,000 from the sale, all of it tax free. The smaller home she found cost $150,000. That left $100,000 that could be used to subsidize her husband's care because her own monthly pension and Social Security income were barely enough to cover her expenses.

Herb's son estimated the $100,000 would be gone in four to five years. For his father to be able to remain in Cedar Village after that, and to avoid having to go on Medicaid (and perhaps be moved somewhere else), the $100,000 had to last as long as possible. Therefore, he put it in the safest, risk-free-rate-of-return investments available to help the money grow. Herb's son also sold the rental properties at an "as is" loss and added the small amount of cash realized from the sale to the investment pot for his father's care.

As of this writing, Herb's Alzheimer's has progressed to the point where he must be moved to the special care section of Cedar Village, where his average monthly expenses will rise to about $7,200. Most of the $100,000 is gone; there is just enough left to cover Herb's expenses in the special care section for about a year. For his wife to be able to preserve some cash of her own and not see it all go to her husband's care, leaving her with nothing to live on, the only option is for Herb to move, after the year is up and the $100,000 gone, to a facility that accepts Medicaid payments. When that happens, of course, the State of Illinois will want whatever assets may be left over in Herb's estate as reimbursement for any monies it has spent on his care. Furthermore, given the new "look back" rules for Medicaid, the State of Illinois has the ability to go back nearly five years to determine reimbursements; it can investigate whether Herb had gifted his wife and children any money during this time that might in the future have been used for Herb's care. If the state determines those gifts were made in order to "defraud" the State of Illinois, Herb's wife and children could be forced to pay all that gifted money back, with interest, as well as face civil and perhaps criminal charges and fines.

Reality Check

Parental Myth: "Our portfolio is doing well enough; we can buy our way into a nursing home when the time comes."

Fact: What if there are no beds available at that time in the nursing home your parents *want*, assuming they haven't outlived their money in the meantime and made the possibility of choice moot?

The one blessing of Alzheimer's, of course, is that Herb himself is "blissfully" unaware of any of this.

One of the tragedies of Parent Care is that many adult children are "blissfully" unaware of the details and cost of the various options of Parent Care.

A Private Affair

So, how does a smart university professor like Herb Pennington wind up putting himself, his wife, and his son in such a financial noose? By not sharing his financial situation and not doing it early on with the adult children or caregiver, he put the family in danger of financial ruin.

The fact of the matter is that unless you know what assets your parents have and where those assets are, you won't be able to arrange things to maximize their use and to protect those assets as much as possible while not running afoul of the myriad federal and state Medicare and Medicaid rules and regulations. Not only will your parents not have any money to pass on to you, but you may end up facing financial ruin by having to subsidize their care out of your own income and investments pocket or be responsible for reimbursing the state for what it has paid out. The money conversation is your first line of defense against these scenarios.

Money is not the easiest topic to talk about with parents. They probably kept you out of that discussion while you were growing up, and it may be a difficult habit for them to break now. This is especially true of parents who grew up during the Great Depression. They belong to a generation with an emotional hangover from the worst financial disaster in our country's history (so far). For many people of that generation, there will never be enough of anything to make them feel totally secure financially. They will likely take their fear of growing old without money, a place to live, or enough food on the table with them to the grave. Money to this generation is a private issue — talked about in private, counted in private, and given away in private.

Another source of reluctance on the part of parents to talk about money with their adult children (or most other family members and friends for that matter) is that in the United States especially we tend to measure success in life almost solely by the amount of money we have accumulated during that life. Your parents may feel that they have not done well enough and be embarrassed to share that with you. Or they may feel that they have done so well that if they gave you a peek at what you might inherit then you would quit your job, throw caution to the wind, build up inventories of tanning oil and sun glasses, and generally join the ranks of the world's ne'er-do-wells.

For whatever reason your parents' financial status has been closed to you, your job now is to crack open that door with the money conversation and gather the following critical information:

- How much in cash and other assets do your parents *actually* have?
- How much do they owe and to whom?
- How well is your parents' money working for them?
- Do they work with a financial advisor and who?
- What are their investments and how are they doing?
- What's not working about their money?
- What changes need to be made to correct that?
- What's possible and what isn't?
- How are the assets titled?
- Do they have legal documents?

You will gather this information in two phases. The first is the money conversation itself, where you will use the CARE system to get at the more emotional issues your parents have concerning money and their financial situation. The answers you get here will enable you to dig deeper and collect the specifics about their financial situation and where their assets are located. In order to do this, you will need the latest statements from their bank(s), brokerage firm(s), insurance company (or companies), and so on. Once you have these statements, you will be able to record such information as asset location, title account numbers, ownership, and other details. You need to have the most complete picture possible of where your parents are financially *right now*.

Having that picture is vital because your parents cannot begin to select a care facility — whether it is to bring care into the home, remodel the home or go to a retirement home or nursing home — until they understand what they are able to pay on a monthly basis for that facility and for how long. They and you won't

---

TIP! When Lips Are Sealed Tight

If you are dealing with parents who are in complete denial about their financial situation and are totally unwilling to discuss this aspect of their lives with you, you have three options. The first is to acknowledge that this is a smoke-screen, offer to help them organize their affairs, and try to get them to see that without knowing what they have, what they will need, and what they want, you may not be in a position to help them when the time comes. The second option is to exit stage left. Yes, I did say "exit." Parent care responsibilities are so huge, so draining, that if your parents aren't willing to meet you even halfway on the money issue, then they will simply have to live with the financial consequences of their noninvolvement. And you will at least have a heads-up that their finances are probably in poor condition, so you can prepare for the fallout from their default decision.

The third option is to get an elder law attorney involved. If you sense mental incompetence and you have to intervene for their safety, you may go through the process of getting guardianship of your parent.

---

know whether the family home is an asset or a liability, whether the amount of Social Security income they receive can be treated as "mad money" or if it must be depended upon. They won't know whether they can afford to give away that Rembrandt or if they'll have to sell it for hard cash to live on. Your parents didn't accumulate all they have in one night, so understand that you aren't going to grasp their financial picture in one night either.

The Money Conversation

1. Challenges

"Mom and Dad, let's (or could we) discuss some of the financial challenges you think are ahead of you with regard to the process of growing older or needing long-term care."

What you are trying to get straight to with this question is whether your parents feel confident about their financial situation (and why) or whether the uneasiness they may be demonstrating about even discussing the subject is an attempt on their part to mask a deep anxiety they feel over their money situation. Here is how some of the responses might get:

- "We think we have enough for our future care, but we're not sure and don't know how to find out."
- "Our money is scattered in several banks and investment firms. We don't have a fix on where it all is ourselves."
- "We don't know if our assets are earning enough for us to be able to live the way we will want to and still be able to leave you kids something."
- "We don't know what to do or where to invest our money to make it grow to what we'll need."
- "We have a financial advisor named _____ that knows our money situation and you can call him/her when the time is right."
- "Money is private and we are not comfortable talking about it."
- "We are afraid that if you know how much money we have you may not want us around…"
- "We have saved so little we are embarrassed about our money situation."
- "We know how much we have, where it all is, and have organized and planned everything out. We'll show you."

Wow! If you get this last response, thank God that you were born into your family, and you can spend your life working on world peace or world hunger because you've just freed up the next twenty years!

2. **Alternatives**

"Mom and Dad, let's discuss some of the options that you think might be available to you in dealing with the financial challenges we just discussed."

Your parents may need some nudging here, particularly if they are in denial or unaware that there may be a problem with their money situation. If so, they may find it difficult to consider their options. Here are some of the options I've heard expressed:

- "Cross our fingers and just hope for the best."
- "Organize our affairs to find out where we stand."
- "The Lord is going to take care of matters…" (Kevin's dad used this one.)
- "Maximize the financial potential of what we have."
- "Find other sources of income or make our money grow."
- "Keep making our own financial decisions about our current and future care."
- "Enlist our children's help to determine our financial picture and prospects."

This last type of response is an open invitation to proceed directly to the fact-finding part of the money discussion before moving on to the final two CARE questions. If you decide to finish the conversation before moving on to the fact-finding, that's OK too. It will all depend upon how well you "read" your parents; sometimes it's best to strike while the iron is hot.

If you do proceed to fact-finding, use the fact-finding tool below to record the pertinent financial data on your parents that you will need later on for analysis, strategizing, and decision making.

> ## TIP! Easy Does It
>
> The process of gathering financial information from your parents can go smoothly or it can be frustrating and maddening, depending upon how you approach it. To achieve the first result, proceed in a way that is open and invitational, not judgmental. You don't want to cause your parents to feel any embarrassment. For example, don't go after the facts about their cash flow and investments like the cops on TV's *Law & Order*.

3. Resources

"Mom and Dad, let's think of some financial resources that you are familiar with already that we could use to help you maximize your options and minimize the effect of these challenges."

The purpose of this question is to start your parents (and you) on the road to thinking about financial strategies, such as: how to transform current wealth into different assets and income streams; how to combine those streams and assets in a way that will maximize return (plus growth as well, if possible) while minimizing risks; and how to ensure that their money lasts as long as they do (with some left to be passed on to their beneficiaries). Coming up with a list of resources that can be tapped to help in the strategizing process is a key step, and the number of resources is probably limited only by your parents' imagination.

Some of the responses you may hear:

- "I spent some time in the military...I wonder if they offer any help."
- "We bought this Long Term care policy...let's see how much that pays."
- "Maybe it is time for us to visit some senior communities to see if we like them?"
- "I have my social security and pension."
- "We have our house paid off, how can we use the equity."

- "I have the 100 acres of land that I got from my parents...maybe we could sell that."
- "I wonder if we should remodel the house and stay at home as long as we can."
- "Maybe we could put a small retirement cottage behind your home and stay there."

Parent Care Solution Financial Fact-Finding Tool

	Value	Location
Cash on hand		
Checking accounts		
Certificates of deposit		
Money market accounts		
Stock mutual funds		
Bond mutual funds		
Individual stocks		
Individual bonds		
Annuities		
Cash value life insurance		
Gifts		
Real estate equity		
Art		
Antiques		
Jewelry		
Rare coins		
Collectibles		
Heirlooms		
Profit sharing plans		
SEP		
SIMPLE		
401(k)		

Other qualified pension plan(s) _____ _____

Loans _____ _____

Reverse Mortgage _____ _____

Line of credit _____ _____

Total Assets: $ _____

Broadly speaking, these resources may include people such as your parents' accountant, attorney, realtors, banker, and broker plus financial resources such as cash, bonds, real estate, business interests, pensions, retirement funds, and so on.

> ## **Keep in Mind!**
>
> Don't forget that family itself can be a huge resource to leverage in this situation. I helped subsidize my father's care for nearly five years. It's easy to complain about having to do it, of course, but when you begin to feel that way, consider this: Add up the cost of caring for you for the first eighteen years of your life, plus all those times afterward that you needed (and got) that "little extra" to help tide you over until payday, catch up on your credit card debts, or take care of unexpected house or auto repairs. Only after the amount you have shelled out to help subsidize your parents' care begins to exceed the amount they shelled out for you for those eighteen years or longer will you really have some cause to complain.

4. Experience

"Mom and Dad, think about the long-term care experience you would ideally like to create for yourselves as a result of the financial decisions you will have made, and tell me what that experience would look like."

What you are striving to come up with here is the ideal picture of your parents' future care situation, fiscally speaking, *from their point of view.*

In other words, as if the money was not an obstacle. Here are some of the responses to this question I have heard:

- "We would like to know that we have enough money to stay in our home and live a normal life without worrying about food or necessities until we absolutely have to move."
- "We would like not to be a burden on anyone, especially our children."
- "We would like to know that we would not have to live in lesser circumstances or experience a lower quality of life and care than we have now."
- "We would like to know that we can live out our lives in dignity, with as much autonomy and independence as is humanly possible."
- "We would like to know that if we do run out of money, caring for us will not drain the coffers of our children or our community."

For some parents, of course, approximating this picture will require coming up with millions of dollars a year in income or assets. For others, it will require as little as the cost of the least expensive compact car, in terms of their net worth. With your fact-finding completed and everything now out on the table, you are ready to help your parents find out which column they come closest to falling into, and how to begin planning for, and creating, the experience, they desire.

Developing Money Planning Strategies

Keeping Principal Intact (as Much as Possible)

What you are trying to do in this chapter is get a feel for how long your parents will be able to sustain themselves in a facility (by which I mean their current home as well as any future retirement community, assisted-living, special care, or acute care situation) without:

1. Beginning to deplete the principal on their assets
2. Going completely broke and losing all control over their future care situation while saddling you and/or the government with the bill

To find these things out, you will need to calculate how much your parents will be able to safely withdraw from their assets over time.

There are many financial software programs available to help you and your parents assess their portfolio under a multitude of scenarios, conditions, and factors.

Some software and money websites to consider:

www.mint.com
www.emoney.com
www.quicken.com
www.microsoftmoney.com
www.dinkytown.com

Or just use an Excel spreadsheet to get their financials in order or just a legal pad. The important thing is to know your parents' financial picture in details.

While perhaps this might be an interesting exercise from an intellectual standpoint, and even fun from the point of view of "financial planning as a video game," in the end you will still be left with the following question: where do things stand now and where will they stand tomorrow?

As a result of conducting the fact-finding expedition earlier, you may already have a fix on where your parents stand now in terms of their total assets (the principal). If not, now is the time to find out, using the fact-finding tool. After that, get a rough fix on the second part of the question — how much your parents can withdraw over time without having to eat into principal — under the following scenarios. For each one, base your calculation on the asset total you came up with using the fact-finding tool, coupled with the markets' average earnings-growth per annum over the past century; i.e., 5 to 7 percent.

- **Real-case scenario:** Total assets minus 50 percent of historical growth average, or 4-5 percent. This means your parents can withdraw 2-3 percent from earnings each year without eating into the principal. Bear in mind, however, that if the markets flatten out or go down (as happened, for example, from 2000 to 2003 and again from 2007 to 2009), then your parents will not be withdrawing from earnings but from the principal.

· **Worst-case scenario:** Total assets minus 100 percent of historical growth average. This means your parents' average 4-5 percent withdrawal per annum will be eating directly into their principal *right from the beginning.*

· **Best-case scenario:** Total assets minus 20 percent of historical growth average. In this case, your parents' portfolio will be growing in the range of 7-8 percent per year. They should plan on withdrawing no more than 4-4.5 percent to keep the principal intact.

Some analysts may consider these formulas to be overly simplistic. But all of us having watched our parents' life savings disappear in a four-year bear market, my level of assurance in the prognostications of most analysts is less than zero. The fact of the matter is that in the last years of a person's life the cost of care will equal almost 20 percent of that person's health care expenditures over his or her entire life up to that point. Any calculation based on assumptions about the future should always be considered with caution and common sense, of course. But the bottom line is that keeping things simple works. The name of the money planning game is fundamentally this:

1. Watch what your parents' money is earning.
2. Watch what your parents are spending.
3. When 2 exceeds 1, your parents are spending more than they are bringing in, a financial plan that is stressful on the family in the short term and catastrophic in the long term.

Conducting an Easy Money-Hard Money Analysis

Your parents' goal is to maximize both income and growth. At some point, they will have to turn the growth into some type of income to pay their bills. This is where what I call the "easy money-hard money" concept comes in.

Think of your parents' assets as breaking down in two different ways: easy money and hard money.

Easy money assets are those that:

- Are easily accessible via a phone call, check, or debit card
- Are easily transferred from one account to another
- Produce little or no income tax liability from their use
- Does not affect long-term capital growth potential.
- Easy money assets include: cash, checking account, savings account, money market accounts, stocks that can be sold and in cash in three days, and bonds.

Hard money assets are those that:

- Are difficult to convert to easy money
- Are not quickly or easily sold
- Have an income tax bill attached to their sale
- End the potential for long-term capital growth
- Hard money assets include: a business, land, rental properties, a home, and timber.

The rule of thumb is that the closer an asset gets to being made of bricks and mortar, the more difficult liquidation of that asset becomes. Use the following Easy Money-Hard Money Decisions Tool to analyze which of your parents' assets is which and to determine how many months of care your parents' assets can sustain. Start by inserting the values you came up with earlier during your fact-finding expedition into the appropriate easy money or hard money column.

Conducting Your Analysis

Steps for easy money analysis

1. Total all the easy money amounts.
2. Divide the total by the amount required monthly.
3. You may have to research options in your area to get the exact cost of home care, assisted living care, or dementia care. Some sites to help with this step include: www.aplaceformom.com and www.seniorlivingguide.com
4. If possible see if there are any "non-profit" facilities in your community. I (Kevin) found one in Conway, South Carolina

and lowered my mother's monthly expenses from $4,500 to $3,000.

5. Determine the number of months available.
6. Assume it doesn't earn anything.

Steps for hard money analysis

1. Total all the hard money amounts.
2. Divide the total by the amount required monthly.
3. Determine the number of months available.
4. Assume it doesn't earn anything.
5. Then you may prioritize these assets and then of options and strategies and timelines as to when and how these may be sold.

The total number of easy money months plus total number of hard money months equals the total number of care years your parents' current financial picture will sustain. You will now know how hard your parents' portfolio must work to improve their long-term financial situation so that the experience they want can be realized.

The Parent Care Solution Easy Money-
Hard Money Decisions Tool

Easy money		Hard Money	
Cash on Hand		Real estate equity	
Checking accounts		Tangibles	
Certificates of deposit		Art	
Money market accounts		Antiques	
Stock mutual funds		Jewelry	
Bond mutual funds		Rare coins	
Individual stocks		Collectibles	
Individual bonds		Heirlooms	
Annuities (can have surrender fees)		Pension plan	
Cash value life insurance		Profit sharing plans	
Gifts		SEP	
		SIMPLE	
		401(k)	
		Other qualified plan	
		Loans	
		Loans	
		Reverse mortgage	
		Line of credit	
Total easy money		**Total hard money**	

Which money to access first:

Once it is time to start paying the bills the question is asked, which money do I spend first? And how do I arrange the money so that it is there to pay the bills?

Order to consider may be this:

1. Pay from current income such as pension, social security, and dividend and interest income.
2. Take money from non-IRA accounts in the form of dividends and interest and invade principle if needed.
3. Then tap non-qualified annuities. These instruments are taxed on a LIFO method…last in first out. Which means the first money out will be taxed until you get back to principle.
4. If you have stocks in a gain position, you may take them next as the gains will be taxed at capital gains rates.
5. Then consider money from IRA's or 401(k) plans that are taxed as ordinary income.

Protecting Assets, Privacy, and Inheritance

In the future, the funding requirements for Medicare and Medicaid will almost guarantee that federal and state governments will be looking for reimbursement of funds expended on behalf of the elderly. This reimbursement will come either from the assets of the person's estate or from assets that have been transferred to children in an attempt to avoid those assets being taken by the government. In fact, technology platforms are now in place with the ability to file constructive liens on the part of the state and federal government from the time of death until an estate is distributed, to recover monies expended on the part of the deceased. In some instances, states are pursuing the children of Medicaid-dependent parents to recover monies that were transferred in order to care for those parents.

It is important to understand here that deliberately and purposefully transferring assets or rearranging one's financial affairs with the intent of defrauding Medicaid is illegal and punishable by law. Nevertheless, every citizen does have a right to organize his or her financial affairs for the purpose of maximizing accumulated life's wealth and transferring as much as possible of that wealth to his or her children and community with a minimum amount of interference from the state or federal government.

I believe that if you design a comprehensive financial strategy with long-term goals of cash flow maximization, income tax reduction, investment planning, retirement maximization, and wealth-transfer (estate) planning, and if you review and update that plan periodically to accommodate changes in law and circumstance, not only will your plan help you accomplish your financial goals and objectives, but you will survive any scrutiny about transfers that occurred as part of that plan.

It is the responsibility of each of us, not only to plan for our own financial success, but also to be responsible for helping our parents continue to be successful in their older years. There will always be a percentage of our population that will not plan for anything: breakfast, career, vacation, or even its own well-being. But that percentage is undoubtedly not reading these words, which are not intended for them anyway. They are intended for those of you who are willing to take the responsibility and be accountable for the destiny of your parents' care and your own as well. For these reasons, it is important that asset protection, privacy protection, and inheritance-transfer planning be initiated as early as age sixty, which means *immediately* if your parents (or you) are now over sixty. Here's what to do:

1. Set specific goals, based on your easy money-hard money analysis, for the accumulation your parents will need so that they can start setting aside those amounts now. The savings can come from a salary, part-time job, or other sources of revenue. If the analysis says that your parents will not have enough without financial support from you and other sources, no matter what they do, the answer is not to surrender to a default solution *but for them to do the best with what they have.* There are only two variables to consider: income and expenses. If there's too much expense and not enough income then the options are to decrease the expense or to create more income while keeping the expense constant.

2. Take advantage of all legal structures and documents (see part 3) available for safeguarding assets, privacy, and the transfer of wealth. Furthermore, consult with an elder care attorney well-versed in the intricacies of Medicaid and Medicare law to enable your parents to protect as many of their assets as possible while still complying with the letter of the law. For a list of such

attorneys throughout the country, visit the National Academy of Elder Law Attorneys Web site at www.naela.com.

Avoiding Medicare and Medicaid Pitfalls

Medicare and Medicaid planning reminds me of those commercials on television where you see a driver in a hot car careening down a scenic but precarious mountain road and a disclaimer flashes on the screen saying, "closed course, professional driver — do not attempt this with your own vehicle." If your analysis shows that your parents are or may be candidates for governmental assistance for their future care, it is *critical* to seek out an estate and elder law attorney who specializes in this area. Medicare and Medicaid are complicated systems that are constantly undergoing governmental changes, and their application varies from state to state. But here are the basics.

People sometimes confuse Medicare with Medicaid. Yes, both are programs for the elderly, but Medicare pays for the costs of hospitalization and medical care, not for long-term care in skilled nursing or assisted-living facilities. Medicaid pays for that. Also, Medicaid pays care providers directly and not the recipient and it is a needs-based program, which, even though federal, allows the individual states to establish their own eligibility and administration standards. Be aware that not only do laws vary from state to state but offices within each state may have their own standard as well. Now you see why I emphasize the need for an attorney experienced at navigating this maze.

All applications for Medicaid have to be made with the appropriate state agency. Though each state will have different priorities, all require the following:

1. **Proof of Residency (and Citizenship)**
2. **Proof of Eligibility,** for which there are several qualifying tests:
a. Category test: Applicants must be sixty-five years of age (or older) and in need of long-term care due to age, blindness, or physical or mental disability. A forty-year-old may qualify too, if he or she is blind or permanently disabled.
b. Income test: congress has established a minimum income, below which it believes no elderly American should fall. This

minimum is called the Social Security Income (SSI) standard, and it varies annually based on the consumer price index. The *maximum* amount of income an applicant can receive and still receive Medicaid is *three times* the SSI standard.

- Income for Medicaid purposes includes all money received on a *regular basis*, such as pensions and other retirement plan income, Social Security, and annuity payments.

- It may not matter if an applicant's income exceeds the current SSI standard for eligibility if the applicant lives in a "medically needy" state or in a state where excess income is not an impediment to qualification. Parents should contact their local Medicaid office to determine their state's eligibility standards.

- Income is separated according to whose name appears on it. This means that an applicant's income is attributed solely to him or her while all income in a spouse's name (called a community spouse) is attributed to both spouses. Income in both names is attributed equally to each spouse. In 1988, Congress passed the Medicaid Catastrophic Coverage Act (MCCA) to avoid impoverishing the community spouse due to the expenses of the other spouse needing care. This means that even if the community spouse's income is greater than the spouse applying for Medicaid, he or she does not have to share that income with the other spouse. But if the community spouse does not have sufficient income of his or her own to meet what's called the Minimum Monthly Maintenance Needs Allowance (MMMNA), then the community spouse may be entitled to some income from the spouse applying for Medicaid. Be aware that there are additional Medicaid provisions for hardship situations, as well.

c. Resource test: An applicant's assets are categorized as either exempt or countable. Here's how the distinction works:

- **Exempt Assets.** An applicant can own an unlimited amount of these, which include: A home (as long as the applicant, spouse, minor or disabled child lives there — be on notice however that the state may place a lien on it for reimbursement of expenses or to recover expenses from the estate of the applicant); an automobile (if used for employment or medical treatment transportation, if the vehicle has been modified specifically to meet the requirements of the applicant's particular circumstances, or if there is a spouse); household items (almost all furniture, furnishings, artwork, etc.); personal effects (usually subject to a $2,000 limit); medical equipment needed by the applicant or spouse; burial needs (funeral plot, vault, casket, headstone, plus money for expenses set aside in a burial fund or a life insurance policy of less than $1,500 in face value); tools (used for a trade or business); a maximum of $2,000 per case ($3,000 if both spouses apply).

- **Countable Assets.** These include everything that can be converted to cash but does not fall into the exempt category, such as: real estate (other than a home or if the home is held in a trust); retirement assets like IRAs, 401(k)s, or any other deferred compensation (While some states treat tax-deferred balances as exempt, most will look at whether the account owner could demand the balance. If so, the balance — minus any applicable tax liability — will be countable. There are exceptions for mandatory IRA distributions past age 70 ½ and for annuities with certain irrevocable elections made inside those plans); liquid or cash equivalents (checking and savings accounts, stocks, bonds, mutual funds, and cash value life insurance); promissory notes (land sales contracts and trust deeds, though "accountability" will depend on whether there is a demand feature within the note).

- **Unavailable Assets.** These are assets that are not capable of being converted to cash — for example, real estate owned with someone else or unmarketable property owned with other parties. Applicants may be required to produce evidence from time to time to substantiate the unavailability of these assets.

<u>**Keep in Mind!**</u>

The "resource test" becomes more complicated if only one spouse is applying for Medicaid benefits. Title to property is largely irrelevant here, since all "countable" assets will be pooled whether they are in the husband's name, the wife's name, or joint. The Community Spouse Resource Allowance (CRSA) under Medicaid law does provide some protection, so be sure to consult the attorney advising your parents about this.

"Spend Down" Strategies

Once an eligibility analysis of your parents' income and resources has been completed and their Medicaid qualification has been determined, the next focus is how to "spend down" certain assets. The intent here is not to defraud Medicaid but to enhance your parents' quality of life as well as to preserve other assets and income for transfer to family members and future generations. The viability of these strategies for "spending down" assets will vary depending upon whether you are dealing with one parent (single parent) or two (married parents), as follows:

- **Single Parent Strategies:** These strategies revolve around what to do with countable assets in excess of $2,000.
  a. Purchase a fixed annuity. This essentially converts a resource asset into an income asset, guaranteeing a consistent income stream from this source while at the same time letting other assets grow. This strategy will only work if the payout election period is certain and the recipient dies before that period ends. Otherwise, the state might attempt to recover any remaining unpaid payments. There are lots of traps for the unwary here, like excessive fees and charges, so beware of them (or make sure your advisor is). The annuity marketplace is fairly competitive and the costs are becoming more transparent, so don't overlook this "spend down" opportunity. Fixed annuities are long-term investment vehicles designed for retirement purposes. Gains from tax-deferred investments are taxable as ordinary income

upon withdrawal. Guarantees are based on the claims paying ability of the issuing company. Withdrawals made prior to age 59 ½ are subject to a 10% IRS penalty tax and surrender charges may apply.

b. Give half and keep half. Gifts have an effect on Medicaid eligibility. Gifts, per se, are not illegal. They may, however, affect the waiting period for benefits, sometimes called the "period of ineligibility" or "penalty period." Within certain parameters, there is an almost unlimited gift exclusion to family members such as a minor child, spouse, permanently disabled child, sibling with an equity interest in the home, or an adult child living with and providing care for the parent. Otherwise, the strategy here is to give away a calculated amount while holding back enough to cover the cost of care until the waiting period expires.

c. Prepay funeral and burial expenses.

d. Pay off all debt and credit cards.

e. Liquidate qualified or tax-deferred plans (for example, IRAs, 401(k)s, etc.) and prepay the tax liability. If taxes will not create a whole new set of problems, the liquidation strategy should not be overlooked.

f. Hire family members to provide care. This strategy has to be pursuant to a written agreement between the parties, and the family member(s) receiving payments for care provided should know that these payments are *taxable income*.

g. Pre-purchase medical equipment and supplies that will be needed.

h. Pre-purchase consumer items the parent will need, such as clothing, a television, room decorations, magazine subscriptions, books on tape, and so on.

·   **Married Parents Strategies:** A couple may "spend down" using all the same strategies as a single parent, plus some additional ones. For example, unlimited assets can be transferred between spouses without being counted as gifts. Here are some others:

a. Purchase a larger home.

b. Put money into an existing residence by either paying off the mortgage (if there is one) or making needed improvements.

c. Purchase exempt assets such as an immediate lump sum annuity. As long as the payout option is not changeable and the payments are not assignable, an annuity that pays a certain amount is exempt in many states. Yours could be one of them.

Keep in Mind!

As noted earlier in this chapter but well worth repeating here: All state agencies have a right under Medicaid law to "look back" five years into an applicant's financial affairs at gifts made to or from a trust to determine if the state should be reimbursed. Under Medicaid law, the "look back" period for gifts made by the applicant to individuals is 35 months.

Recovering Costs: A Guaranteed Way Not to Go Broke

One of the most difficult challenges in caring for aging parents is coming to the realization that not only do they not have enough money to pay for the duration of their care, but they also do not have enough money to cover the *current* cost of their care. Children in this situation are faced with an incredibly difficult choice: to watch their parents spend themselves into insolvency or to step up to the plate and divert sorely needed savings and retirement plan contributions of their own in order to help their parents out. This is the classic "heads you lose, tails you lose" dilemma. But it can now be solved, allowing both parents and offspring to recover the confidence to move forward. Here's how:

My solution is called The Parent Care Cost-Recovery Strategy, and it provides a viable alternative to the traditional "heads you lose, tails you lose" dilemma. It involves insuring the lives of parents with either an individual policy on each parent or a second-to-die policy on both parents. The owner of the policy can be the one paying the premiums or anyone else in the family who is contributing to the current support of Mom and Dad and may need to recover those costs. The beneficiary of the policy can be anyone the owner of the policy deems appropriate. The proceeds of the policy can first be used to pay back the monies spent for Mom and Dad's care, with the balance used to replace any inheritance that was lost due to the high costs of care incurred. In some instances, these proceeds will result in the creation of an estate and an inheritance where none previously existed. The benefits of using life insurance in this situation are that the insurance proceeds, if properly structured, arrive untouched, untaxed, on time, and guaranteed.

Some people have expressed a certain discomfort with this strategy because they see it as profiting from the parents' demise. But consider this: (a) buying a life insurance policy on your parents certainly doesn't create or hasten that demise, which is inevitable; (b) your parents I'm sure would rather that you recover whatever you've spent caring for them than go broke and have to pass your retirement and future care needs onto your own children.

The question to really keep asking yourself as you consider this strategy is not "Am I profiting from the death of my parents?" but "If my money is paying for my parents' care, whose money will pay for mine?" If you already have a trust fund, are really tight with a wealthy Auntie Mame, or have married into the Hilton family, then the question is moot. But for most of us, the Parent Care Cost-Recovery System is a sound and worthwhile alternative.

So, how do you go about the recovery? There are five steps:

1. Using the easy money-hard money and income-resources analyses you conducted with your parents, determine if you will need to contribute to your parents' care now or in the future.
2. Determine how much you will need to contribute and for how long.
3. Calculate the impact diverting these monies will have on your own retirement and future care needs.
4. Determine how you will pay for the insurance premiums used to recover these monies.
5. Determine who will own the policy and who will be the beneficiary (or beneficiaries).

Putting It All Together

Among several reasons for our avoiding the money conversation is this one: the fear of what we might find. It is possible that our parents aren't as well-fixed financially as we thought (or were led to believe), and since we may not be where we would ideally want to be either, this knowledge makes us feel as though we are about to experience a car wreck that we can do nothing to stop.

But here's another way to think about what the money conversation may reveal. It's not what we find out that's the problem; it's what we want to believe is true, and isn't, that is the problem.

The minute you have a realistic picture of your parents' financial situation, you can begin to help them alter that picture. Even if your parents have little or no prospect of creating another dime of income for their future care — and you are barely making ends meet yourself — a car wreck is not inevitable. There are government programs like Medicaid to step in and help. That's why those programs exist. But before your parents can take advantage of such programs, they must be able to demonstrate that they qualify for them by determining the exact status of their financial situation. It is avoiding the money conversation that truly puts your parents' future care and your fiscal future in harm's way. Here's how things should work.

Bob and Crystal Taylor are solid working-class folks living in Omaha, Nebraska, and have recently retired. Bob ran a small restaurant (Taylor's Tin Cup Diner) and Crystal was an English teacher in the Omaha public school system. Their daughter, Ashley, and her husband, Max, live in Kansas City, where Ashley is an executive secretary for the Kansas City Gas Company and Max owns and operates Max's Tire Emporium. Ashley and Max do very well financially and have no concerns about their own retirement and long-term care. But Ashley didn't really know what her parent's financial situation was; she could only speculate. She knew that while growing up she always had nice clothes, the family always took wonderful summer vacations; and that when she graduated from college she had no student loans to pay off. Her folks had even helped her and Max out with the down payment on their first home and then forgiven the note. Therefore, Ashley assumed they were financially OK. But, just *how* OK? To find out, she engaged her parents in the money conversation.

Ashley's father has $250,000 invested in his profit sharing plan, plus he owns the building his diner is in, which is worth approximately $450,000 and is debt free. Based on his earnings, he is entitled to almost $1,300 per month in Social Security income. Both parents carry $250,000 worth of life insurance. The family home is worth $325,000, with no mortgage debt, and they own their cars and have no consumer debt.

Ashley's parents shared with her that in a couple of years they would like to downsize to a smaller residence close to her, in Briarwood Retirement Community in Kansas City. To do this, they will purchase the smaller home for about $250,000 and pay cash for it, leaving them with about $50,000 for an emergency fund. By pooling their savings together, they can live comfortably on Social Security alone yet have access to almost $5,200 per month without eating into their principal. This is as far as their thinking and calculations had taken them. But what about further down the road, when assisted living or acute care might be needed?

One of the things the money conversation revealed Bob and Crystal Taylor had not done, even though they had talked about doing it, was purchase long-term care insurance. Their daughter encouraged them to make an appointment with their insurance agent to discuss the matter, and she went along. It turned out that since her parents wanted to be sure they would have enough for their future care without assistance from anybody and yet still be able to pass on substantial assets to their daughter and grandchildren, long-term care insurance was an excellent investment for the couple. They committed to a policy for each of them.

The Taylors also made a commitment to meet with their lawyer and update their estate documents to take into account the purchase of long-term care insurance and other changes that had occurred since the documents were originally drawn up (when their daughter was a child). Even though these were basic documents, there was a need for updated health care directives and a redrafting of the Taylors' powers of attorney to name their grown daughter and her husband as dual holders of their powers of attorney. With just a few changes and some good strategizing,

Bob and Crystal have now fully organized their affairs in such a way as to provide a maximum amount of financial security for themselves and a minimum amount of financial difficulty relating to their future care for their daughter and son-in-law. And everyone now feels a sense of confidence about what lies ahead financially. That confidence could only grow out of having the money conversation, not by avoiding it.

Dos and DON'Ts of Financial Parent Care Planning

DO's

DO make sure you know exactly where your parents are financially.

DO make sure you know where all of their financial assets are located.

DO know the names of your parents' accountant, attorney, and banker, and how to contact them.

DO estimate what it's going to take your parents to live on in their long-term care situation.

DO take responsibility for planning your parents' long-term care finances.

DO make sure you have the legal documents you need to talk on your parents' behalf and make the needed financial decisions.

DON'Ts

DON'T let your parents try to put off talking about money with you and be assertive if you need to do so.

DON'T take their word for it that their finances are OK.

DON'T assume that someone else in the family will financially rescue them — or you.

DON'T bank on the government (or anyone else) providing all the necessary funds for your parents' long-term care.

DON'T wait until the s—t hits the fan to try to figure all this out.

DON'T ruin your financial future because your parents are under prepared.

5

THE PROPERTY CONVERSATION

Useless Appeal

There is an interesting corollary between personal property and sibling relationships. Both start out new and shiny. Over time, some wear occurs, resulting in little nicks. As the years pass, the nicks turn into cracks and the glue that once held everything together begins to yellow and harden and pull away. If enough stress is applied at a certain moment, the entire piece can crumble from the weight it has endured all these years. Time and circumstance have combined to create the ideal conditions for that collapse.

In the same manner, sibling relationships that have endured for years can suddenly be torn asunder by a picture, a hope chest, or a wedding ring that, in the stress of the moment that accompanies a parent's death, goes to "someone else." As a lawyer, financial advisor, and gatekeeper for families in the parent care area, we have seen this happen over and over again. Case in point: the Albright family of Albuquerque, New Mexico.

Bill Albright was the owner of Albright's Market, a combination convenience store and gas station. Bill had one of the largest collections of Anasazi pottery in the Southwest, having inherited part of it from his father, an amateur archeologist, and acquired the balance of it as a result of his own Saturday expeditions into the desert with his son, Bill Jr. Even though nothing was written down, Bill Sr. had indicated by his words and his actions that if something ever happened to him, then Bill Jr. was entitled to the pottery collection.

Neva Albright, Bill Sr.'s wife, was an amateur painter and photographer. Neva had achieved national recognition for some of her photographs and paintings of the Southwest. At a showing in Santa Fe, the owner of a Washington, DC, gallery had bought nearly $50,000 of her work at wholesale for his own gallery. Dotty, one of Bill and Neva's two daughters, had always helped her mother organize and catalog her works. According to Dotty, Neva said that when something happened to her, Dotty could pick out what she wanted from the work and let her siblings have what was left to divide among themselves.

Neva Albright passed away four years ago, and her husband followed a year later. Their estate plan left everything to each other. The Albrights' attorney gathered the four children (Bill Jr., Dotty, Sam, and Elizabeth) together shortly after their father's memorial service to read his last will and testament. It was their father's intent to divide everything equally among the children, including bank accounts, the family home, personal property, and the convenience store. He had a clause in his will that said if they could not agree, the attorney would make the decisions, and they would have to abide by them. What happened next is the kind of nightmare that the property conversation is designed to circumvent.

The siblings went to their parents' home after the reading of the will. There, Sam asked Dotty and his brother if everything in the house had been left the way it was when their father died. Bill Jr. said that he had taken the pottery collection from the gas station since his father had promised it to him, and Dotty indicated that she had taken the photographs and paintings her mother had specifically given to her. Sam and Elizabeth got furious and began accusing their siblings of cheating them out of the chance to choose equally among this property, saying there was no hard evidence that either parent had singled things out for Bill Jr. or Dotty to take; the will alone controlled that. It did not help the situation that the spouses of all the parties were also present. A shouting match followed that resulted in Sam and his wife, and Elizabeth and her husband, storming from the house, vowing to "get a lawyer and make sure we get what we're supposed to."

Reality Check

Parental Myth: "There's not really all that much stuff. Your mother can sort through it and get rid of it quickly when the time comes."

Fact: Sure she can, beginning with the thirty-seven years of *Popular* Mechanics underneath the workbench in the garage, then the same-size piles of *Woman's Day, Redbook,* and *National Geographic* in the den. And those are just the magazines of which they accumulated the fewest issues!

Sam and Elizabeth felt the pottery collection and the paintings and photographs possessed as much monetary as sentimental value, if not more. They were concerned that their siblings had "cherry picked" the estate of the most valuable assets and thought that, therefore, they were entitled to an equivalent amount -- in dollars if not in property itself. Their attorney sent a letter to Bill Jr. and Dotty, demanding that they immediately return the objects they had taken or provide an appraisal of those objects and send the equivalent in cash. The appraisal value of the pottery collection in Bill Jr.'s possession and the artwork in Dotty's home was in excess of $200,000. When their siblings received this news, they got even more furious and accused Bill Jr. and Dotty of cheating them by manipulating their father and mother.

Negotiations quickly broke down. Bill Jr. and Dotty refused to relinquish control of either the pottery or the artwork, citing their belief that their parents wanted them to have these things and that the "divide equally" clause in the will meant to divide everything that was *left*. Sam and Elizabeth were equally adamant, claiming that not only had they been deprived of the right of choice, they had been robbed of nearly $50,000 apiece -- their share of the appraised value of the assets their brother and sister had taken.

Sam and Elizabeth filed a lawsuit against their siblings for return of these assets, money damages, and attorney's fees. The suit accused Bill Jr. and Dotty of fraud, deceit, collusion, conspiracy to defraud, and named their spouses as well. Bill Jr. and Dotty filed a countersuit, accusing Sam and Elizabeth of intent to defraud, collusion, unfair dealing -- and naming their spouses as well. During the course of the next two acrimonious years, interrogatories were submitted and depositions taken. Temperatures ran so high that a special trustee was assigned to take over the management of the estate, and the family home and all belongings were put under lock and key. Each party involved in the lawsuit was exposed to questions about personal finances, employment history, relationship with his or her spouse, and whether they gambled or were addicted to drugs. Neighbors, employers, and friends of the parties were interviewed about them and deposed under oath, as well.

Almost three years after the filing of the lawsuits, a trial was held in probate court in Albuquerque. After two weeks of deliberation, the probate judge rendered his verdict. The court decided that the pottery in Bill Jr.'s possession was in reality the property of the state, since it had been found on federal land and was of historical value. The court ordered the items to be sent to the New Mexico Museum of Natural History in Albuquerque, and Bill Jr. was charged a $1,000 fine for each item in his possession -- *plus interest* on each item, dating from the time it was taken from federal land almost fifteen years earlier. His total fine: $120,000.

The court also determined that since all four children were equally entitled under the will to receive the pottery, they were *jointly liable* for the fine.

In the matter of the artwork, a court-ordered appraisal determined it to have grown in value due to the resale of several of the paintings and photographs the DC gallery owner had purchased. Thus, Dotty was ordered to pay her siblings $25,000 apiece for the art she had taken.

Meanwhile, during a court-ordered examination of the convenience store and surrounding land, it was discovered there had been a petroleum spill on the property shortly after Bill Sr. purchased it, about which he had done nothing. And so, the New Mexico Environmental Department along with the Environmental Protection Agency ordered the property to be cleaned at the inheritors' expense and that the store be closed until approval was given by the state that the cleanup had been successfully completed. The cost of the cleanup, which was to be borne equally by the four siblings, was estimated at $150,000.

While the court's rulings could be appealed, the high courts in New Mexico (as in many other states) usually affirm the decisions of the probate judge, rendering any appeal virtually useless.

Reality Check

Parental Myth: "Our grandkids will want this to remember us by."

Fact: Think carefully. When was the last time they got a phone call from the grandkids to say "hi," let alone to express fondness for a particular heirloom?

Powerful Pull

The Albright family saga defines the kind of extreme relationship collapse and financial disaster that can befall the average family over the property issue. Miscommunications and misunderstandings occur under the best of circumstances, in even the closest of families. Under the worst circumstances, such as the death of a parent and the disposition of his or her possessions, miscommunication and misunderstandings between siblings can exacerbate an already emotionally charged situation into becoming a road to hell -- or to court, which in the Albright case turned out to be the same thing.

In such situations (again, the Albright case is a good example), the problem is not the property itself but the *beliefs*, the *expectations*, and the *feelings of entitlement* the respective parties have concerning that property -- in other words, the emotional and other bonds they have to it and how those beliefs, expectations, and feelings of entitlement can affect and even overpower their thinking process.

That ring, watch, or necklace Mom wore, and that hammer, hat, or radio of Dad's, can exert a tremendous pull on siblings. Conversely, that same property can exert a powerful hold on Mom and Dad as well, for another important reason.

As we age, we experience a gradual loss of control over so much in our lives, ranging from our health and ability to take care of ourselves in our own homes to the ability to make simple decisions about our daily affairs. Our possessions remain a last bastion of control for us. No, we can't take them with us to wherever we go after we're gone, but we can come close -- by using them to exercise our last-minute control to punish or reward those we leave behind.

This chapter, however, is not about the "why" behind our respective connections to family heirlooms or the control issues that impact our thinking about property. I'll leave that to psychologists and social scientists to address. Rather, it is about the "what" and the "who" -- in other words, the disposition of that property so that the feelings of all the parties involved can be managed in a way that avoids the road to hell (or court)

The Property Conversation

The options your parents have regarding disposal of their personal property boil down to these three:

1. Make a will or create a trust for disposing of it after they're gone
2. Write a Memorandum: This is a list of your personal items and who you want them to go to when you pass. Many wills mention the memorandum, but many do not take the time to write them out.
3. Start giving it away now
4. Do nothing

The third choice, what I call the default position, is the natural inclination of most people. The reason for choosing it depends mostly upon whether they are parents or offspring:

- As offspring, we want to avoid conflict with those we were hatched from by forcing the issue and to avoid the even greater potential for conflict with those we were hatched with, who may not see eye to eye with us about who gets what.
- As parents, doing something -- whether it's choose one or two or a combination of both -- is tough physically, mentally, and emotionally, with seemingly little or no payoff other than the realization that "at least it's done!"

Therefore, the default position of doing nothing is the easier route for everybody, at least in the short run. But in the long run, it is the hardest and most painful for all concerned.

When Dan's father became incapacitated with Alzheimer's and had to go into a nursing home, he was abruptly faced, at the worst possible time, with having to spend almost an entire week of ten-hour days going through all the possessions (not to mention papers) in his dad's house, room by room, drawer by drawer, file by file, to inventory everything that was there, and make sure nothing was missing that was supposed to be there or that in the process he didn't toss anything one of his siblings might want. "I've been exhausted in my life", he said, "but never as much as when I tackled that job". Not only was he emotionally spent from strolling down memory lane while going through all that stuff of his Dad's, he suffered mental fatigue from sorting it and from the paranoia he felt as he did so, worrying about "What if I screw up?" Having the property conversation with his dad early on could have spared him all that -- and would certainly have given him dad the "say" he would have preferred in his pre-Alzheimer's days as to who got what.

OK, so here's the common scenario: Your folks are getting up there and may or may not have started contemplating the idea of downsizing their lifetime accumulation of stuff and getting it under control. They have long been very clear about what they want to do with some of their property but are mostly unsure, or completely indecisive, about what to do with the rest. Here's how the property conversation might go with them.

1. Challenges

"Mom and Dad, tell me what crosses your mind when you think about having to move and what to do with all of your stuff."

Some common -- in fact, the consistently *most* frequent -- responses you will get include:

> ### TIP! When to Have the Property Conversation
>
> My rule of thumb: have it the minute your parents give you a clue that they may be open to it. Clues can range from the frustrated cry of "I can't find anything in this mess!" to the more clearheaded and practical, "You know, your father and I have been thinking about downsizing and would like some help deciding what to keep and what to give away." The first clue is quite common; the second comes most often from parents resembling the couple that lives in Pleasantville, whose neighbors on one side are Ozzie and Harriet and on the other, Rob and Laura Petrie. But it happens. Absent any clues at all, have the conversation no later than two to three years before you anticipate your parents being unable on their own to inventory their possessions and decide what to do with things and to whom they should go.

- "We don't know how much to keep and how much to give away in terms of furniture and clothing."
- "We don't know how to divide the things we didn't want among you children."
- "We don't know what to do with what was left over."
- "We don't know how to begin."
- "We don't have the energy to sort through everything ourselves."
- "We are not able to agree what we wanted to keep and not to keep."
- "We don't know who should get Grandmother's rocking chair after we're gone."

2. Alternatives

"Mom and Dad, let's discuss some of the options that you think might be available to you in dealing with the property challenges we just discussed."

As noted earlier, the options your parents have are pretty clear, but to get them to start moving on this issue, it is important for them to actually see and express for themselves what their options are. Here are some typical examples of options parents offer:

- "Do nothing until the last minute so the decision making will be easier."
- "Decide everything now and get it over with."
- "Decide about what we can now, and put off deciding about the rest until a better time."
- "Let someone else decide for us."

Reality Check

Parental Myth: "Everything can be rearranged to fit in our new home."

Fact: Perhaps -- if they are "downsizing" from their current abode, not to a smaller house but to a mini-warehouse for the elderly. And for a retirement community or an assisted-living/special care facility, here's the rule of thumb about what will fit: one-third to one-half (max) of their things; some of their belongings from when they were toddlers, for nostalgia's sake, plus the addition of a Lazy-Boy -- maybe.

---

3. Resources

"Mom and Dad, let's think of some resources that you are familiar with already that we could use to help maximize your options and minimize these challenges."

Once they get going on this question, here are some typical examples that will tumble from their lips:

- "Hire an organizer to help determine how much space we have, then select the furniture and clothing we want -- with the remainder of both going either into storage, to charity, to our children, or to the Dumpster."
- "Select the things we want, invite the children over to pick out what they want, and just give the rest of it away."
- "Charitable organizations from the Salvation Army to the Humane Society are always looking for donations."
- "A journey of a thousand miles begins with one step'? The first step can be to decide what to do with a single chair and then to do it."
- "Where there's a will, there's not only a way, but the energy to get there, not to mention help from others to assist us once they see us actually doing something."
- "As a couple, we haven't always agreed on everything, so when we don't agree, we just get on with it and get past it like we've always done."
- "We can leave Grandmother's rocking chair in our wills to all our children to share and share alike -- and until then enjoy rocking in it ourselves."

4. Experience

"Mom and Dad, think about the long-term care experience you would ideally like to create for yourselves as a result of the decisions you make about your property, and tell me what that experience would look like."

Reality Check

Parental Myth: "When the time comes, we'll just have a big garage sale and get rid of everything ourselves."

Fact: By the time people reach their golden years, most have accumulated enough "stuff" to require the services of a professional liquidator to dispose of -- and a young one at that. They should hire one instead to do this for them and save themselves, and you, tons of time and a severe headache.

Here are some typical responses:

- "We have all our things organized in a way that is useful for us."
- "We kept what we wanted and are no longer burdened with not knowing what to do with the rest."
- "Our place is outfitted with things of ours that are comfortable and familiar."
- "The valuables we have but aren't using and want to pass on are all safely stored away and protected, so we don't have to worry about losing them or having them stolen."
- "We were able to manage the whole process without getting exhausted, irritated, or having it turn into a big production."
- "We were able to do a little at a time over several months to let us get used to the idea and ease into it."

The Property Decision System

The property conversation will move your parents toward, at the very least, thinking about making a decision with regard to their possessions.

TIP! It's About Making a Transition, Not About Packing

The property conversation is not about deciding to move to a smaller home or an institutional care facility (see chapter 6, "The House Conversation," and chapter 7, "The Professional Care Conversation"). It is about helping your parents prepare for that decision by getting leaner and meaner with their possessions *now* before a move becomes necessary. Avoid assuming that answers will come easily and that decisions will be as quick and precise as a surgical strike by a Special Forces team. Be patient. Your mom and dad will be dealing with a lifetime's accumulation of cherished keepsakes and other personal treasures, favorite tools and even appliances, plus all the memories these things will trigger as they prepare for upcoming transitions.

The next step is for them to actually start making decisions. This consists of two phases: (1) taking inventory of what they have; and (2) assigning a value to each item and determining what to do with it.

Kevin's Property Experience

My back still hurts thinking about it. I moved my mother four times in less than two years. I moved her from her 1500 sq. foot home to a 600 sq. foot independent apartment, to a 400 sq. foot assisted living, to a 300 sq. foot dementia care. I had boxes that filled my garage that took over a year after mom's passing before I went through them all.

The property conversation is an important conversation in the task of parent care.

I have devised a property-decision system that provides the tools necessary to complete both tasks in an efficient and organized manner, whether you will be working proactively (that is to say, with your parents in anticipation of an imminent transition) or retrospectively (after your parents are gone).

Tool number one is the Parent Care Property-Description Tool. This is used to identify each of your parents' possessions, room by room, category by category. Once the inventory is taken -- whether that's three weeks from now or three months from now -- the Parent Care Property-Decision Tool is used for estimating the value of each item as well as deciding and, most important, documenting what's to be done with it. For example, will they be holding onto the item or giving it away, and if the latter, to whom or where and when? The decision tool makes this task far more manageable than it may otherwise be.

The information gathered with these tools will also be tremendously helpful down the road, when it comes to settling your parents' estate. At that time, you may be called upon to provide state and local authorities with a final inventory and accounting of your parents' possessions.

Your parents have the option of using these tools on their own (many parents want to) or with your help. If they opt to go solo, however, be sure to check in with them regularly to find out how much progress they've made. If all the information has been collected and the decisions made and documented, be sure they tell you where the sheets are stored. If there has been no progress or it has become stalled, you can offer to jump in and assist. In the end, remember this: you can prod, but you can't force.

The Parent Care Property-Description Tool

Use this tool to go room by room in a systematic way, to catalog and inventory the key items you will be giving away. Granted, there will be objects in the rooms besides the ones that are intrinsically valuable, so remember, it's not necessary to go off the deep end and list everything (e.g., "blue throw rug from Target"). The idea is to create a record of your parents' possessions -- what they have and/or may have had at a certain time and who has it now -- so that locating and distributing those items will be an easy, straightforward task when your parents are gone. I suggest breaking the project up into mini projects by floors, so that it won't seem as daunting, and doing it as soon as your parents are close to making a change in their residence -- i.e., contemplating putting the house on the market to move into a retirement community or professional care facility.

List all items

First Floor	What is stored	Where placed	Stored by whom
Foyer			
Hallway			
Living Room			

Den			
Kitchen			
Great room			
Closet			
Bath			
Laundry Room			

List all items

Second Floor	What is stored	Where placed	Stored by whom
Foyer			
Hallway			
Living Room			
Den			
Kitchen			
Great room			
Closet			
Bath			
Laundry Room			

Hallway			
Bedroom #1			
Bedroom #2			
Bath			
Linen Closet			
Garage			
Basement			
Attic			

Other			

List all items

Personal Items	What is stored	Where placed	Stored by whom
Jewelry			
Art			
Antiques			
Watches			
Tangibles			

Assuming the property is significant and they have not made a decision about to whom it should go, this tool will assist your parents in working through that process. By asking themselves the following set of questions about each item, they will be able to determine: (a) what the property means to them and therefore what it would mean to the person they give it to; (b) who else they may want to have the item in case their first choice can't or won't accept it; and (c) to avoid promising the same item to more than one person so any potential disputes will be resolved in advance.

TIP! Helping Parents Decide What to Do with "Stuff"

Naturally, your parents will want to keep as many of their things as possible, such as watches, jewelry, clothing, pictures, and some items of furniture, wherever they go, up to and even including an acute-nursing or special care situation. So, start with that premise and work backward, asking of each item:

1. If we stay in our current residence, would we like to keep it?
2. If we stay in our current residence, would we like to give it away now, and to whom?
3. If we stay in our current residence, would we like to store it now to give away at a later date?
4. If we move, would we like to keep it with us?
5. If we move, would we like to give it away now?
6. If we move, would we like to store it now and give it away at a later date?
7. Would we like it given away at our death, and to whom?

Here's the set of questions for them to ask about each item, and how they might be answered:

- **What does this mean to me?** This pocket watch belonged to my dad and his dad before him. My dad carried it to work every day, and I remember as a child seeing it hang from a key chain around one of his belt loops. I can remember the sound of it clinking as he walked through the house. It was one of the first ways, when I was little, which I learned to recognize my dad was home from work.
- **What do I want it to mean to the person who receives it?** I have worn this watch of my dad's ever since he left it to me when he died twenty-five years ago, and every year I take it out on New Year's Day to set the time for the New Year. It is significant

99

because it connects me to my dad. I would like my daughter to have it for the same reason, so that she can use it to remember the times we had together.

· **Who else might enjoy this if my first choice is unwilling or unable to accept it?** If my daughter does not want to accept it, then I would like it to go to my nephew Anthony. He has always been a favorite of mine and would treasure it on my behalf the same way I treasured it on my father's behalf. I would like him to pass it on to a son or daughter of his.

· **How do I want this resolved if there is a dispute?** I don't think there will be a dispute, but if there is, I would like my daughter to have the watch no matter who is upset, as long as she wants it. If she doesn't want it, and there are two or more relatives who do, I would like their names put in a hat and the name remaining in the hat after the drawing gets to keep the watch.

· **What is my ultimate dispute-resolving wish?** My ultimate wish is that there is no dispute. But if there is one and it cannot be resolved, then I would like the watch sold and the proceeds evenly divided according to the other terms of my estate plan.

The Parent Care Property-Decision Tool

Having worked through the tough decisions on these items of personal property, use this tool to spell everything out for future reference: item, location, description, value, how the item will be distributed to the recipient, whether the recipient has been notified, and so on. In this way, there will be no doubt about what goes to whom.

Current location				
Piece of property				
Description				
Approximate value				
Prior decisions	Yes	To whom	Do they know?	How?
	Date			
Prior decisions	No	To whom		
	When?			

Averting "Nuclear Winter"

Prior to filling out a property-decision sheet for each item, parents can ask you and your siblings what you would like to take now or be assured of receiving later, and spell that out on the sheet. If nobody expresses any wants now, the property's ultimate disposition thus becomes your parents' decision all the way, and once they document it, you have to live with it.

As an added step, however, your parents can label items with the names of the people to whom they are or will be going -- or even videotape themselves pointing to things as they specify, "Betsy, this, this, and this go to you when you want them," and send copies of the tape to each of the offspring or other family members. It's tough to argue about Mom and Dad's intentions with that kind of evidence.

TIP! Valuating Property

Everyone's mom and dad has inherited something from their own moms and dads, or picked something up at a flea market, that Uncle Stan says will "someday be worth a fortune." If your parents, or you, suspect an item has resale value, not just sentimental value, and the suspicion is not just based on wishful thinking or Uncle Stan's analysis, have the property appraised and get its resale value established. Look under "appraisers" in the phone book for a listing of local estate appraisers. These appraisers will be able to establish not only the property's current resale value but whether that value is likely to increase and whether the item should be insured to protect its value for future recipients. The bottom line: If you think an item has resale value, get it insured, and designate a recipient. If it just has sentimental value, gauge the degree of that value by who is the *most* sentimental about the item, and designate that person as the recipient.

Of course, every family seems to include at least one sibling (or spouse of a sibling) who is a staunch conspiracy theorist no matter what the evidence. My advice if you have such a sibling or spouse in the family is to let them choose first, last, and often. Pick your battles. Unwillingness to compromise can lead to nuclear war within the family; even if you win, it will be "nuclear winter" for the rest of your life.

TIP! The Four Rules of Conflict Resolution

Unless there is clear and convincing evidence that the other party would rather rub you out than come to an agreement, assume that the person is acting in your interest on this matter, and say that it is your intention to act in a similar manner. Then follow these four guidelines for collaboration:

1. Show up ready to settle.
2. Do what is necessary to settle.
3. Never bluff.
4. Be polite.

These rules are like my Scout knife -- thoroughly dependable, but if not, you will know PDQ (and so you won't waste a lot of time).

Dividing Property without Instructions

In the event your parents don't (or can't) make any property decisions, how do you divide their property with no instructions from them? Here are some possible scenarios to consider:

- Arrange a family meeting where each family member will stand up and openly state what possessions he or she wants. If such a meeting isn't possible for logistical reasons, each family member can put his or her wants in writing and send the list to whomever your parents have appointed executor of their estate.
- If two family members want the same item, these are the options: (a) assuming it's not an "I've got to have this or die trying" situation, one party can opt out -- yes, it does happen in some families that when two people want something but one clearly wants it more, the other will stand aside because it doesn't matter as much to them; (b) the two parties can put their names in a hat and a disinterested third party (someone not keen to have the item him or herself) can make the draw; (c) They can hire a professional mediator and abide by his or her decision; (d) they

can sue each other over the item, go to court, and let all hell break loose; (e) they can share the item, if possible -- for example, let's say the property is a vacation home left by your parents with no instructions to whom it should go (this happens more often than you would think), or the language of their will states that it should go "to all our children" -- the interested parties can then set up a timeshare arrangements; (f) they can sell the property and divide the proceeds of the sale -- a method that tends to work best with big-ticket or bulk items, such as automobiles, homes or other real estate, jewelry, furniture, and clothing.

Recognize this: when two family members really, *really* want the same item, even with the best outcome to a dispute, there are bound to be some hard feelings on the part of the one who didn't prevail. It's just human nature. Hopefully, that person will simply nurse his or her wounds, move on, and not let them fester into anything worse. To those who do prevail in any dispute, and do get to take home Dad's fishing rod, know this: at some point in your own future care situation, you will have to weigh what happens to that fishing rod next and how you want that decision to come out.

Using a Professional Mediator

If you reach the stage where you need a professional mediator, trained by or belonging to such organizations as the American Arbitration Association or the Society for Conflict Resolution, to resolve who gets Mom's needlework or Dad's high school diploma, you have reached the stage where you are about to step into a huge mess of relationship goo. Litigation is probably the final course of such action, so you might as well try a professional mediator first. In effect, he or she is the warm-up act to the "Big Litigation Show" you are about to experience if the mediation doesn't succeed.

In fact, once litigants have filed suit, our justice system will often require them to take a swing by the mediation station before going to court in the hope that a decision can be reached there. Today's swamped courtrooms, overworked judges, and aggressive attorneys pretty much assure that if every lawsuit filed were actually tried, the parties' day in court would come sometime in their grandchildren's lifetime, not theirs.

This is especially true if the property is real estate, where all sorts of factors must be considered by the court, such as the location, value, future appreciation, personal use value, legacy value, commercial versus residential zoning issues, and so on. The court will look at three likely strategies for resolving the dispute:

1. Can one party buy the other party out now or over time?
2. Can the property be sold and the proceeds divided?
3. Can the parties share in the ownership and benefits until 1 or 2 can be accomplished?

DOs and DON'Ts

DO make sure you have the time to help your parents see this through.

DO encourage your parents to make these decisions now instead of later.

DO let your siblings know what is going on.

DO consult an attorney if you aren't sure what to do.

DO voice your opinion.

DO ask for help from family members.

DO document anything you take for yourself and your parents' permission to take it.

DON'T make all the decisions yourself about what should be done with the property.

DON'T treat your parents like children -- it's their stuff and their life.

DON'T tell your parents what they can and cannot keep.

DON'T minimize the value of their things to them even if you're right.

DON'T ask for everyone's opinion on everything.

DON'T sell anything without your parents' approval, and document all aspects of the sale.

DON'T think for a moment you won't be criticized along the way.

DON'T second-guess yourself.

Courts as a rule are reluctant to order property sold when there are other strategies to be utilized, even if those strategies are inconvenient. There are costs to the sale, dangers of lost value due to a forced sale, tenant's rights, etc. The courts would much rather you figure this out than ask them to. Judges are, for the most part, overworked, underpaid, well-meaning civil servants who face a daily barrage of issues that would drive a wise man crazy. The last thing they want to ponder on a Friday is whether you or your brother Bob should have the house.

So, in the event of a dispute over an unassigned item of property, ask the family members who are in disagreement -- or with whom you are in disagreement -- if they are open to a neutral third party listening to both sides and making a decision that both parties agree to be bound by. The courts will love you for this. And you can avoid a family feud.

Resources for Organizing

National Society of Professional Organizers   www.napo.net

Professional Organizers in Canada   www.organizersincanada.com

Resources for Conflict Resolution

Academy of Family Mediators   www.mediators.org

American Bar Association Dispute Resolution Section   www.abanet.org

American Arbitration Association   www.adr.org

Association for Conflict Resolution   www.acrnet.org

<u>Resources for Senior Moving</u>

Gentle Transitions   www.gentletransitions.com

Move Seniors   www.moveseniors.com

Aging Care   www.agingcare.com

<u>Moving for Seniors: A Step-by-Step Workbook</u> by Barbara H. Morris and Carol Cornette

<u>Don't Toss My Memories in the Trash - A Step-by-Step Guide to Helping Seniors Downsize, Organize, and Move</u> by Dellaquila, Vickie

<u>Sell Keep or Toss? How to Downsize a Home, Settle an Estate, and Appraise Personal Property</u> by Harry L. Rinker

6

THE HOUSE CONVERSATION

A Man's Home Is His Castle

John and Edna Williams have lived in the same neighborhood in Columbus, Ohio, for the last forty years. John retired ten years ago from Procter and Gamble as a senior vice president in marketing, and Edna retired eleven years ago as a fifth-grade teacher in the Columbus city schools. Over the past ten years, they have traveled, spent time with their grandchildren, and attended classes at the local community college, taking courses in everything from photography to bird-watching. In fact, the last ten years have been everything they dreamed retirement would be.

At seventy-five, John is beginning to slow down a bit, and Edna, while a bit more energetic, is feeling her family history of arthritis begin to take effect. Their home of forty years is a typical split-level of the kind found throughout much of Ohio, with about 3,500 square feet counting both levels. Soon after their children were born, they put in a swimming pool connected via a stone patio to the deck leading out from their family room. John occasionally swims, on really hot days, but for the most part the swimming pool is, as John puts it, "a really great place to throw money into."

<hr>

<u>Reality Check</u>

Parental Myth: "We can just have someone live with us. There are lots of people who are looking for room and board at a reasonable price and would be happy for the opportunity."

Fact: While there may be lots of people looking for a place to room and board at a reasonable price, I can assure you -- and you in turn can assure your parents -- these people are not looking for a full-time elder care job to go with it!

<hr>

The house's current roof is about fifteen years old, and the guttering was replaced about twenty years ago. Here and there you can spot places on the windows that need a little work, like some caulking and paint. Generally, the brick exterior is in good condition. The kitchen, remodeled fifteen years ago, is more than adequate for their cooking needs, and maintenance, such as painting, has been reduced to the kitchen, bedroom, and bathrooms that John and Edna occupy. The other rooms are kept closed, except when their kids and grandkids come to visit. For the most part, John and Edna live in about 1,100 square feet of the 3,500-square-foot house.

Up until last year, John did most of the yard and shrubbery maintenance himself, but last fall he injured his back while spreading pine straw and fertilizer -- just a silly accident that left him unable to pick up even a bale of pine straw for over six months. This past summer, he had to hire one of the neighboring boys to mow the lawn and trim. John and Edna would like to stay in their home as long as they are able since they own it free and clear, which is a great source of financial security for both of them. But John's back injury prevents him from moving between floor levels without help from his wife. Since she's not getting any younger either, they have wondered aloud to each other whether they should consider selling the place and relocating to Merrywood, a combination retirement home and assisted-living facility for people in transition, located nearby. It provides twenty-four-hour medical attention, communal and individual dining, and a recreation center for the almost daily socials and "senior connections" activities it offers.

Reality Check

Parental Myth: "There's no reason for me to leave my home when I get old because I have family and friends who have said they will stop by and check on me."

Fact: Yes, your mom or dad will be checked on -- some of the time. But there won't be visitors dropping by all of the time. And accidents suffered by the elderly in their homes seldom occur when it's convenient for their visitors.

Edna is more open to the idea than John simply because there would be lots of new folks for her to share ideas and engage in activities with, but John complains that he would have to give up his woodworking -- even though he hasn't been in his woodworking shop for over a year. (You never know, he insists, when he might want to get down to building that china cabinet he's been working on in his head for years.) This complaint, however, is just a mask for his real feelings. He loves his house even though it's getting to be too much for him, and he knows that it is. He realizes there is no way he can stay there if he suffers a major health crisis (cancer, for example), but has convinced himself that such a thing happens only to "other people." And even if it were to happen to him, he tells himself, he'd somehow figure out a way to cope. After all, he says, what's the point of having your grandkids come to visit if you can't treat them to a swim in the pool?

If you haven't yet gone through a similar experience with your own folks, or walked in John and Edna's shoes yourself, recognize this fact: *you will.*

The family home is full of shared memories: it holds a special place in the hearts and minds of our parents and in our own if it happens to be the home we grew up in. Even if it isn't a longtime residence and there is little or no generational history connected with it, it is a symbol for our parents of their self-sufficiency and continued independence, a dream we all share. It is estimated that as many as 86 percent of all Americans say they want to be able to stay in their own homes for as long as they can as they progress through their senior years, no matter how financially or physically difficult or impractical that might be. This makes it all the more difficult for any of us to suggest to loved ones like John, much less persuade them, that like it or not, for their own sake as well as the sake of others, they might have to consider moving to an assisted-living residence or nursing facility some day. It's like asking them to give up their last refuge from Father Time.

Reality Check

Parental Myth: "We don't have to be in a hurry about this; when the time comes we'll know it and we'll just do what we have to."

Fact: Congratulate your folks on their unique ability to predict the future. Let's hope the future agrees with them.

It's a Woman's Castle Also

The house dilemma is not restricted to families with two aging parents. The fastest growing group of homeowners in America is single women. Statistically, women live longer than men, so it follows that most women outlive their husbands. Today, the average widow in the United States is sixty-three years old and is projected to live almost twenty years beyond the death of her spouse. While remarrying is certainly an option, statistically the odds are in the ballpark of fifty-to-one against this happening. And even if she does, the odds are statistically in her favor that she will outlive her second spouse as well. In other words, it's a better than even bet that whether she started out single as the owner of her castle or not, she will wind up that way, with all the responsibilities falling on her shoulders alone.

Mary Simpson is a perfect example. Mary is sixty-one years old. Her husband, Bob, fifteen years her elder, passed away a year ago from diabetes. She had been taking care of him for five years, seeing him through all the complications of his disease -- a series of amputations, loss of vision, and eventually kidney failure. She has spent the last year recovering emotionally and financially from the ordeal.

Until Bob died, they had been living comfortably on his $4,500-per-month pension. At his death, however, the pension was cut in half. Fortunately, he had maintained a $250,000 life insurance policy, which was paid to Mary upon his death, to make up the shortfall. Their $350,000 house was owned free and clear, and Bob had amassed a $500,000 investment portfolio in the last years of his career as his salary increased. In addition, at age sixty-five, Mary will be able to collect a small $500-a-month pension of her own from her earlier working years. On the surface, it would appear from all points of view that Mary has her housing situation licked for the foreseeable future.

But let's look a little closer.

Provided she could remain in the same community, still be close to her children, and maintain her church ties, the idea of downsizing from the 4,200-square-foot, three-story home she and her late husband had shared for years is not unappealing to Mary. But she is not open to retirement-community living and is not ready for assisted living. If she were to move, a smaller home even in the 1,800- to 2,600-square-foot range will require an investment of $220,000 to $400,000, and for the most part she will be responsible herself for the yard work and other maintenance associated even with new home ownership.

Mary was diagnosed two years ago with Parkinson's disease and early-stage multiple sclerosis, facts she had kept from her late husband and her children throughout his illness. But now the mild tremors in her hands are becoming stronger and more evident, letting her know that whatever housing option she chooses, special considerations must be taken into account. For example, whether she conserves money by continuing to live in her present home or opts for the expense of a newer but smaller one, the hallways and stairways in each will have to be wheelchair-accessible to accommodate her physical needs. Kitchen cabinets, closets, and other storage facilities will have to be accessible to her from a potential sitting position, as well. Appliances offering easier accessibility will have to be purchased. In order to continue driving, she'll have to buy a new car equipped with special foot controls or specially adapted hand controls, or will have to get her current auto outfitted with them. Bathing, grooming, and showering requirements must suit her present circumstances and be made flexible enough to respond to her needs in the future in the event that her physical condition deteriorates. Mary has some big challenges facing her: all of a sudden home ownership as a single woman, even a financially comfortable one, no longer looks like such smooth sailing.

Reality Check

Parental Myth: "My children have told me that they would like to buy the house from me to make sure I get the maximum value for it without having to do a lot of repairs."

Fact: Children and third-world countries share a similar philosophy about paying full price for anything. They prefer not to. And even if the children of an aging parent are willing to pay full price, they may have a financial advisor (a.k.a. their spouses) who says no.

And Mrs. M's Castle, Too

A declining birth rate, fairly steady divorce rate, and a tendency toward cohabitation in lieu of marriage has compounded the dilemma by adding extended families to this parent care issue, as well.

Consider Dan and Lois Wallace. Dan is a fifty-one-year-old Bank of America senior vice president. His wife Lois, forty-eight, works as a partner in a large local accounting firm. Together they gross about $220,000 a year, enough to pay their $2,500-a-month mortgage, $1,100-a-month car payments, $1,500-a-month private school tuition, and $10,000-a-year contribution to the college education of Dan's children from a previous marriage. Dan's mother died two years ago and his aging, widowed father is now living with them -- a tense but tolerable situation. So where does this "extended family" stuff come in?

Recall the words *previous marriage* from the last paragraph? Dan was married before. His first wife died nearly ten years ago from cancer. He was very close with her mother, a widow, and has remained so ever since. In fact, he has continued helping out his ex-mother-in-law financially, even after remarrying, and his wife, Lois, has no problems with this since she gets along fabulously with "Mrs. M" (Dan's affectionate nickname for the woman). Currently capable of living alone, Mrs. M will do fine in her present housing situation, but Dan worries about her as she ages since she has no siblings and her daughter was an only child. While open to continuing to help out Mrs. M in any way they can, Lois does not see how, with Dan's elderly father already living with them, Mrs. M could come to live with them also, or how they could assist her more financially -- especially since Lois's own parents aren't getting any younger either.

Now in their seventies, Lois's folks are generally in good health except for her dad's increasing forgetfulness. Hoping that it's not serious but deep down suspecting it is either dementia or Alzheimer's, she prays they can live in their home for a few more years before she has to help them consider other options. Since her mom has already declared that she will never move to a retirement home, Lois assumes that it is her responsibility to take in her mother just as Dan did his father!

Welcome to the twenty-first-century American family, where the image we once held of the traditional family unit -- man and woman, first marriage, two kids and a dog, white picket fence -- now represents just 12 percent of American households. The other 88 percent is made up of second and third marriages, with or without children, same-sex unions, widows, and widowers, all living in a variety of housing situations ranging from Mom and Dad in a house that's getting too big for them, Mom or Dad living alone, plus extended families from two, three, sometimes four sets of relationships and generations living alone or sharing space together. Whew! That's a lot of people with a lot of big-time choices to make about housing -- and a lot of complexities to deal with in making those choices.

An Emotionally Charged Issue

Staying in one's home becomes a huge challenge when people get older, especially if a debilitating illness strikes. The majority of homes in America built before 1980 were not designed to accommodate the needs and accessories that often come with old age, such as wheelchairs or walkers. Electrical systems in older homes were not designed to handle the AC requirements of the many different pieces of medical equipment needed for today's elderly, who are living longer lives, often in infirmity.

<u>Reality Check</u>

Parental Myth: "From a psychological standpoint, it's really better for me to be in my own home than in a care facility with a lot of strangers."

Fact: Yes, I've heard the same thing said about solitary confinement. The truth is, the elderly who subscribe to this myth think they will always have the ability to come and go under their own steam, embracing the outside world or retreating from it as they please. But then they suddenly find themselves in a wheelchair, unable to leave their home without special assistance, and the place becomes a prison.

And for seniors suffering from spells of dementia or a crippling disease like Alzheimer's, health issues combine with logistic and security concerns as well. For example, a door left unlocked at night or a wrong turn at the end of the garden could spell the difference between life and death.

In spite of all the practical reasons for doing so, engaging parents in the issue of what to do if and when their castle becomes too much for them is so emotionally overcharged it's like asking them to consider what will happen if they get divorced. Divorce is a hypothetical every married couple may be willing to acknowledge but few will want to indulge much time speculating upon.

There are so many ancillary decisions connected with the stay-or-leave strategy of the house decision, as well as so many by-product decisions that are no less stressful to make, it's no wonder families put off having the house conversation. As I wrote at the beginning of this chapter, it can be an emotional roller coaster.

So, what can you do to get your parents to sit down and face this issue with you? How can you get them to open up their feelings to you so you can develop a solution together?

The House Conversation

The CARE process is a perfect vehicle for getting into a discussion about the house issue. It gets parents thinking about a future when they are no longer living in their house but elsewhere, and to envision that future in a way that will make them feel good about it.

Keep in mind that you are not asking them to make a stay-or-move decision now, although quite often they will feel inclined to start the ball rolling after going through the house conversation with you. That is why I've included a useful house repair checklist tool and resource list at the end of this chapter for you and your parents to use when that ball starts rolling.

However, if your parents feel you are *pressing* them to make a decision now, it will typically lead to such responses as: "I'm never leaving here. They'll have to carry me out!" "I could never get this house organized enough to be able to sell it." "Who would buy this old place anyway?" And they will shut down on you emotionally, ending all hopes of a fruitful discussion for the time being.

Your objective is to get your parents to reflect on what events or other triggers would prompt them to reconsider living where they are now, and to articulate their feelings to you. For example, an offhand comment from Dad like "there seem to be a lot more steps in this house than there used to be" will tell you a lot about where his head really is on that score. The CARE process will help you smoke this out.

How to make my house senior friendly:

Certified Aging-in-Place Specialist (CAPS)

The Certified Aging-in-Place Specialist (CAPS) designation program teaches the technical, business management, and customer service skills essential to competing in the fastest growing segment of the residential remodeling industry: home modifications for the aging-in-place. www.nahb.org

1. **Challenges**

"Mom and Dad, tell me what crosses your mind when you think about continuing to live here in your own home and taking care of it or moving elsewhere if it would make life easier."

The idea here is to uncover what troubles them most deeply about the prospect of continuing to live on their own in the house as they grow older or having to move to an unfamiliar location in their golden years. The responses you get will be as varied as there are styles of houses.

Typically, what will emerge from these responses is an expression of overall panic at the prospect of losing control over some, or many, aspects of the house issue -- for example, not knowing when to make a decision about the house, and perhaps making it too late, thus getting stuck with costly last-minute repairs or having to sell at a financial loss.

DOs and DON'Ts

However extreme or overboard some of their concerns and anxieties may seem to you, DON'T minimize or dismiss them. To your parents, these worries are substantial and very real. Your role is to help them transform these challenges into a set of realistic possibilities for achieving a positive experience. It is up to them to minimize or dismiss what worries they may have about staying or moving by exposing those worries to the light of day and weighing them without feeling judged.

Here are some of the most commonly expressed concerns and anxieties that cause parents to put off making the house decision:

- "The house is in need of so many repairs."
- "The market is soft. We'll lose so much money if we sell!"
- "After commissions, taxes, and bank costs, we wouldn't have anything to live on if we sold."
- "We are not leaving this house...we can bring in help."
- "We have great neighbors that will keep a check on us."
- "We have each other and that is all we need..."
- "Where would we go, everything is so expensive?"

The responses you get from asking the challenges question will assist you and your parents in developing a list of every fear they have about *making* a decision regarding long-term housing. Once those fears are exposed, they can be addressed.

A typical list of challenges raised by this question might look like this:

- Can't sell
- Too little money
- Too many repairs
- Bad market
- Tight credit
- Bad local borrowing
- No place to go

- Expensive future repairs
- Expensive current repairs
- Won't maximize value
- Will never see you

What do you do, now that your parents have acknowledged their fears of making a decision about staying in the house or moving out, and have spelled those fears out for you? The next step is to find out what options they see that will enable them to address these challenges and create a positive outcome.

2. **Alternatives**

"Mom and Dad, let's discuss some of the options that you think might be available to you in dealing with the challenges we just discussed."

The goal here is to shift the focus from apprehension over thinking about the housing issue to what your parents might gain. Some of the alternatives they come up with will surprise them. For example:

- "Sell the house and pocket the money to increase our other savings and investments."
- "Rent the house and use the extra income to supplement our new-home needs."
- "Remodel the house to allow a caregiver to occupy it jointly."
- "Take out a reverse mortgage and stay in the home."
- "Sell the home to one of the children and let them pay us payments."

From these and other responses, you will be able to compile another list -- this one of the realistic possibilities your parents have (and are now able to acknowledge) to enjoy as good and perhaps even more rewarding, a life by making a decision about the house rather than avoiding the issue.

3. **Resources**

"Mom and Dad, let's think of some resources that you are familiar with already that we could use to help maximize your options and minimize these challenges."

By posing this question to them, your parents will begin to recognize that they have many more resources at their disposal, both of their own and outside the family, to help them with their house decision. For example:

1. Get the house appraised to determine its true market value.
2. Have a handyman service preview the house and come up with a suggested repair list.
3. Contact a home health care agency to do an assessment of what it would take to alter the house to allow them to stay there as they age.
4. Contact a local property-management company to see what their house may rent for.
5. Contact a caregiver's association to see what the cost and requirements of a live-in caregiver would be.

4. **Experience**

"Mom and Dad, think about the long-term care experience you would ideally like to create for yourselves as a result of the housing decisions you will have made, and tell me what that experience would look like."

Keep in Mind

Your parents' decision to leave their castle is an acknowledgement of the cycle of life. It is their statement to the world that they are entering the next phase of the human experience. Like many of life's transitions, it will bring a mixture of sadness and joy. There will be a temptation on the part of your parents (perhaps even yourself) to emphasize the former and ignore the latter -- in other words, to see this transition as a conclusion that says something is over. But it is not over; it has simply become *different*.

Your parents may need some prompting here to get them going. This is, after all, a difficult question to answer even if one has been considering the prospect of leaving one's home. Contemplating leaving is a whole lot different from actually doing it. But once your folks have exposed the reasons why they feel they cannot leave (the negatives) and put them out on the table, it becomes easier to open their eyes to the positives.

Once you get started, you will be surprised at how hard it will be for your folks to stop coming up with more and more positives. This is because they will now recognize the pluses in their life and the circumstances that make facing the house decision less troubling. In turn, this will empower them to want to make a decision because they will now feel emotionally prepared to confront the issue.

Some of their responses to the experience question might go like this:

- "We no longer have to worry about the upkeep and maintenance of the grounds and the structure."
- "We are able to travel without worrying about something happening while we are gone."
- "We don't have to set aside money for maintenance and repairs."
- "We're able to increase the money we had invested in the house."
- "We don't have to worry anymore about our children disagreeing over what we do."
- "We have more time to do more things for ourselves."

From typical responses such as these, you will be able to develop a list of positives that will help spur your parents to action. I call these positives "experience accelerators," and some of them might be:

- Marketable location
- No mortgage debt
- Have maximized existing potential
- Willing to move

These accelerators, when put on paper in black-and-white, will help your parents minimize the fears they have about confronting the house issue, much less deciding it, and maximize the things that excite them about resolving that issue. They will thus be in a positive frame of mind to make a decision now -- whether the actual move will be a month from now or a year from now -- so that you can work together to plan for it strategically.

Think about the story of John and Edna that began this chapter; if they and their children had engaged in the house conversation using the CARE process, they would have reached a consensus together that, for the moment at least, there's no reason for John and Edna to have to pack up and find new digs right away. Other than spending a little bit of cash for pool maintenance and perhaps hiring somebody for yard work, they're fine economically, certainly for a few more years. As for John's woodworking shop, that's his vision of the ideal. With a bit more procrastination, he may avoid going in there altogether. But by keeping the workshop idea alive in his mind, he is creating a psychological hedge that provides him with hope for the future and a way to anchor his current life.

Largely because of John's personality, he and his wife Edna will very likely stay in their current dwelling longer than they should, until illness or infirmity strikes one or both of them and they have no other choice but to move to the Merrywood nursing home and assisted-living residence they've been considering. But if they had gone through the CARE process and made the decision to stay in their home for as long as possible, they would have been able to plan for that eventuality rather than being suddenly faced with it.

> ### Keep in Mind
>
> Cell phone technology may be the next best thing to being there, but it isn't the same as being there, and for seniors *being there* is what counts. A sense of community is important throughout our lives but especially as we grow older. The idea of moving out of their house or apartment into a nursing home produces great anxiety in the elderly if they see it as severing the web of connections -- familial, social, medical, legal -- they have established over the years and disrupting their sense of community.

To Sell or Not to Sell

For many seniors, the home is their greatest source of equity and potential income in retirement. Whether they access that income through a reverse mortgage (see chapter 4, "The Money Conversation"), a line of credit, selling the home so they can afford a move to smaller, less expensive quarters, or by renting out a portion of the home for income purposes, the vast majority of seniors may have to depend upon their castle to support themselves in some way in their later years, no matter how well-fixed they may otherwise be.

Let's say the consensus is that moving elsewhere -- apartment, assisted-living residence, or other type of care facility -- is the best option. The obvious next question is whether to sell the house, rent it, or hold on to it. Working through this question really involves just a few straightforward considerations, after which even Hamlet would have little difficulty making up his mind:

1. Is the market favorable or unfavorable to sell?
2. How long will it take?
3. If your parents sell, how much can they get?
4. If they rent, how much expect to pay?

For help with these and many other questions regarding your home contact a professional who specializes in seniors' needs and who understands the housing market in your area. They should understand your specific care needs and other housing options that may be available.We have designed a process called The Parent Care Housing Solution™ and have trained professionals called Parent Care Housing Specialists™ to help you navigate this complicated and confusing issue. To find a list of our trained professionals visit www.parentcaresolution.com.

If your parents don't need the equity from a sale to live on, or rent money to get by, they may want to hold on to the home so they can come back to it if, for example, their facility stay is not permanent, or they may want to keep it for future generations. In this case, they will want to preserve that equity for as long as possible. This can be done in several ways.

One is to transfer the house into a residence heritage trust. This is an irrevocable trust that holds the real estate as a fractional or interval-ownership asset used by family members as, for example, a second home or community retreat, whereby they contribute equally to its upkeep and maintenance. Any competent attorney can set up such a trust; the trick is to provide safeguards against potential inter-sibling bickering and rivalry.

Alternatively, the house can be sold and the equity placed in a family heritage trust. This is another irrevocable trust that can be designed to survive generations. The trust principle can then be invested for growth or income (or both) to meet the needs of family members as they arise.

In the final analysis, the "stay or go" decision is really about safety. Parents may want to stay in their home but may not be safe there for a number of reasons: injuries from falls, inability to come and go, inability to follow a medicine or food regime required for their health, or a myriad of other daily financial or personal-management issues. It is important to understand that no parent except those in the most fragile physical or mental state will ever cheerfully give up their independence. At some point you must exercise that judgment for them. They will probably be angry at first, and you may feel unappreciated and perhaps overwhelmed with self-flagellating guilt for "taking their home." If so, just remember this: your responsibility here is not to make them happy but to make them safe.

A Seller's Checklist

Most contracts for selling a house require that an inspection be made and accepted by the buyer prior to sale. To avoid surprises once a decision is made by your parents to sell their house and move, use the following tool before putting the home on the market. It is designed to help your folks get an idea of what they need to do to maximize the investment, the market value, and the equity in their home.

A member of the National Association of Realtors, a certified appraiser, or another marketing specialist in the real estate field in your parents' area can then take the information you gather on this form and determine which repairs and other maintenance activities would be the most valuable to undertake to preserve or maybe even to increase the home's market value.

The Parent Care
<u>House Repair Checklist Tool</u>

Item	Fair	Good	Excellent	Repair	Estimate
Roof quality					
Windows					
Frames					
Sills					
Doors					
Frames					
Locks					
Body					
Walls					
Paint					
Plaster					
Wall Coverings					
HVAC					
Plumbing					
Kitchen					
Bath					
Exterior					
Fencing					
Guttering					
Sprinkler System					
Appliances					
Refrigerator					

Stove				
Microwave				
Insulation				
Pavement				
Tiling				
Kitchen				
Bath				
Patio				
Pool				
Electrical				
Indoor				
Outdoor				

Checklist to make Your Home Senior Friendly:

Household Tips

A home that's perfectly convenient for people in their 50's and 60's can actually become an obstacle in their 70's and 80's. The first tip in making your home more senior-friendly is to simply eliminate clutter- one of the best solutions in preventing accidental falls. Also be sure to move lamps. Extension and telephone cords out of pathways and remove any throw rugs that slide or tape them down. Another good tip is to add lighting everywhere. Seniors need twice as much light to see clearly as someone in their 40's. Full-spectrum bulbs are a good option because they can reduce glare. Also consider replacing round doorknobs with levers, and light switches with illuminating rocker switches. They're easier to use for those with arthritis. And to better accommodate wheelchairs or walkers you can easily widen your doorways (two inches) with inexpensive offset door hinges. It's also wise to have handrails installed in hallways and wherever steps are present.

Bathroom

More home accidents happen in the bathroom than any other room.

Some solutions to consider:

- Bath/shower: Add non-skid mats both inside and outside the bath/shower to reduce chances of slipping and falling. Install grab bars for additional support (they come in all styles and colors). And consider getting a hand-held, flexible shower head and a bath/shower chair for bathing comfort and safety.
- Sink: If you have arthritis or limited hand strength, replacing twist knobs with lever handle faucets can make a big difference.
- Toilet: If you have problems with leg strength or balance, adding a raised toilet seat extender (it adds two to four inches) and grab bars next to the toilet will make getting up and down a lot easier.
- Other tips: Install a water-resistant, wall-mounted phone in or near the bath/shower in case of a fall. To avoid burning yourself, add anti-scald devices or turn down the water heater to warm or 120 degrees. And don't forget a nightlight for those middle-of-the-night trips to the bathroom.

Kitchen

This is another room that can cause a lot of physical stresses on the body. Some correctable areas include:

- Lighting: Brighten up your countertops with easy-to-install under-cabinet task lighting
- Cabinets: Replace cabinet and drawer knobs with D-shaped handles. They're more comfortable to grasp for those with arthritis. And replace cabinet shelves with sliding, pull-out shelves – this lets you access items much easier

Appliances: If you're in the market for new appliances, choose a refrigerator-freezer with side-by-side doors, so everything you use regularly can be placed at mid-shelf range. Dishwashers with a drawer design are easier to load and unload.

· And have it installed on a raised platform to eliminate bending over. Stoves that open from the side are easier to get into because you don't have to lean over a hot door. And a countertop microwave is also easier to reach and safer versus one above the stove.

· Extras: Install a peg board with hooks for pots, pans and utensils that's easy to get to, as opposed to bending over to retrieve them from lower cabinets. And get a "reacher" (18 to 36 inches) to reach items on high shelves.

Outside

Install motion sensor lights outside the front and back doors and driveway so you're never in the dark. Put a small table or shelf outside the entrance to hold packages while you unlock the door (remote control door locks are also available at moderate prices). And for walker or wheelchair users, there are easy-to-install add-on ramps for the front steps and mini ramps to go over high entrance thresholds.

Savvy Tips: For more information on senior home modification tips, including where to find products and contractors to install them, visit www.homemods.org. Visit www.savvysenior.org

Resources

American Institute of Architects   1-800-242-3837
www.aia.org

Contractors   Check with State boards for all projects over $500. They are required to have a license.

Handymen   The Handyman Connection
www.handymanconnection.com
Home Owners Club of America
www.HOCOA.com

Interior Designers   American Society of Interior Designers (ASID)
1-800-755-2743
www.asid.org

Remodelers   Division of National Association of Homebuilders
1-800-223-2665
www.nahb.org
Look for CAPS certified professionals

Repairmen   Home Advisor
(www.homeadvisor.com)
Check out their project Calculator

A Continuing Conversation

Older people can get along quite nicely in their homes for some period of time if they have a little extra help. That help really comes in two forms: at-home nonmedical care and at-home medical care. Sometimes the two types of care come into play simultaneously.

At-home nonmedical care includes outside and inside house maintenance and upkeep, grocery shopping, minor repair work, errands, driving assistance, laundry, dry cleaning, etc. At-home medical care can run the gamut from having someone stop by to make sure medicines have been taken to a range of treatments such as physical therapy, respiratory therapy, at-home dialysis, diabetic care, blood pressure/ cholesterol checking, speech therapy, rehab work, dental care -- you name it. When you consider the range of both medical and nonmedical at-home services that are available, one may ask why the transition to a care facility would be necessary at all. I address this question in the next chapter, "The Professional Care Conversation," but let me just reinforce the idea here that care facilities do play a vital role, especially in the later stages of life when more demanding care needs present themselves.

7

THE PROFESSIONAL CARE OR LEVELS OF CARE CONVERSATION

The Care Continuum

To stay or not to stay? That is the question your parents will have started on the road to deciding, with your help, by the conclusion of the previous chapter, "The House Conversation." If the decision is not to stay in their current home but to move to a smaller house or apartment in the not-too-distant future, they will have begun thinking about the process of doing that as well -- again with your help. The house conversation does not end here, however. It is a progressive conversation that continues with the next stage, the professional care conversation, because the question of whether "to stay or not to stay" will crop up again as the years roll by and your aging parents come to need additional and more sophisticated care and attention on a professional level.

The professional care facility experience in the United States moves along a broad continuum that looks like this:

Non-Medical Home Care
Medical Home Care
Retirement Community
Assisted living
Special care
Nursing care

Acute nursing care
Hospice
Internment

As a person moves along this continuum in the aging process, the need for professional care and services of different kinds increases accordingly. More specialists are brought in, more complex systems are encountered, and, therefore, more complicated health maintenance options must be considered. If you are having the professional care conversation, then you and your parents recognize that they are somewhere on that continuum right now. The purpose of this conversation is to learn where, so they will be able to make the facility-housing decision that is best and most appropriate for them.

Reality Check

Parental Myth: "All care facilities are alike so it really doesn't matter which one I choose."

Fact: Care facilities are as different from each other as are the people who staff them and the people who live in them. I have visited so-called top-ranked professional care facilities and walked away from them with an impression of coldness and distance. I have visited Medicaid-run facilities and experienced the opposite. And vice versa. Care facilities are micro-communities with their own culture and language. It's important for parents to have a sense of whether they can connect with that culture and language.

Types of Facilities and Care:

The professional care conversation is just not about doing a building inspection. It is about the kinds of care facilities available, what each of them offers, and how they conform to the needs and expectations your parents have. For example, if your parents love art, southwestern colors, and spacious, clutter-free rooms, moving to a facility with institutionally painted walls, tile floors, and indoor/outdoor carpeting will not be all that conducive to their continued mental (and, therefore, physical) health and well-being. Conversely, in the latter stages of Alzheimer's, it's difficult for an individual to differentiate between a luxury hotel room and a closet, so the impact of their environment on their mental health and well-being will be less important. Proximity to family and simple availability of space in the facility of choice are part of the professional care equation as well.

Here is where you and your parents will get down to the nitty-gritty of spelling out the structure of care they want and will need delivered by the facility they are considering, and the level of support required to deliver that care:

- **Non-Medical Home Care and Medical Home Care:** The trend today is for seniors to get help at home for as long as possible. This is preferred and a more economical way to grow older. Non-Medical care (often referred to as custodial care) provides services like taking parents shopping, buying grocers, lite house work, running errands, help them dress, and remind them of medications. This care can be helpful to extend the length of time that a parent can stay at home. When the parent needs medical care such at a daily IV or medicine by injection a medical home care provider can be brought into the home.

- **Retirement Community.** A retirement community (or sometimes referred to as Independent Living Community) most resembles the traditional neighborhood or community in which your parents have probably lived, except that all the inhabitants are your parents' age or older. Modern retirement communities are much like planned unit developments where there are numerous support services, recreational opportunities, and community creation situations. Medical services, nursing staff, pharmacies, even a mini hospital can be found in most modern retirement communities. While some retirement communities offer full facility integration (retirement community to nursing home), the vast majority of such communities are segmented according to lifestyle and health capabilities. Probably the most well-known national retirement community model is Del Webb Sun City, found in various cities throughout the country.

- **Assisted Living.** Assisted-living communities offer quasi-independent living within a single structure concept, with shared common areas such as dining and recreation, while allowing the residents who are able, to occupy single or double apartments within the facility. Usually round-the-clock nursing care is available with a physician on call. Mobility is usually an issue, so many assisted-living communities have a variety of planned outings and opportunities for the residents. Two well-known national assisted-living models are Brighton Gardens and Sunrise Assisted Living.

- **Special Care.** Special care is a euphemism for pre-nursing-home care. In this situation, a resident is usually afflicted with a chronic illness such as Alzheimer's disease or Parkinson's that renders the person a danger to him- or herself and others. Twenty-four-hour nursing care and staff attention are present, with either an off-site physician on call, or, at larger special care facilities, a full-time physician on staff. Special diets and meds are the norm in this type of facility. Again, Brighton Gardens and Sunrise Assisted Living are examples of facilities that offer these stand-alone capabilities, thus providing the ability to transition the resident from the assisted-living side to the special care side within the same facility as the need arises.

- **Nursing Care.** Nursing care is the choice when a senior requires the administering of specific medications and therapies of a medical nature and is unable to do this him- or herself or with the help of a family member. Nursing care may be accomplished through at-home medical care organizations, whereby visiting nurses or therapists stop by the patient's home and administer whatever is needed of a medical or therapeutic nature. Many seniors prefer to have this type of care rather than relocate to an assisted-living or special care facility. This type of care usually suggests a medical condition that is stabilized but has the potential to deteriorate and demand additional therapy that can only be provided at a facility.

- **Acute Nursing Care.** Acute nursing care is provided in facilities such as hospitals and state-run or private nursing homes because the person's mental or physical condition is in such a serious state of decline that the presence of twenty-four-hour down the hall medical attention is required. While there are many private acute nursing care facilities in the country that accept private-pay patients, the vast majority of such patients are dependent on Medicaid from the federal government distributed through the states.

- **Hospice.** A hospice is almost exclusively concerned with the terminally ill. The emphasis here is on acceptance of the inevitable and keeping the person as comfortable as possible. Great attention is paid to helping the individual organize his or her affairs as well as helping family members achieve closure. Many terminally ill patients may choose to remain at home until the end; hospice accommodates this choice by making at-home visits to give medicines, aid in personal hygiene, provide companionship and conversation, and even help out with the shopping.

- **Internment.** The final resting place of the individual after services or cremation. Many seniors prefer to make these arrangements themselves years in advance so as to relieve the family of this burden during a time of grief and stress.

- **Continuing Care Communities.** These communities typically offer three levels of care on one campus. They allow you to stay in one location as your level of care increases, without the stress of moving from one facility to the next. They most often include Independent Living, Assisted Living and Special Care. Some even offer Hospice Care.

Meet the Weinsteins

Douglas and Joann Weinstein, a couple in their early seventies, have decided to leave their family home of nearly twenty-five years and make the transition into a retirement community called Seven Springs Village, which is typical of many communities now available throughout the United States for housing our country's elderly.

They have selected Seven Springs Village because it offers, all in one location, every level of professional care they will ever need, beginning with the freedom of the retirement community experience, followed by the opportunity to transition to assisted-living apartments, a fully staffed special care unit, and then, when and if required, a hundred-bed nursing facility with acute care capabilities, located in a small corner of the development.

The Weinsteins will first be going into the independent-living section of Seven Springs Village; its housing options range from small-lot, ranch-style homes and zero-lot-line homes to quadruplex arrangements with separate porches but shared communal areas. As the Weinsteins are still able to drive, they have chosen one of the ranch-style homes with a single-car garage. In this particular section of Seven Springs Village (which, by the way, is a completely gated, secure community) they will be able to enjoy walks, a community social center, and access to an on-staff registered nurse, dietician, and physician available 24/7.

In this independent-living section, the Weinsteins will have the option of shopping for groceries at the Seven Springs food market and cooking for themselves, taking their meals (breakfast, lunch, and dinner) at the Seven Springs dining facility, or having their meals delivered via Seven Springs catering, a food service available to them at several different price levels depending on the types of meals chosen and the frequency with which they are delivered. In addition to these amenities, Seven Springs provides on-site classes on a variety of subjects, plus other educational opportunities as well as daily outings and weekly excursions for all but those who are bedridden or too infirm to participate.

All yard work and maintenance of their new quarters is attended to by Seven Springs Village staff and included in the Weinsteins' homeowner's dues. Furthermore, as homeowners, they can sell their ranch house to whomever they want, whenever they want, and move elsewhere at any time. For example, should the couple's level of independence change and their health deteriorate, they have the option of selling their ranch house and paying a monthly care fee to transition to the Seven Springs assisted-living home and receive all of the same amenities and a greater level of care. The option also exists that if one spouse can no longer live independently, but the other is able to, the latter can stay on in the ranch house while the other can move to a small apartment in the assisted-living section, and both parties can still remain in close proximity to one another.

Another very important reason that Douglas and Joann Weinstein are choosing Seven Springs is that Douglas has a family history of both Parkinson's and Alzheimer's. He is concerned that should he develop either of these diseases -- or, God forbid, both of them -- that he not be separated from Joann by having to move to another care facility. Seven Springs offers all the levels of medical care and attention Douglas will ever require, all in one locale.

Seven Springs Village is an excellent choice for the Weinsteins because it will enable them to transition from their existing home to similar surroundings without experiencing the stress of a dramatic change in environment. At the same time, they will be relieved of many of the day-to-day burdens that are becoming increasingly difficult for them to handle as they age. Seven Springs, like many other care centers being built across this country, is designed to fully accommodate the developmental path of aging seniors and to respond to their changing needs.

The Weinsteins would not have made the decision to transition to a professional care facility let alone have chosen Seven Springs Village if it hadn't been for their two children, Rachel and Adam, who had attended one of my seminars. Having observed the difficulties their aging parents were increasingly having living totally on their own, Rachel and Adam decided to initiate the professional care conversation with them. The conversation got their parents to focus on the challenges they would face in moving from their longtime home to a professional care facility from a holistic point of view, by considering the experience they would want to have as they moved along the care continuum through each phase of the transition process.

Here's how the conversation between Rachel, Adam, and their parents, Douglas and Joann Weinstein, was structured, so that you can adapt it to your situation.

1. **Challenges**

"Mom and Dad, tell me what goes through your mind when you think about needing some form of elder care in the future."

The Weinsteins:

- "Not knowing what's available to us."
- "Not knowing how to plan for what might happen to us down the road. A facility that is good for us now may not be good for something that happens to one of us later."
- "Not being locked into a decision that we couldn't change if we needed to."
- "Keeping as much of our freedom as possible and not having to give up all our decision-making abilities."
- "Not having our money so tied up that we'd lose everything if we changed our mind."
- "Not knowing what type of care we need -- or will need as we age."
- "Not being separated from each other if one of us becomes ill."
- "Not being too far away from our temple and all of our friends."
- "Not being able to leave anything to you kids because we've spent it all on housing ourselves in our dotage."

1. **Alternatives**

"Mom and Dad, let's discuss some of the options that you think might be available to you in dealing with the challenges we just discussed."

The Weinsteins:

- "Keep physically fit for as long as possible so we can stay put."
- "Use a service like Home Instead Senior Care to help us with grocery shopping, housekeeping, yard work, running errands, and other things that are getting to be too much for us."

- "Find a caregiver to live with us."
- "As long as you kids can stop by every now and then and check on us, that wouldn't be so bad."
- "If there comes a point when we cannot take care of ourselves or can't remember to, then we'll just trust you kids to decide what's best for us."
- "We do love seeing you and whether that's here or someplace else, we want to stay in close touch."
- "Maybe a retirement community to start with; we would want a facility that allowed us to live pretty normally unless or until we were really sick."
- "No place where there are just sick people all around, unless we're in the same boat."
- "If we get really sick, we could go to one of those assisted-living places like your Auntie Yentl. They let her alone in her apartment except when it's time to eat, and even then she doesn't have to eat unless she wants to. They even let her keep her cat and dog as long as she can take care of them."

2. **Resources**

"Mom and Dad, let's think of some resources that you are familiar with already that we could use to help maximize your options and minimize these challenges."

The Weinsteins:

- "If resources include money, then we have the money to live most anywhere we choose."
- "We could do research on our own and look to you kids to help us 'surf the Net' for more information."
- "Get recommendations from friends who have already made this decision."
- "Our attorney has lots of experience helping people with these types of decisions, as does our accountant."
- "We know somebody that we can talk to who may have an ownership interest in one of those assisted-living communities."

3. Experience

"Mom and Dad, think about the professional long-term care experience you would ideally like to create for yourselves as a result of the decisions you will have made, and tell me what that experience would look like."

The Weinsteins:

- "We would like to still feel as independent and in control of our lives as we do now, but without all the headaches."
- "We would want to feel safe, but not like Big Brother is keeping us under twenty-four-hour surveillance."
- "We would like to be with people who are like us, who are interested in the same things we are, and who don't define every day as either AD or BC ('after disaster' or 'before calamity')".
- "We may look and sound old and be a bit unsteady on our feet, but we still look forward to every day. So, we would want to feel that we have moved to a place where we are not just waiting to die and having the occasional visitor drop in to see if we did."
- "We love life and each other and want to be able to continue doing both even if we can't live on our own."
- "If we eventually do have to go into a special care type of place, we would still want our surroundings to be as upbeat as possible."

Choosing a Facility -- the Critical Questions to Ask

Once your parents understand the level of care they need and want, use these questions to assess the list of appropriate care facilities you are helping them to consider. Give each facility a yes or a no for each question.

> ## <u>Keep in Mind!</u>
>
> The subject of professional care may have a multitude of meanings for your parents. It may mean the actual physical day-to-day care they will want and need -- from seeing to it that they get their morning coffee and newspaper to making sure they take their daily meds to changing their soiled undies. It may also mean the emotional attention your parents want from you at this stage of their life but may not be able to articulate. In fact, the most challenging, the most sensitive, and ultimately the most rewarding part of the care conversation will be the decisions you make with your parents about the expectations they have of you and how you will be able to meet those expectations. (See also in the book: The Attention Conversation on page 159).

When you are finished, the facility (or facilities) with the most checks in the yes column goes to the top of your list.

1. **Do the buildings and the grounds create a good impression?**
   Yes [ ] No [ ]

Here's an easy clue to look for on this one: If the building is in need of repair, the grounds are not kept up, and the grass is chronically too high, it is almost a given that the kitchen will not be in much better shape in terms of upkeep and cleanliness. It is easy to see that grass needs mowing, but not so easy to spot E coli on a countertop. Therefore, go with the law of integration: the way the outside of the facility looks is probably the way it is managed inside.

2. **Is the floor plan easy to understand and follow?** Yes [ ] No [ ]

If *you* have trouble finding your way around the place, your aging parents will have a progressively tougher time of it, which can be dangerous in the event of a fire, power outage, or emergency. The physical layout of the facility should be free of complexity, making it easy to find the residence area, dining room(s), main exits, fire exits, administrative offices, and public restrooms. Listen to your own instincts: if *you* think you should be dropping breadcrumbs to find your way back from the tour, imagine the trouble your parents will have.

3. **Are all the important rooms in the facility wheelchair-accessible?** Yes [ ] No [ ]

Mobility is essential for residents to experience full integration into, and enjoyment of, their life in a care facility. All the rooms in the facility -- not just the resident's room, dining room, and activity room -- should be fully accessible by wheelchair since this will ensure accessibility to residents requiring any other type of mobility aid, such as a walker or just a cane, at any stage in their residency. If there is a platform at the front of the facility for loading and unloading wheelchair-bound residents, be sure there is an awning over it. Trying to maneuver a wheelchair-bound family member into a waiting vehicle while exposed to the elements is guaranteed to transform what is already a stressful moment for all concerned into a potentially full-fledged disaster. There should also be ample attendant staff to help assist residents with indoor and outdoor mobility.

4. **Are elevators and ramps available for the physically challenged?** Yes [ ] No [ ]

While Congress has mandated a number of improvements care facilities must make in this all-important area, many facilities are still playing catch-up. Make sure there are ramps throughout the facility that will enable wheelchair-bound residents access to all vital locations. Elevators should be large enough to allow a wheelchair-bound resident and an attending staff member easy maneuverability inside. Ask the director of the facility to show you the route wheelchair-bound residents must take in an emergency should the elevator system fail -- or in the event of a fire, when residents are typically warned *not* to use elevators. Employ your common sense here and pretend that you are a wheelchair-bound person using the facility on a daily basis or experiencing an emergency.

> ## Reality Check
>
> **Parental Myth:** "By the time I go there, it won't matter at all what the facility is like; I won't know anyway."
>
> **Fact:** Nothing could be further from the truth. Elderly patients in care facilities may not remember who you are or why you came to see them or the names of the staff treating them or the time of day, but they respond every bit as you and I do to a kind word, a gentle touch, a hug, or other gesture of connection from you and from those treating them.

5. **Are all essential shelves, closets, and storage spaces easy to reach?** Yes [ ] No [ ]

A resident's physical abilities decline over time, so drawers and shelves for storing clothes, closets for hanging jackets, and so on should be within easy reach even if not used on a daily basis. Bathrooms should be roomy enough to keep soap, shampoo, toothpaste, grooming supplies, and other items easily accessible. A nightstand by the bed with a couple of drawers for various items is also a plus. While it's easy to say that things can be stored out of the way under the bed, imagine how arthritic knees and hands are going to react to retrieving those things when needed. And in memory-impaired residents, things out of reach or out of sight under a bed may as well be located in deep space.

6. **Are floor surfaces skid proof and floor coverings securely fastened?** Yes [ ] No [ ]

The floors of a care facility should be clean and well-scrubbed, but not slick and dangerous. If a resident is allowed to bring floor coverings such as a throw rug or a carpet for his or her room, make sure the policy is that these coverings be installed with the utmost safety in mind, since this ensures every other resident must follow the same policy too. Throw rugs should be placed on nonskid matting and be free of frayed or upturned edges. Carpets should not be too thick or of a weave that might cause a shuffling resident to trip and fall. Housekeeping staff should monitor floor conditions in residents' rooms at all times.

Ask the management what policies and procedures are in place for preventing risk to residents in the event of hazardous situations such as spilled water or food items. A puddle of water or mashed potatoes thrown on the floor by a resident and not detected right away are, like spilled orange juice or grapes dropped in the aisle of a supermarket, accidents waiting to happen. Every facility should have portable barriers similar to the concrete barriers used on interstate highways to keep residents out while floors are being cleaned, messes eliminated, or minor maintenance completed.

7. **Is there an abundance of natural and artificial lighting?**
Yes [ ] No [ ]

Proper lighting throughout the facility -- in common areas, residents' rooms, dining halls, hallways, dayrooms, restrooms, and so on -- is an important consideration. Your parents may be entering the twilight of their lives, but that doesn't mean they should have to live in the dark. Each resident's space should have sufficient natural light available to them from a window as well as artificial light from ceilings, nightstands, and wall outlets. Wattage and color output should be appropriate to the resident's needs. Some residents are ultrasensitive to fluorescent light. Many times, bedside lamps or reading lamps are too dim or too bright, and not easily adjustable by the resident. Many female residents find it difficult to apply their makeup under fluorescent light conditions. Also, beware care centers that mimic the institutional feel of lighting at KGB headquarters or the interrogation rooms on *Law & Order*. It's a downer to visitors and residents alike.

8. **Is the facility clean, fresh smelling, and free of odors?**
Yes [ ] No [ ]

The way a care facility smells tells you a lot about management philosophy. All care facilities should have a policy of checking at least every hour on residents who are prone to soiling themselves. Not only is wearing a soiled garment uncomfortable to the resident, it's a health hazard and an unpleasant olfactory experience to the resident and everybody else, as well. There will always be the natural aromas of food or coffee in the air as well as the smell of cleaning agents used in keeping the facility spotless. But it's the intensity of those aromas and smells that counts. Beware of care facilities that smell like the county landfill or a Pine Sol manufacturing plant. That means something is *definitely awry.* Flowers should be present in communal rooms and allowed in residents' rooms. There should be air fresheners in every bathroom, common shower, and bathing area. Closets should be free of soiled clothing, and food should not be left on serving trays or in rooms for an extended period of time.

9. **Are heating and air-conditioning units capable of handling individual usage and facility demands?** Yes [ ] No [ ]

In South Carolina, where we live, the temperatures in the summer can hover near the 100 degree mark for over a month. A lesser heat wave claimed nearly seven hundred lives, primarily the elderly, in 1995. Thus, it is imperative that the heating and cooling systems in residents' rooms are capable of adjusting to such extreme conditions as well as accommodating the temperature requirements of each resident. This flexibility is important because for every resident who complains the room is too cold, another resident will claim it's too hot. This is not as important a consideration in retirement communities as it is in assisted-living, special care and nursing home situations where temperature extremes can cause accelerated dehydration. Ask the facility manager or supervisor about the capacity of the building's heating and cooling systems should demand run high in conditions of sustained extreme cold (zero degrees for a week or more) or extreme heat (100 degrees for two to three weeks). Also find out the emergency backup plan for replacement power should utility service fail. Forewarned is forearmed, as the saying goes.

10. **Are handrails installed in appropriate places such as hallways and individual bath units? Yes [ ] No [ ]**

I remember walking with Dan and his father in his care facility one day, when out of the clear blue his right leg gave way. Were it not for the railing along the corridor wall, he would've suffered a nasty fall. While it is impossible to imagine any care facility in our post-OSHA and ADA age not being equipped with adequate handrail and other support devices, I suspect there may still be some relics around.

There should be handrails installed throughout any special care unit and strategically placed in assisted-living units. All railings and similar support devices should be firmly fastened without any give or play.

Bathrooms for all residents should have supports enabling them to steady themselves if need be and to bear their entire weight for short periods.

11. **Are there clear fire and emergency escape plans with exits clearly marked? Yes [ ] No [ ]**

The disaster movie *The Towering Inferno* made an indelible mark on my young psyche when I saw it back in 1974. It impressed upon me that even the best-designed structures are subject to catastrophe under extreme circumstances, when things often don't work as planned. Always think the unthinkable about the care facility you are considering. Exits should be clearly marked, and the residents should be able to understand the facility's exit strategy well enough to explain to *you* what they are to do and where they are to go in the event of a fire or natural disaster such as a tornado or windstorm. There should be enough staff on duty to assist each resident if need be in the event of an evacuation, as well. Never just assume that management has thought about these things and has a plan in place. Ask for specifics.

12. **Is the facility financially solvent? Yes [ ] No [ ]**

While most facilities will be reluctant to let you look through their income statements and balance sheets, if you ask they will usually reveal how many months of operating cash reserves they have on hand in the event of emergencies. The local Better Business Bureau is another source for determining how solvent a facility is because there you can find out if it has been the subject of any fiscal complaints or litigation. Also check any records of lis pendens ("suit pending") in the files of your local courthouse to see if the facility is subject to creditor claims or actions. You can also use your own eyes as a resource to gauge how flush a facility is just by eyeballing how cash is being spent in the place.

If the facility appears to be understaffed given the number of residents, if the furniture and fixtures are unduly worn and the supply closet bare, you can guess pretty accurately that the facility is operating on a tight budget.

A less traditional method of getting a fix on the money situation is to ask management what the facility's "rolling resident occupancy rate" is. Residents, you see, are a source of cash flow; just as in a motel or hotel, the ability to provide services is dependent on occupancy and room rate. The higher the occupancy and room rate, the more services will be available.

My *favorite* nontraditional method of monitoring a facility's cash flow status, however, is to pop in at mealtimes and see what's being served. The fresher the vegetables, the greater the variety of protein sources, and the more natural the starches and carbohydrates, the better the facility's cash flow and overall solvency probably are. Here are a few clues: no matter how well-cooked, broccoli is never beige; there are more parts to chickens than just wings; and a slice of ham is not translucent if held up to the light.

13. **Is the facility adequately staffed and in good standing with regulatory agencies?** Yes [ ] No [ ]

Without sufficient support staff at the facility, you will find yourself making countless trips to the emergency room at the hospital to retrieve your parent after treatment for problems of as little seriousness as an attack of gas! All states have guidelines as to the appropriate number of staff per resident a facility is required to maintain. Like the FDA's recommended daily allowance for vitamins, however, these are *minimum* standards.

Each facility should have enough staff members to ensure the following: (1) if a staff member fails to report for duty, a substitute can be found and on the job before that staff member's shift is over; (2) there is enough staff to ensure that baths, daily cleanings, and resident meals are served on time and without unnecessary delay; (3) that all medicines are dispensed with the frequency and in the dosage expected per documentation.

Furthermore, there is absolutely no excuse today for inadequate background checks on all current personnel and those applying for future openings. The Internet allows even the oldest of care facilities to easily ascertain information -- from past pedophiliac acts by individuals, to prom dates -- on almost any individual.

14. **Is there a registered dietician or nutrition expert on staff?**
Yes [ ] No [ ]

Whether it's a retirement or assisted-living community, special care unit or nursing home, expert nutrition and meal advice is critical to the health and well-being of residents. The elderly often find themselves caught in a "perfect storm" of nutritional conundrums: little or no appetite to begin with, plus mandatory medicines that kill appetite, plus declining physical abilities that limit exercise and decrease appetite.

> ### TIP! Interacting with Staff
>
> I have seen the offspring of the elderly in assisted-living, special care, and acute care facilities treat staff members as if they didn't exist or as if they were their parents' personal servants. These staff members are typically underpaid, overworked, and often completely unappreciated for the services they perform. As someone who has helped serve meals and clean up the dining room on weekends along with staff throughout Dan's father's five-year stay at a care facility (I still help out at this facility on weekends), I know for a fact that most of the folks working there are angels in disguise. Most people are not up to the task of doing for one day what these folks do every day. So, unless you see a staff member commit a terrible infraction, ease up.

These combinations are recipes for disaster. A registered dietician or nutrition expert on staff at the facility will make sure that your parents are eating enough, eating the right things, and eating responsibly in relation to their current physical state and medical protocols -- for example, that diabetics do not have free-range access to the dessert bar and that Alzheimer's patients aren't allowed to eat like lumberjacks when they can't remember when they last ate (which was twenty minutes ago).

15. **Does the facility maintain an in-house nurse or available physician on call 24/7?** Yes [ ] No [ ]

Granted, having nurses and physicians always on call is expensive, probably the most expensive line item in a care facility's budget. But they are a must. Ideally, there should be a registered nurse or physician on staff 24/7 at acute care facilities. If not, find out what the response time is for the nurse or physician the facility has on call 24/7. With today's cell phones, pagers, and Blackberries, response time should be close to immediate. But if the response is a recording that says, "You have reached the medical offices of Doctors We Don't Give a Flip, please leave a message and we'll get back to you as soon as we can during normal office hours," look for another facility.

TIP! Emergency Services Policy

Most care facilities have access to emergency medical personnel through the 911 system or speed dial to the emergency room at the local hospital. If the hospital is Boston General, the process is going to be a little more complicated than if it's Mayberry General and Aunt Bee who answers the phone there. The local fire and police departments are often staffed with EMTs as well, who can perform on-site diagnostics or at least transmit the vitals to the people who can diagnose. The larger consideration is the facility's policy for using emergency services. In a health care environment shell-shocked by an onslaught of malpractice litigation, a knee-jerk response policy is more often the rule than the exception. A severe headache demands less acute treatment than a heart attack, but they both require a reasonable response policy. Emergency transport and treatment are expensive. But in the end it is better to err on the side of caution and send someone to the ER unnecessarily a couple of times than to not send him or her there the one time it is critical to do so.

---

16. **Is the nearest acute care facility or trauma center close enough to provide fast response?** Yes [ ] No [ ]

Most populous areas in the United States offer relatively fast access to an acute care or trauma hospital by highway or air ambulance. A good rule of thumb is for the care facility you choose to be no more than thirty minutes to an hour away from a trauma center and to have excellent transport capabilities (an ambulance equipped with state-of-the-art technology and not Bob the night-man's Explorer with seats folded down to spread Dad out on an army blanket). Response time will vary from location to location depending upon availability and weather conditions. Conversely, if the local EMT response time is always "We'll get back to you after dinner and see what we can do," consider a care facility with better capabilities and trauma center connections.

17. **Does the facility offer a written plan of care and have the flexibility to adapt it to the residents' changing needs?** Yes [ ] No [ ]

A written care plan is important for several reasons. First, it spells out the type of care provided to elderly residents so that you, the layperson, can get a pretty good idea of what your parents can expect to receive. Second, a written care plan will usually stipulate that you are allowed to meet the staff or the managers supervising the staff who will be providing that care so you can ask questions. This written plan is what I call the "parent operating system" (POS) for your folks while under the facility's care. Make sure to go over it with your parents carefully. And take the initiative to get updates so that you will know if the POS has been modified. A sudden change in your parents' physical or mental state as a result of such a modification could prompt a change in their medical condition that will need to be addressed in a change of medical protocol. Do not just assume that everything is happening according to plan or that if a change occurs, or is required; the facility has the ability to flex and is right on top of things.

The Ten Warning Signs of Negligence and Neglect

In a care facility where there are dozens, sometimes hundreds, of patients all suffering from various complaints, ailments, and illnesses to different degrees, one cannot expect a perfect record of care all the time. Why not? Environment is one reason - it's a care facility, not the Four Seasons. Staffing is another reason. Care facilities are staffed by wonderful, dedicated people with the best of intentions. But overcrowding, overwork, and stress take a toll. Expect the ball to get dropped from time to time. But there is a vast difference between your dad not having his pitcher filled with fresh water one day and his being medivacked to a trauma center due to acute dehydration. Look at trend lines. One day without a bath could mean your mom slept late, didn't want a bath, or was too difficult to handle that day. An entire week without a bath means someone isn't doing their job.

Warning Sign 1: *Your parent's personal hygiene is not being attended to on a daily basis.*

Oily hair, food particles in the teeth, and body odor are sure signs that bath time and brush time are being neglected. Pay particular attention to toenails and fingernails, as they are more disease-friendly than almost any other part of the human body. Toenails, especially in diabetics, can be a source of infection and disease if not trimmed properly.

Warning Sign 2: *Your parent is noticeably losing weight.*

This could be a function of a number of things: not eating, not taking in enough calories, improper diet, onset of diabetes, depression, or undetected cancer. Any weight loss noticeable enough to get your attention should be getting the staff's attention first.

Warning Sign 3: *Your parent is always asleep, listless, or unaware of your presence when you visit.*

These symptoms could be signs of a deteriorating physical condition, excess or inappropriate medicines, depression, lack of exercise, or perhaps even an unbearable roommate. It's normal for the elderly to have good days and bad days -- and more of the latter the older they get. But unless your mom or dad is in the final stages of a chronic, fatal illness, it's not normal for them to be having a bad day every time you visit.

Warning Sign 4: *Your parent complains of mistreatment by staff.*

Granted, older people complain more than young people (except for seventh-grade girls, who complain all the time in my experience as a parent), but even older people are not inclined to complain constantly *unless there's a reason.* Sure, they will create mountains out of molehills just to get attention or spawn tales of mistreatment and how "awful this place is" simply because they suddenly may not want to be there. But don't assume this is the case. *Investigate* all *complaints of mistreatment!* Somewhere between "the food here stinks" and "Nurse Betty came at me in the shower with a knife," there may be an element of truth worth pursuing.

Warning Sign 5: *Your parent has unexplained, frequent, and unusual bruising or pressure marks on the body.*

Nursing home abuse and neglect are staple fodder for newspapers, periodicals, and made-for-TV movies. And the reason why, is that such abuse occurs -- more frequently than we would like to believe. Imagine being in a room with your elderly father or mother bitching about everything to the tenth power. Multiply that by the number of other residents in the facility, all of them bitching about everything to the tenth power as well -- all day, every day. Some environments are just conducive to abuse. But that's no excuse for it.

Warning Sign 6: *Your parent's personal belongings keep vanishing.*

Disappearing socks or underwear, a missing wristwatch, a vanished ball cap can be the result of several things: your parent's laundry got mixed up with that of another resident; your parent left it in a room he or she was visiting but can't remember which room; it was stolen by another resident; someone visiting your parent's roommate picked it up and put it away thinking it was the roommate's; some of the facility's staff members have light fingers. The way to prevent all this from happening is to print your parent's name on each item he or she takes to the facility

> ### <u>TIP! Keeping Tabs</u>
>
> Presumably, you wouldn't leave a toddler off at day care and not check back for weeks at a time to see if he or she were safe and healthy. Well, the same goes for your parents at a care facility. The best way to make sure they are being well taken care of is to see and talk to them frequently -- and to regularly check on the care facility's treatment protocol to see that their program of care is being adhered to. If you cannot physically visit your parents often, then call them at least weekly and follow up with a telephone call to the staff member in charge of administering your parent's care. There is no excuse for not staying in touch with your parents at their care facility and keeping up on their physical and mental well-being, no matter how far away it is from you.

or adds while living there. Keep an inventory of these items and run a periodic check to make sure all are present and accounted for. If not, check with the laundry service to see if it has the socks or underwear that disappeared. Keep an eye peeled for a resident wearing your dad's missing shirt or a staff member with his vanished Seiko.

Warning Sign 7: *Your parent keeps going AWOL.*

Most care facilities are required to log a resident out and in again when he or she goes off premises and returns. Unauthorized departures must be logged, as well. No matter how good the care experience may be, at some point most residents, especially of nursing homes, will come to view the place as more of a prison than a refuge because they're unhappy, scared, bored, or abused (or think they are). Thus, a door left open becomes an invitation to, and an avenue of, escape. In the early days of Dan's father's stay with Alzheimer's, he was aware enough to know that he didn't want to be where he was but not aware enough to remember why. He would loiter in the hallway by the exit doors to the special care unit, and when someone went in or out, he would use his cane to hold the doors open so he could slip away. If your parent keeps trying to "escape" (and is succeeding!), confront the staff right away as to how and why.

Warning Sign 8: *There are increasing unexplained medical and maintenance costs.*

All medical procedures and costs should be itemized for you by the care facility on a separate bill or included as part of your overall statement. Be sure to ask during the initial interview what past increases for basic services have been and what the facility anticipates rate increases to be in the future. Many facilities charge a premium for special care sections for patients with Alzheimer's or Parkinson's disease and other debilitating diseases. Also, in some cases, an expensive drug may be prescribed with the best of intentions but will prove to have little staying power, or may not work at all, yet routinely continue to be prescribed -- and routinely you continue to pay the cost. In my father's situation, for example, he was given a prescription for a costly memory-improvement drug that in the end seemed to have no effect at all. Review any drug recommendations in consultation with your parent's physician.

Warning Sign 9: *Your parent's skin is overly dry and cracking.*

There may be a number of explanations for this: dehydration, the temperature in the facility is kept too hot, the air is too dry and the resident needs a humidifier, lotions or creams are not being applied to your parent's skin to ease the problem. A good care facility will have a dermatologist available for consultation in the event you and/or the staff notice undue dryness on your parent's hands, elbow joints, or around their eyes. Keeping skin lubricated is often overlooked in older residents, but dry, flaky skin can be the breeding ground for nasty infections.

Warning Sign 10: *Your parent complains of chafing or rash in the buttock area, or you observe the presence of small ulcers on the back and legs.*

Bedsores are not a medieval phenomenon. They occur almost routinely in the elder population, especially those who are bedridden for extended periods. Most facilities will have a protocol for making sure that immobile or bedridden residents are shifted frequently so that pressure sores or ulcers do not develop. Rashes and irritations often appear around the buttock and groin area on both men and women due to incontinence and sitting in soiled undergarments for extended periods. Candidly, in any modern care facility there is no justification for the presence of bedsores or the irritations described. If you see your parent developing them, confront the nursing supervisor or the facility's director of physical therapy *immediately.*

TIP! It's Not Just About
<u>Holidays and Birthdays</u>

Typically, when they reach the point where professional care is required, what the elderly need most to sustain them are the three *c's*: connection, community, and conversation, especially with the children whom they brought into this world. Statistically, the average stay in an extended care facility is between four and six years. Step up your visitation scheduled to include more than just birthdays and holidays.

What to do if I notice Neglect with my parents' community?

1. Discuss the concerns with management and staff and document your findings? If this continues, let me know actions will talk place.
2. Contact your state ombudsman to report your concerns.

What Does an Ombudsman Do?

Long-term care ombudsmen are advocates for residents of nursing homes, board and care homes and assisted living facilities. Ombudsmen provide information about how to find a facility and what to do to get quality care. They are trained to resolve problems. If you want, the ombudsman can assist you with complaints. However, unless you give the ombudsman permission to share your concerns, these matters are kept confidential. Under the federal Older Americans Act, every state is required to have an Ombudsman Program that addresses complaints and advocates for improvements in the long-term care system.

This is the contact for South Carolina:

State Long-Term Care Ombudsman
A. Dale Watson, State LTC Ombudsman
Lt. Governor's Office on Aging
1301 Gervais Street, Suite 350
Columbia, SC 29201
Work: (803) 734-9900
Website: http://www.aging.sc.gov

If you live in other states you can find your office at:
www.ltcombudsman.org/ombudsman

You may consider an attorney who works with bringing cases against assisted living or nursing homes. You can do an internet search for "nursing home abuse lawyers" and find those in your area or visit www.martindale.com.

National Resources for
<u>Locating a Professional Care Facility</u>

Home Instead Senior Care   www.homeinstead.com

Retirement Living Information Center www.retirementliving.com
                203-938-0417

Senior Resource   www.seniorresource.com

American Association of Homes and www.leadingage.org
Services for the Aging   202-783-2242

Adult 55+ Communities   www.seniorhomes.com

Covenant Retirement Communities www.covenantretirement.com
                773-878-2294

WEBB Active Adult Communities www.delwebb.com
                800-808-8088

A Place For Mom   www.aplaceformom.com

8

THE ATTENTION CONVERSATION

Remember the words to the Cat in the Cradle? The words read:

Cat in the Cradle by Harry Chapin

A child arrived just the other day...He came to the world in the usual way. But there were planes to catch, and bills to pay. He learned to walk while I was away. And he was talking before I knew it and as he grew, he said, "I'm gonna be like you, Dad, you know I'm gonna be like you". And the cat's in the cradle and the silver spoon, little boy blue and the man in the moon. When you comin home, Dad, I don't know when, but we'll get together then, you know we'll have a good time then. My son turned ten just the other day He said "Thanks for the ball, Dad, come on let's play; can you teach me to throw?" I said, "Not today, I got a lot to do". He said "that's okay" and he walked away but his smile never dimmed and said "I'm gonna be like him, yeah you know I'm going to be like him". And the cat's in the cradle and the silver spoon little boy blue and the man in the moon when you comin home, Dad. I don't know when, but we'll get together then, you know we'll have a good time then. Well he came from college just the other day so much like a man I just had to say, "Son, I'm proud of you, can you sit for a while?" He shook his head, and he said with a smile, "What I'd really like, Dad, is to borrow the car keys. See you later, can I have them please?" And the cat's in the cradle and the silver spoon little boy blue and the man in the moon. When you comin home, Son? I don't know when, but we'll get together then, Dad, you know we'll have a good time then. I've long since retired, my son's moved away. I called him up just the other day. I said "I'd like to see you if you don't mind". He said "I'd love to Dad, if I could find the time. You see my new jobs a hassle, and the kids have the flu. But it's sure nice talking to you, Dad, it's been sure nice talking to you........" And as I hung up the phone it had occurred to me he'd grown up just like me, my boy was just like me.............And the cats in the cradle and the silver spoon little boy blue and the man in the moon. When you comin home, son, I don't know when, but we'll get together then, Dad, we're gonna have a good time then.

The song is about the journey of life and how busy we can get and how we wished we could have more visits with the people we love. One of the key conversations with parents is to define the frequency, level of attention, and method of attention they would like. Without this conversation, the relationship between parent and children can be filled with manipulation and the feeling of falling short with the level of attention. With this conversation, parents and children can have a healthy relationship with attention that meets the needs of the parents.

The Speed of a Computer Chip

We love the story of John Glenn when he returned from space and was asked: "As you sit there with the rocket getting ready to launch you into space....what were you thinking?" He said, "I couldn't stop thinking that this rocket was built by the lowest bidder. A funny comment, but here is another truth about that trip. Some believe that we have more technology today in our wrist watch than they had to take them into space.

Technology has certainly changed many things in our world and much of our world has been impacted by the technology that came directly from the space program. With knowledge and some training many seniors can do much more with technology to stay in touch with their adult children and grandchildren. To better use technology, we may have to overcome some mental hurdles and get some additional training.

Reality Check

Parental Myth: "Seniors want to hang around playing shuffle board but don't want to learn or use technology."

Fact: Pew research project says that as of April 2012, 53% of American adults age 65 and older use the internet or email. Though these adults are still less likely than all other age groups to use the internet, the latest data represent the first time that half of seniors are going online. After several years of very little growth among this group, these gains are significant.

As of February 2012, one third (34%) of internet users age 65 and older use social networking sites such as Facebook, and 18% do so on a typical day. By comparison, email use continues to be the bedrock of online communications for seniors. As of August 2011, 86% of internet users age 65 and older use email, with 48% doing so on a typical day.

Looking at gadget ownership, we find that a growing share of seniors own a cell phone. Some 69% of adults ages 65 and older report that they have a mobile phone, up from 57% in May 2010. Even among those currently age 76 and older, 56% report owning a cell phone of some kind, up from 47% of this generation in 2010.

Reality Check

Parental Myth: "Young people think that communication with their grandparents via email is too old fashion."

Fact: Some grandchildren may be embarrassed with close contact with their grandparents, but I think the numbers are very few. Many would welcome the ability to email or text their grandparents. Many young people would think their grandparents are the coolest around....especially if the grandparents bought them the technology in the first place.

From Reel to Reel to Flash drive...

It is hard to imagine the change that has occurred in technology in our parents' lives. Many of them sat by the radio and listened to President Roosevelt's fireside chats and updates about our soldiers during World War II. After the war, they saw dramatic changes in radios, appliances, cars, airplanes, electronics, and then the invention of the computer chip. Many seniors embraced the changes as an improvement of the American way of life.

A few seniors prided themselves in the statement, "I don't have a computer and I don't want a computer." For some, the computer was a step too far, a luxury, a gadget that was not worth the money or the time it would take to learn how to operate it. While some don't want to learn, an education in what a computer can do could help seniors to be open to learn how a computer can bridge the communication gap.

TIP! Choose a Facilitator

Teaching your parents about the computer may be a task that requires more time than you have. However, many community colleges or tech schools offer beginner computer classes. I bought mom her first computer and encouraged her to sign up for the computer class. She learned the basics of the computer and then used the computer to print out things for her Sunday school class. About the time we started to send more emails, was the time she began to decline mentally.

Technology and Communication Conversation

1. Challenges

Challenge with Attention:

"Mom and Dad, as we think about staying in touch in the future, what are some of the challenges that you see that we could face?"

Here are some of the responses you may get to this question:

- "You are busy...and think you will forget about me..."
- "You live three states away..."
- "I would love to see you every day and get a hug....but I know that is not possible."
- "How can we find a balance between my expectations or desires and you living your life?"
- "You may not take the time to write a letter or send me a card..."
- "I may not see you as often as I like..."
- "You have grown kids with family now and they may want to see you on the holidays."

Challenge with Technology:

"Mom and Dad, as we think about staying in touch in the future, the computer can be a great tool for us to communicate; what challenges do you think we may face in using the computer and technology to stay in touch with each other?"

Here are some the responses you may get to this question:

- "Computers are very expensive...we can't afford one of those..."
- "We are just too old to learn about these modern computers..."
- "Young people waste too much time on computers....we don't have time to waste." (this one may be true)
- "I wouldn't even know how to turn a computer on...much less...operate one..."
- "I see no reason at this age...since I am not working why I need a computer..."
- "I will leave technology to another generation..."
- "I can send a letter the old fashion way or just make a phone call."
- "I am open to learn...if you will teach me..."
- "I would like to learn to connect to the grand children in their language..."

<u>Reality Check</u>

Parental Myth: "The Computer has no practical use for me as a senior..."

Fact: Showing a senior the practical uses of a computer can often change their mind on why the computer would be a great thing for them to have and learn.

1. **The Computer can increase communication:**

   If seniors can see the use for email, Skype, and an active blog or website as tools to increase their contact with the grandchildren, they may be motivated to learn how to use the technology.

3. **Research Tools:**

   The active seniors of today use the internet to research travel plans, investigate their hobbies, stay current with news and sports, and even listen to their favorite music.

4. **Mind Games:**

   The internet also has a number of mind game websites that can help seniors strengthen their minds. Websites like lumosity.com can provide regular exercises for strengthening the mind.

Two best nights…

I (Kevin) had just set up my iTunes account and learned how to download music and make a CD. So after dinner, I took Mom and Dad into my study and sat them down. I said, "Let's take a walk through your life of music. I want you to tell me about some of your favorite musicians and artists of the 30's, 40's, 50's and to the present." When I got them started it was amazing. I learned about Glenn Miller, Johnny Reeves, Johnny Cash, Charlie Pride, and a host of others. I learned about Polka music and other dance music I had never heard. At the end of the night, I had their collection of music all on one CD. They were amazed and cherished the CD for several years to come.

On another night, with my mom, we sat in my office and I asked her to tell me about some of the funniest comedians she could remember. We spent the night laughing to the humor of Red Skelton, Phyllis Diller, Carol Burnett, Bob Hope, and others. These were two uses of technology that helped me connect with my parents in a very memorable way. You may want to try it with your parents.

2. **Alternatives**

Conventional Methods:

"Mom and Dad, as we consider our alternative about how to give you attention and us stay in touch, what alternatives should we consider?

Answers you may get:

- · "I would like for you to call me at least a couple times per week."
- · "I would like an old fashion letter once in a while."
- · "I would love it if you would have the grandkids surprise me with a card from time to time."
- · "I would like to see you if possible on or around the holidays."

- "I would be willing to help pay your way to come see me on your birthday."
- "I would be willing to learn technology if someone would teach me."

Technology:

"Mom and Dad, let's discuss some of the options and ways that you may use technology, the computer, and the smartphone to make our ability to stay in touch more enjoyable..."

This conversation will let you know how much exposure your parents have had with the computer. Does the computer intimidate them or are they comfortable?

One way to get them comfortable is to show them the various things you can do with a computer. Show them several things like:

How the internet works...

Many times we assume that everyone knows what the Internet is all about. However, to someone who is brand new to the computer, you may want to explain that the internet is a system of wires and networks that allows us to access unlimited information.

You may start by showing them how www.google.com works. Begin by searching in their areas of interest. You might search for new cars, or how to garden, or how to do home repair, or look at some of the golf or cooking sites. If you can find their hot button it can be a catalyst in getting them excited about using the computer.

How to send and receive emails...

Show your parent how to set up an email account through folks like aol.com, gmail.com or yahoo.com. Send an email to the grandchildren (your children) and show Mom and Dad how the technology works. I know that many of you seniors know more than all of us about technology so don't let me sound overly bias that all seniors don't know technology.

Explain to Mom and Dad that you and your children would love to start sending pictures and emails on a regular basis. Some parents will then take this to the next level with Facebook and even their own family website.

How Skype works...

For many of us, seeing is believing; that is why Skype.com has quickly caught on as a means to add a face to a voice. Work with your parents to set up a skype account and then get the computers and or cameras needed to make the technology work. Skype can be a great tool for parent care so you can actually hear and "see" how your parents are doing. The grandparents who live far away will also get a big thrill out of seeing the grandchildren on skype on a regular basis.

How www.youtube.com works...

A key part of aging is maintaining memories from the past. I am amazed at all the videos you can pull up on www.youtube.com. Help your parents make a list of "favorite singers of the past" or "favorite TV shows" of the past or "favorite comedians of the past." Once your parents know how to search things on www.youtube.com, they can virtually entertain themselves for hours and remember the great moments of their lives.

How smart phones work...

Many seniors have cell phones. Some think that the "smartphone" is an expensive luxury and for some that may be true. However, show them what smartphones can do and how they can be used. One of the most important may be how a parent could find their way home with google maps or how we can locate them with the phone if they are lost.

How a family website can be created.

There are a number of websites on the internet that provide posting for a family to have their own website. This is a place where you can post family events, photos, memories and the like. Such a project could be a great hobby for a parent and an invaluable resource of information for the family. Some may also get into the family tree and enjoy such a hobby at websites like www.ancestry.com. Technology can trim many years off the building of family ancestries.

How Facebook works...

More and more seniors are learning the magic of Facebook. Don't assume your parents will not like it. Show them how and watch what happens.

Another use of Technology

When I (Kevin) first relocated my mom to Columbia, South Carolina, I put her into an independent living community. It worked well for about a year and then I began to notice mom declining in some areas. She was putting her clothes on backward or inside out. I would call her at 10 a.m. and she was napping and I believed that she was not sleeping well at night. I felt I needed another set of eyes to monitor the situation.

I talked with a friend who owns a security company. We agreed to install two cameras in her room so I could sign on from the internet and monitor mom's activity. In less than a month my suspicions were confirmed. Mom was getting up at 1 or 2 a.m. and starting to get dressed to go to breakfast. I would call her and sometimes be able to coach her back to bed. Other times she would leave her room and I would have to call the front desk at the community and ask if they would escort her back to her room. After several weeks of monitoring and watching, I was sure that it was time to move mom from an independent living community to an assisted living community. Technology gave me a set of eyes to monitor parent care in real time. This technology was invaluable.

---

3. Resources

Conventional Method:

"As we define the right level of attention, communication, and contact.... what resources do you think we might consider?"

Responses:

- "I would be willing to pay for the grandchildren to come spend time with me..."
- "I am willing to pay for gas money for you to come and stay in a hotel."
- "I would be willing to pay for your smartphone and mine if you will call me and stay in touch."

Technology:

"Mom and Dad, as we think about getting more comfortable with computers and technology, can you tell me what currently you have in resources and how we can help find other resources?"

As you have the technology and communication conversation with Mom and Dad, you will want to seek out these answers:

1. Do they currently have a computer?
2. How old is the computer?
3. Have they taken classes on the computer? Are they willing to take classes on the computer?
4. Where are classes taught in your area?
5. Can they type?
6. What other technology do they have or need?
7. You may discuss: a digital camera to send pictures, a camera for Skype, an iPod or iPad, a mini video recorder, and an upgraded computer.
8. How much money do they have or are they willing to put into technology?
9. What kind of cell phone do they have?

4. **Experience**

"Mom and Dad, think about us using technology to stay in touch...how often and in what ways would you like for us to stay in touch with you?

Some parents and children talk daily.....some monthly.....some weekly... some once per year...some not at all. How often do you and your parents talk?

When you ask this question you may get:

- "We don't want to be a bother to you."
- "I know how busy you are and I respect that."
- "I only want to call when it is an emergency."
- "You have your own family and your own life"

It is hard, but important to communicate to parents, that they are not a bother and that you want to communicate with them as much as possible. Coming to some agreement on the various ways that technology can help you stay in touch can make for a closer relationship with your parents.

Send them a Song

My positive mom (Kevin) recently blessed us with her version of using technology. She is quite a good singer so she put together a list of her favorite Christmas music and went to a sound studio in Orlando, Florida and recorded about 15 Christmas songs. The CD featured her picture, the title of the CD and the listing of all the songs. Listening to it while she is still alive brought tears to my eyes. I know that it will be a family treasure for years to come when she is no longer with us. Technology like this can allow parents to communicate to their children and grandchildren for generations.

Technology in the Right Hands

A client of mine recently lost his father at age 88 very suddenly. As hard as it was for him to lose him, he said, "You know, if I have to go, I want to go the way my Dad did." I said, "What do you mean?" he said, "Dad went ice skating on Tuesday, drove his Porsche on Wednesday, and then died at his computer on Thursday. His wife had called down to the computer room in the basement and when she got no answer, she discovered he was gone. Sign me up to exit at my computer, using it as a tool to enrich the lives of others."

Technology can add years to your life…I wish you well on your parent care journey and I hope you will add the technology and communication conversation to your parent care conversations.

Best Websites to Learn about the Internet and Computers:

http://www.gcflearnfree.org/internet
http://www.skillfulsenior.com/index.php
http://www.bbc.co.uk/webwise/guides/what-is-the-internet
www.good50.com
http://www.microsoft.com/about/corporatecitizenship/citizenship/
giving/programs/up/digitalliteracy/default.mspx

9

"The Identity Theft Conversation"

Trust with Verification

I was at church one Wednesday night about fifteen years ago and a gentleman came up to me and asked, "Kevin, have you ever heard of identity theft?" I thought he was one of the conspiracy theory guys who was one fry short of a happy meal. I responded, "I don't think I have; can you explain it to me?" He said, "That is when someone takes your social security number, your address, your date of birth, and driver's license number and they become you." I said, "Do what!?" He went on, "then they can take out loans in your name, clean out your bank accounts, and destroy your credit." I listened cautiously that night, but since then I have verified just how real identity theft is and how damaging it can be. Enter our parents "the greatest generation." They come from a world where you sat on the front porch and drank lemonade. Everybody knew their neighbor so they didn't bother even locking their doors at night. To think that a total stranger would take their identity and then do them harm was unthinkable! So having the "identity theft" conversation has become more important than ever in the parent care conversations.

Reality Check

Parental Myth: "Identity Theft has never happened to me or anyone else I know…does this really happen to people?"

Fact: Visit the www.ftc.gov website and on the front page you will see the link "identity theft". When you go to the next level you will find an abundance of identity theft occurrences and how it has become one of the most frequent complaints for the federal trade commission.

Reality Check

Parental Myth: "I am not going to be applying for credit…why should it matter to me?"

Fact: One of the reasons that seniors are the most vulnerable for identity theft is that they are not doing much activity with their credit. They don't use it and many don't check it. If they do not have a monitoring program in place, their information can be used for quite some time without discovery. That is why it is important to have the "identity theft" conversation to prevent a breach and to have a monitoring system in place for the future.

Know the Kinds of Identity Theft

When you think of identity theft, many only think of financial identity theft, that is when someone steals your personal information to violate your financial matters. However, identity theft goes well beyond the financial.

The 8 Types of Identity Theft

There are several types of identity theft. Knowing what to do if you are a victim of identity theft starts by knowing what type of identity theft you are dealing with.

Financial Identity Theft

When we hear the words "identity theft", we usually think of credit reports and bank accounts. This is called <u>financial identity theft</u>. We hear about data breaches like TJ Maxx (<u>47.5 million credit cards</u>) and Heartland Payment Systems (130 million credit cards) regularly. Our faith in our financial institutions is shaken. Some of us are thinking about stuffing our money in the mattress again. If an identity thief gets access to your bank account, you will want to read up on the <u>Electronic Funds Transfer Act</u> (<u>EFTA</u>)

Insurance Identity Theft

<u>Insurance identity theft</u> is a "new" type of identity theft. Although the problem has always existed, it presents specific problems for the victim that must be addressed independently from other types of identity theft. Of course, all types of identity theft have the potential (or even likelihood) of bleeding over into other types. Generally speaking, <u>insurance identity theft</u> tends to be a concern when you are a victim of <u>medical identity theft</u>, and could also show up as <u>financial identity theft</u>.

Medical Identity Theft

The World Health Organization said this is "the information crime that can kill you." (<u>Read the full publication here (PDF)</u>.) It's not just the most dangerous form of identity theft, it's also one of the hardest to fix. There are very specific areas you will want to look into when you are a victim of <u>medical identity theft</u>, and they are in general vastly different from dealing with any other type of identity theft.

(As a side-note, there is a lot of <u>misinformation</u> concerning the <u>Medical Information Bureau</u> (<u>MIB</u>) when it comes to medical identity theft. Keep in mind that, despite the name of the organization, MIB Group has almost nothing to do with medical identity theft – although if you are a victim of insurance identity theft you may want to consider checking your free MIB report.)

Criminal Identity Theft

Criminal Identity Theft is just as difficult as medical identity theft in terms of resolving the problem. Like medical identity theft, criminal identity theft has a way of coming back to haunt you, even after you think you have the problem resolved. The easiest way to find out if this has happened to you is to get caught speeding. The officer who stops you will run your license and registration. If there are warrants out for your arrest, she/he will give you a pretty set of matching silver bracelets, and free public transportation.

Driver's License Identity Theft

This may be the easiest form of ID theft to commit. Your purse/wallet gets stolen, and your driver's license gets sold to someone who looks like you. Then it's easy for them to get other forms of ID in your name. This type of ID theft spreads to others, especially criminal identity theft.

Social Security Identity Theft

There are millions of people working in America who don't want to pay taxes. It may be an illegal immigrant, a deadbeat parent, or a paroled criminal trying to shake their past. Your SSN may be the most valuable piece of personal information a thief can steal.

If someone steals your social security number, uses it to secure a job, and then they owe taxes and do not pay, you will have the challenge of your life. While the Social Security Administration isn't required to tell you about all these jobs, the IRS will want you to pay the taxes. This can be a tough battle, too. For a non-government agency, the IRS has unbelievable power. Expect a lot of hoops to jump through here. Although it's gotten easier over the past few years, the process is still time consuming.

Synthetic Identity Theft

This is the "latest thing" in the ID theft world. The thief will take parts of information from many victims and combine it. The new identity isn't any specific person, but all the victims can be affected when it's used. It will show up in the areas above, so look to those sections for additional information.

Synthetic identity theft has also been used to describe any act in which the criminal attempts to convince someone they are another person, real or fictional. This careful wording is no doubt reactionary to the US Supreme Court ruling that an illegal immigrant has not committed a crime unless he/she knew the SSN they were using belonged to an actual citizen.

Child Identity Theft

Our kids are a big target for identity theft. Child Identity Theft has become a serious concern in recent times, and there are a lot of articles giving widely varying advice concerning the matter. From a practical standpoint, an 8-year-old won't be looking at his or her credit for at least eight more years, when they decide to get a car and insurance. Sadly, in these cases it is almost always a friend or family member who commits identity theft. This means the parents will usually not want to press charges, and the identity thief counts on that.

The Identity Theft Conversation

1. Challenges

"Mom and Dad, as we talk about identity theft and how it could happen to us all, what challenges might you face in the future in regards to identity theft?

You may get responses like this:

- "How would someone get my social security number and use it for bad?"
- "I never would give my personal information out to a stranger?"
- "Do people really use our information to steal from us?"
- "I have never checked my credit score…is that important to do?"
- "We don't use credit cards; are there other ways thieves could do us harm?"

You want to listen to see if parents understand just how harmful and damaging identity theft can be.

Top Senior Scams

The National Council on Aging offers these
top 10 scams Targeting Seniors:

Top 10 Scams Targeting Seniors

Financial scams targeting seniors have become so prevalent that they're now considered "the crime of the 21st century."

Why? Because seniors are thought to have a significant amount of money sitting in their accounts.

Financial scams also often go unreported or can be difficult to prosecute, so they're considered a "low-risk" crime. However, they're devastating to many older adults and can leave them in a very vulnerable position with little time to recoup their losses.

It's not just wealthy seniors who are targeted. Low-income older adults are also at risk of financial abuse.

And it's not always strangers who perpetrate these crimes. Over 90% of all reported elder abuse is committed by an older person's own family members, most often their adult children, followed by grandchildren, nieces and nephews, and others.

Review our list below, so you can identify a potential scam.

1. **Health Care/Medicare/Health Insurance Fraud**

Every U.S. citizen or permanent resident over age 65 qualifies for Medicare, so there is rarely any need for a scam artist to research what private health insurance company older people have in order to scam them out of some money.

In these types of scams, perpetrators may pose as a Medicare representative to get older people to give them their personal information, or they will provide bogus services for elderly people at makeshift mobile clinics, then use the personal information they provide to bill Medicare and pocket the money.

2. Counterfeit Prescription Drugs

Most commonly, counterfeit drug scams operate on the Internet, where seniors increasingly go to find better prices on specialized medications.

This scam is growing in popularity—since 2000, the FDA has investigated an average of 20 such cases per year, up from five a year in the 1990s.

The danger is that besides paying money for something that will not help a person's medical condition, victims may purchase unsafe substances that can inflict even more harm. This scam can be as hard on the body as it is on the wallet.

3. Funeral & Cemetery Scams

The FBI warns about two types of funeral and cemetery fraud perpetrated on seniors.

In one approach, scammers read obituaries and call or attend the funeral service of a complete stranger to take advantage of the grieving widow or widower. Claiming the deceased had an outstanding debt with them, scammers will try to extort money from relatives to settle the fake debts.

Another tactic of disreputable funeral homes is to capitalize on family members' unfamiliarity with the considerable cost of funeral services to add unnecessary charges to the bill.

In one common scam of this type, funeral directors will insist that a casket, usually one of the most expensive parts of funeral services, is necessary even when performing a direct cremation, which can be accomplished with a cardboard casket rather than an expensive display or burial casket.

4. **Fraudulent Anti-Aging Products**

In a society bombarded with images of the young and beautiful, it's not surprising that some older people feel the need to conceal their age in order to participate more fully in social circles and the workplace. After all, 60 is the new 40, right?

It is in this spirit that many older Americans seek out new treatments and medications to maintain a youthful appearance, putting them at risk of scammers.

Whether it's fake Botox like the one in Arizona that netted its distributors (who were convicted and jailed in 2006) $1.5 million in barely a year, or completely bogus homeopathic remedies that do absolutely nothing, there is money in the anti-aging business.

Botox scams are particularly unsettling, as renegade labs creating versions of the real thing may still be working with the root ingredient, botulism neurotoxin, which is one of the most toxic substances known to science. A bad batch can have health consequences far beyond wrinkles or drooping neck muscles.

5. **Telemarketing**

Perhaps the most common scheme is when scammers use fake telemarketing calls to prey on older people, who as a group make twice as many purchases over the phone than the national average.

While the image of the lonely senior citizen with nobody to talk to may have something to do with this, it is far more likely that older people are more familiar with shopping over the phone, and therefore might not be fully aware of the risk.

With no face-to-face interaction, and no paper trail, these scams are incredibly hard to trace. Also, once a successful deal has been made, the buyer's name is then shared with similar schemers looking for easy targets, sometimes defrauding the same person repeatedly.

Examples of telemarketing fraud include:

"The Pigeon Drop"

The con artist tells the individual that he/she has found a large sum of money and is willing to split it if the person will make a "good faith" payment by withdrawing funds from his/her bank account. Often, a second con artist is involved, posing as a lawyer, banker, or some other trustworthy stranger.

"The Fake Accident Ploy"

The con artist gets the victim to wire or send money on the pretext that the person's child or another relative is in the hospital and needs the money.

"Charity Scams"

Money is solicited for fake charities. This often occurs after natural disasters.

6. Internet Fraud

While using the Internet is a great skill at any age, the slower speed of adoption among some older people makes them easier targets for automated Internet scams that are ubiquitous on the web and email programs.

Pop-up browser windows simulating virus-scanning software will fool victims into either downloading a fake anti-virus program (at a substantial cost) or an actual virus that will open up whatever information is on the user's computer to scammers.

Their unfamiliarity with the less visible aspects of browsing the web (firewalls and built-in virus protection, for example) makes seniors especially susceptible to such traps.

One example includes:

Email/Phishing Scams

A senior receives email messages that appear to be from a legitimate company or institution, asking them to "update" or "verify" their personal information. A senior receives emails that appear to be from the IRS about a tax refund.

7. Investment Schemes

Because many seniors find themselves planning for retirement and managing their savings once they finish working, a number of investment schemes have been targeted at seniors looking to safeguard their cash for their later years.

From pyramid schemes like Bernie Madoff's (which counted a number of senior citizens among its victims) to fables of a Nigerian prince looking for a partner to claim inheritance money to complex financial products that many economists don't even understand, investment schemes have long been a successful way to take advantage of older people.

8. Homeowner/Reverse Mortgage Scams

Scammers like to take advantage of the fact that many people above a certain age own their homes, a valuable asset that increases the potential dollar value of a certain scam.

A particularly elaborate property tax scam in San Diego saw fraudsters sending personalized letters to different properties apparently on behalf of the County Assessor's Office. The letter, made to look official but displaying only public information, would identify the property's assessed value and offer the homeowner, for a fee of course, to arrange for a reassessment of the property's value and therefore the tax burden associated with it.

Closely related, the reverse mortgage scam has mushroomed in recent years. With legitimate reverse mortgages increasing in frequency more than 1,300% between 1999 and 2008, scammers are taking advantage of this new popularity.

As opposed to official refinancing schemes, however, unsecured reverse mortgages can lead property owners to lose their homes when the perpetrators offer money or a free house somewhere else in exchange for the title to the property.

9. Sweepstakes & Lottery Scams

This simple scam is one that many are familiar with, and it capitalizes on the notion that "there's no such thing as a free lunch."

Here, scammers inform their mark that they have won a lottery or sweepstakes of some kind and need to make some sort of payment to unlock the supposed prize. Often, seniors will be sent a check that they can deposit in their bank account, knowing that while it shows up in their account immediately, it will take a few days before the (fake) check is rejected.

During that time, the criminals will quickly collect money for supposed fees or taxes on the prize, which they pocket while the victim has the "prize money" removed from his or her account as soon as the check bounces.

10. The Grandparent Scam

The Grandparent Scam is so simple and so devious because it uses one of older adults' most reliable assets, their hearts.

Scammers will place a call to an older person and when the mark picks up, they will say something along the lines of: "Hi Grandma, do you know who this is?" When the unsuspecting grandparent guesses the name of the grandchild the scammer most sounds like, the scammer has established a fake identity without having done a lick of background research.

Once "in," the fake grandchild will usually ask for money to solve some unexpected financial problem (overdue rent, payment for car repairs, etc.), to be paid via Western Union or MoneyGram, which doesn't always require identification to collect.

At the same time, the scam artist will beg the grandparent "please don't tell my parents, they would kill me."

While the sums from such a scam are likely to be in the hundreds, the very fact that no research is needed makes this a scam that can be perpetrated over and over at very little cost to the scammer.

2. Alternatives

"Mom and Dad, let's discuss some of the options and steps you would take if you were to become a victim of identity theft...."

Responses:

- "I don't know what to do."
- "Where do I turn to get help with the steps?"
- "I already have something in place with my bank."
- "I have a system in place with my property and casualty company."
- "Perhaps I should sign up for a monitoring system."
- "I could research the internet to be more informed about identity theft."
- "I could refuse to give personal information over the phone or the internet without another family member present."
- "I could change my view of the world that the world still works on honesty and a handshake...there are people out there who want to do us harm."

Steps if you are a Victim of Identity Theft

The Federal Trade Commission offers these steps at www.ftc.gov:

Immediate Steps to Repair Identity Theft

If you take action quickly, you can stop an identity thief from doing more damage. Follow these three steps as soon as possible:

1. Place an Initial Fraud Alert
2. Order Your Credit Reports
3. Create an Identity Theft Report

Monitor Your Progress

Resolving identity theft takes phone calls and letters. Create a system to organize your papers and calls, and to track deadlines.

Item	How To Track	Tips
Telephone Calls	Create a log of all telephone calls.	· Record the date of each call and the names and telephone numbers of everyone you contact. · Prepare your questions before you call. Write down the answers.
Postal Mail	Send letters by certified mail. Ask for a return receipt.	· See **sample letters and forms**.
Documents	Create a filing system.	· Keep all originals. · Send copies of your documents and reports, not originals. Make copies of your identification to include in letters.
Deadlines	Make a timeline.	List important dates, including when: · You must file requests · A company must respond to you · You must send follow-up

3. Resources

"Mom and Dad, let's think of some resources that you may be familiar with already regarding identity theft and how to monitor your identity..."

As you begin to explore the resources for identity theft monitoring, here are some of the key programs in the market place:

- Ask your bank what identity theft options they offer

- Ask your property and casualty insurance agent what identity theft protection they have.
- Ask your family and friends what identity theft service they use and if not, why?

List of options to identity theft:

Each of the credit bureaus offer credit monitoring:
www.equifax.com
800-685-1111 (general) or 800-525-6285 (fraud); P.O. Box 740241, Atlanta, GA, 30374

www.experian.com
888-397-3742 (general and fraud); P.O. Box 2002, Allen TX, 75013

www.transunion.com
800-888-4213 (general) or 800-680-7289 (fraud); P.O. Box 2000, Chester, PA, 19022

Note: To "opt out" or remove your name and address from mailing lists provided by these three credit bureaus and other nationwide company (Innovis) to marketers, call toll-free 888-567-8688.

Other Identity Theft Services to research:
www.lifelock.com
www.legalshield.com
www.legalguard.com
www.identityguard.com

Free Credit Report:
www.annualcreditreport.com

Note to adult children: When your parents get signed up on a monitoring system, you may want to also be notified if there is a problem. You may want to review their credit card bills and checking account each month for possible identity theft breaches.

What is the difference between restoration and monitoring systems: Understand that some of the monitory services will alert you to a breach, but it is up to you to solve the problem. A restoration service will monitor and go to work with you to solve the problem and even pay for legal fees.

Department of Consumer Affairs:

Check your state's Consumer Affairs website. They have many resources to help you in the task of educating and teaching you and your parent about identity theft.

Federal Trade Commission:

The Federal Trade Commission website also has some great videos and written material about identity theft. You and your parents can get more information at <u>www.consumer.ftc.gov/features/ feature-0014-identity-theft</u>

Books on Identity Theft:
Identity Theft Toolkit: How to Recover from and Avoid Identity Theft (Reference Series) [Paperback]
<u>John Lenardon</u>

If You Are Me, then Who Am I: The Personal and Business Reality of Identity Theft [Paperback]
<u>J.D. CITRMS John P. Gardner Jr.</u> (Author), <u>CITRMS James D. McCartney CIPPG</u> (Author), <u>Jeffrey M. Omtvedt CITRMS</u> (Author)

THE Silent Crime What you need to know about identity theft Paperback
By Stgeffan McCoy Michael and Schmidt (Author)

4. Experience

"Mom and Dad, thinking about identity theft, what would you like to experience when it comes to keeping your identity secure in the future?"

You may get responses:

- "I would want to know what to expect because this is new to me."
- "I wouldn't want someone to take advantage of us."
- "I would want to learn more about how to protect our private information."
- "I would want to feel safe from these thieves!"
- "I would want to have peace of mind that my assets were protected."

Our parents surely are the greatest generation. They fought, sacrificed, and won the Great War. For them "their word was their bond." They saw…no need for contracts, agreements, or attorneys. With these core values…it is often beyond their comprehension that someone would take their personal information and steal, rob, and pillage them. That is why they need you to "watch their back" and protect them from those who would do them harm. Do your parent care duty and protect them from the identity thieves that seek to part them from their money.

10

THE LEGACY CONVERSATION

What Is a Legacy?

Legacy is about remembering the past in order to make sense of it. Remembering is also about bringing organization to the present so that it transcends the past, and designs a future that integrates all that has gone before, in honor of that past.

History, some might say, is essentially an exercise in revisionism, while legacy falls more into the category of reconstruction: it is a way of identifying and celebrating the progress we have made over the course of our lives. And I guarantee there is not a soul, living or dead, who failed to make some manner of progress during his or her time here on the planet. Being born is by itself a milestone step on the progress path; think of it, 50 million sperm all after one egg-- and yours won out! Learning to speak, to walk, to write, to learn, and to relate, to provide for oneself and others -- all are huge milestones in our personal progress along life's path.

Our legacy is, perhaps, the last step on that path, a summing-up of our life's journey along that path and what that journey has meant to ourselves, as well as what we want it to mean to those who will follow and may even be able to benefit from our having "been here."

Reality Check

Parental Myth: "When I'm gone, I'm gone. I don't care if future generations remember me."

Fact: Of course not. That's why you've got all those albums full of photos dating back to your first-grade graduation and that huge record collection and every cup from Dairy Queen you ever had a date-night sundae in stashed around the house that you say should go to this person and to that person when you're gone. You've kept these things because they're like stored memories of the events, the interests, and the passions that symbolize you. The simple truth here is that parents who make this statement are usually those who want to remember and be remembered the most. My dad said something very much like it in his last years. After I responded, "I know you don't care, but if you did, what would you want everybody to remember?" He talked nonstop for the next hour.

Shattered Legacy

Russell Simpson was the owner of Simpson Products ("Simpson Box" the locals called it), a corrugated container manufacturing company in Austin, Texas. Through his company and on his own, Russell was a big supporter of many local charities as well as the local Methodist church where he and his wife, Ilene, and their three children (two sons and a daughter, all of whom have worked in the family business since graduating from college) attended services every Sunday.

With retirement age looming, Russell Simpson went for his annual physical and was told by his doctor that he had developed an incurable form of cancer; his prognosis gave him about a year. Accepting his fate with the dignity and grace of a man who has lived fully, completely, and is comfortable with his future in the hereafter no matter what form it takes, he immediately went about the business of getting his affairs in order.

He made numerous attempts to talk, one-on-one and collectively, with his three children about what he wanted to happen with the company, the gifts he wanted to make to each of them, and his dream of funding a new wing for the Methodist church that would serve as a combination gym and classroom facility for the kids in the community. But his children were unable to face, let alone talk with, him so openly about his impending demise. On each occasion that he attempted to sit them down for such a discussion, they would either find an excuse to change the subject or reschedule the meeting ahead of time.

Russell went ahead and met with his pastor at the church to discuss his plans for the new wing; based on those discussions, and Russell's assurance that he had the financial wherewithal to bankroll the project, the pastor urged the church board to request proposals from contractors right away in the hope that the new gym and classroom center might be completed in time for Russell to attend the opening ceremonies.

Russell also visited several other organizations -- the Salvation Army, the Humane Society, the Children's Care Center -- to inform them of the donations he would be making to them through his estate, and they too set about making plans accordingly.

Meanwhile, Russell's children remained in complete denial of his condition and all the issues relating to that decision that swirled about them. It was all too painful for them. But then, events took an even more painful and tragic turn.

Two months before Russell was to enter the hospital for his final stages of care, he and his wife Ilene were killed in a freak two-car collision outside of Austin. The loss of their father and their mother at the same time totally devastated the children.

At his death, Russell had yet to finalize his complex estate plan and sign all the required documents. There turned out to be insufficient liquidity in his estate to pay the tax obligations due the government, so the children were forced to bring in a venture-capital partner to raise money to keep Simpson Products in operation and pay the estate taxes. The new partner immediately called a halt to any future donations by the company and refused to honor the financial commitments Russell

Simpson had made to the Methodist church and other charitable organizations. Unfortunately, the Methodist church had committed itself financially to building the new wing and the failure of Simpson Products (and thus the Simpson family) to deliver on Russell's promise put severe stress on the church's budget and cast Russell's memory in a bad light among its board and parishioners. Instead of a monument to Russell Simpson and his philanthropy, the new wing had become a financial albatross around the church's neck, and the good name of Simpson Products was declining rapidly, not just with the church but with the other organizations to which Russell had promised contributions, as well.

Within two years of the deaths of Russell and Ilene Simpson, the venture-capital partner the Simpson children had brought in to save the company merged "Simpson Box" into a larger operation in San Antonio and bought them out. Many employees who had been with the company for years elected not to transfer to the new location for various reasons and thus had to take an early retirement or resign.

Russell Simpson's lifetime of work, commitment, and industry was gone overnight. Surely, this was not the legacy he had in mind for himself, his wife, or his family.

The loss of the Simpson family business, a community company and generous contributor over the years to many community causes, might have been prevented if rather than evading the reality of their father's mortality, the Simpson children had forced themselves instead to sit down with him as he had wanted, to address his legacy concerns, goals, and desires. That is what having the legacy conversation is all about.

> ## Reality Check
>
> **Parental Myth:** "I can take care of managing my own legacy without any help."
>
> **Fact:** Yes, and the paint-by-numbers industry makes a small fortune out of convincing people they can be artists. Remember how the legacy of Russell Simpson got totaled -- and he didn't start out thinking or even wanting to manage his legacy on his own!

As a result of having the legacy conversation, you and your parents will come to understand, and thus be able to act on, their legacy wishes as regards:

- **How your parents view *themselves* and their lives.** Except, maybe, for serial killers, most people want at some point to gain some perspective on their lives. As human beings, we have a deep need to build connections and to establish transitions for ourselves as a way of gaining perspective on how we have lived and what we have achieved along the way. Discussing legacy concerns with your parents builds a connection and establishes a transition that allows a legacy strategy to be designed. Parents who were teachers obviously spent a great deal of their lives in pursuit of knowledge and sharing that knowledge with others. A scholarship in their name for a child -- whether awarded based on need, achievement, or random drawing -- acknowledges their commitment in a tangible way. Similarly, parents who loved and cared for animals all their lives can continue their good work with a gift in their name to the local Humane Society or animal shelter.
- **How your parents want *you* to remember them.** The process of raising children involves making them do things we don't particularly enjoy making them do (and that they often don't like or want to do). This is all part of the experience of transforming children from wild animals into (hopefully) responsible, contributing adults. Inevitably, though, the tensions that arise from this experience will impact the parents' and the

child's respective memories of those key child-rearing/growing up years. As a result, after the parent is gone and the child reflects on those years, he or she may remember the parent a different way than the parent would like. For example, most parents would hope that their kids remember them more for their persistence, courage, and loyalty in supporting the family than for the numerous times they grounded the kids as teenagers for smarting off at them. The legacy conversation is a way of setting the record straight about the lifelong parent-child relationship and gaining some lasting perspective on that relationship so that, for example, parents can *know* their children will always remember them not as the prison guards they on occasion had to be but as the human beings they are -- and always were.

- **How and by whom your parents also want to be remembered.** All but the most reclusive and isolationist among us accumulate friends over the years, and are, thus, part of a larger community -- be it a church, synagogue, Rotary Club, or YMCA. These associations produce relationships that also create memories. Whether it's with a generational family portrait, plaque, award, donation in their name, or whatever, parents may wish to be remembered for the part of their life they shared with those folks and organizations too.

- **What your parents want others to remember them for.** I remember watching Senator Edward Kennedy's eulogy on behalf of his assassinated brother Bobby on television back in 1968. While undoubtedly there were hundreds of ways the senator could have memorialized his slain brother, he did so simply, and powerfully, as a "good and decent man." He then went on to explain what he meant, concluding with the message that his brother "saw war and tried to stop it." I still think of Bobby Kennedy that way. Our parents too want to be remembered not only for who they were and what they achieved in life, but for the many worthwhile things, large and small, they sought to achieve for others and that gave their lives meaning.

The Legacy Conversation

The overall aim of the legacy conversation is not to come up with a checklist of pros and cons about your parent's life as a way of scoring whether that life was well spent or not. It is to continue the process of empowering them to feel the confidence they have built up from the previous conversations and to carry it through to this final parent care issue as well. Your role here is to focus your parents toward thinking about their past and to get them to communicate their thoughts and reflections to you from the perspective of the present, so that together you can start ensuring that legacy by taking strategic action.

Here's how it goes.

1. Challenges

"Mom and Dad, think about how you would like to be remembered and tell me what goes through your mind."

What you are trying to get at here is your parents' view of their history and the struggles they faced, individually and as a couple, while making their way in life. They had bills to pay, children to feed, and jobs to consume their time and attention. There must have been periods when they were feeling on top of the world and periods when they thought they would never get off the bottom. Each situation served to create the people they became and, thus, how they wish to be remembered.

Typically, as parents begin to open up on this, they will share some, if not all, of the following. For some of you, it will not be the first time you have heard many of these things. But it may be the first time you actually *hear* them, and the experience can be an eye-opener. Tales you might hear include:

- The story of their humble or ostentatious origins and how they triumphed over one or the other.
- The story of their first job and the career path they chose (or that chose them) and led to where they are now.
- The story of meeting their mate (your mother or father), falling in love, and creating the family of which you are a part.
- Their moments of joy and heartache from both the work involved and the excitement they experienced in raising a family.
- Stories of the places they lived or visited, and the memories they have of those places.

- Stories about the friends they made growing up and into adulthood.
- Stories of relatives you may not know or remember, who were funny, interesting, or just plain weird characters that contributed to your parents' life experience.
- Favorite anecdotes, favorite times, and specific events they treasure and remember most.

2. Alternatives

"Mom and Dad, let's discuss some of the options that you think might be available to you in dealing with the challenges we just discussed."

During the course of our lives, we all make decisions we wish we could take back or wish we had made in a different way. These missed opportunities and what we learn from them define us as well. But this question is not about brooding over past regrets; it's about helping your parents focus on and appreciate (perhaps even relish) what was -- the things they did well and wouldn't change, which benefited themselves and others because they made those choices -- and not "might-have-beens" that will bathe them in remorse. From conducting thousands of hours of

---

Reality Check

Parental Myth: "I'm no storyteller. Besides, I have no great stories worth telling."

Fact: Raising children, housebreaking a puppy, planting roses, painting a barn, the first car, the first date, the first grandchild -- all are fodder for stories that come out of our lives and the laughs we experience recalling them. My father must have told the story about the longest train he'd ever seen nearly 5 million times in his life, but the last time he told it, I heard something different, something I'd never thought of before. Now that he is gone, I can still hear him telling that story, and the memory of it is a great thing.

---

these conversations, I can tell you this: If you think of the course of your life as the hours from noon to midnight, the things most people would change or do differently in their life if they could would take up the last five minutes, from 11:55 to midnight, to accomplish. The number of "might-have-beens" is barely worth considering, let alone regretting.

In many ways, this conversation will enable your parents to shed any regrets they may still have, by acknowledging the important lessons they have come to understand from the decisions they made (which were right for them at the time), and which can be passed on.

Some typical alternatives that will come up in response to this question are:

- "We would've started a savings and investment plan sooner."
- "We would've taken more vacations to interesting places."
- "We would've not worried so much about things that didn't really matter."
- "We would've spent more time at home and less time at the office."
- "We would've spent more time with you children."
- "We would've been kinder and more considerate of each other."
- "We would've made more friends."
- "We would've worked through our problems rather than giving them short shrift or running away from them."
- "We would've had careers rather than just jobs."

Ethical Will

Parental Myth: "My children really don't care about the events of my life that shaped me and made me who I am…"

Fact: I believe nothing could be further from the truth. All of us have our ways, our "weirdness", our "idiosyncrasies", but where did they come from? An Ethical will allows you to put in writing the fiber of who you are and why. What were the life experiences that shaped your life and being? What where the events that built the character that you are today. I challenge you to write them down and it will be more precious than gold to your heirs. To learn more about writing your ethical will, check out the website: www.ethicalwill.com

---

3. Resources

"Mom and Dad, let's think of some resources that you are familiar with already that we could use to help maximize your options and minimize these challenges."

This question allows your parents to toot their own horn a bit as well as to recognize the contributions to their lives others have made along the way. Face it, none of us would be able to make it in life without the help, the inspiration, and what we learn from others -- even if "others" means those puppies, the guppies, and the hamsters on wheels we grew up with that played a big part in our formative years.

Here are some of the resources parents have said they drew upon in life:

- Books and learning
- Travel
- Different jobs
- Relationships
- Births
- Deaths
- Friendships

- Spirituality and faith
- Financial skills
- Tenacity
- Foresight
- Integrity

Just look at that list. It tells you a lot about those people, doesn't it -- as parents *and* as human beings!

4. Experience

"Mom and Dad, if you were to describe the legacy you would like to create as a result of all the long-term care planning decisions you have made, what might it look like?"

What you're trying to achieve with this question is to get your parents to see their life as an *experience* -- and what they want others to take from that experience about them. You may have to do some prompting here to help them to reflect on their lives from that perspective, which will involve overcoming any tendency they may have toward false or excessive modesty. It is not prideful to want to be recognized and remembered for the good you did in your time on earth *just being you*. I'm sure that while we can all admire and respect the symbolic remembrance and anonymous recognition offered by the Tomb of the Unknown Soldier, few of us would wish to be buried there.

You want your parents to see that while they were finding their own way in life, they were also finding the way for, and even guiding, others -- like yourself.

Their responses might go something like this.

"We always did try to help those less fortunate than ourselves and to show a strong work ethic to you kids because we feel a job worth doing is worth doing well. And so we never gave up on anything or anyone. If we can have some recognition for that, well, it's only human nature to want to have it -- for us, for our children, and for the generations to come."

TIP! Ways of Remembering

Here is a sample of the ways your parents can be remembered tangibly for their life experience. Expand on this list by involving your parents in coming up with their own ways of symbolizing their memory -- then work on making it happen:

1. A room, wing, chapel, etc. in a local hospital.
2. An annual fund-raising event such as a walk, bike ride, or bake sale
3. A festival, gathering, production, or some other type of artsy event
4. A matching-donor pledge program up to a certain amount.

Dan's Story,

It was one of those fall days in the South that is remarkable for its clarity and its color; evening had come, yet the air was still without a trace of humidity.

My dad and I were sitting in rocking chairs on the porch of his care center. It was early on in his bout with Alzheimer's, before the disease had erased his memory of the past, his awareness of the present, and his ability to contemplate the future. At that moment, he was aware -- he was "back" as they say about Alzheimer patients -- no, not exactly back like he used to be but clearly back enough to have a conversation. You see, it is one of the cruel ironies of Alzheimer's that on occasion the brain rights itself, and for brief periods -- hours sometimes but mostly moments -- the afflicted resembles his or her old self before the identity-destroying disease grabbed hold.

The whole idea of a Parent Care Solution Program and its accompanying Parent Care Conversation methodology was still in the incubation stage. But since he was back and aware, I decided to raise the legacy issue, though I didn't call it that at the time. I asked him how he would like to be remembered. After what seemed like an eternity, he responded: "I would like people to say that I was honest, that I cared for my family, and that I always tried to do what was right. Oh, and another thing -- that you could always depend on me."

I asked him which of those he would like to be remembered for most. He replied without hesitation, "That I took care of my family."

I asked him if he had any concerns about being remembered that way, and he said there were times when he had to be tough on us kids when we were growing up, and that he worried we'd remember him mostly from those times, as just this tough, hard guy instead of as a guy who was only tough and hard when he had to be because he believed it was necessary. He was really more than that.

I told him that I thought he had created a remarkable life for himself and our family, and that the very hard, poverty-stricken West Virginia background in which he'd been raised may have been not just the origin of his toughness but the inspiration for him to do well by himself and all of us. That opened the door, and for the next hour he talked and talked about how growing up really poor had helped him to appreciate every little thing. About how he had learned to ride a bicycle without using his hands so that he could keep them warm in his pockets on bitter cold days ("I could ride five miles or more like that," he said). About the war -- I mean the big one, World War II -- where he'd been a sailor on the USS *North Carolina* during the brutal battle for Peleliu, the Japanese front line of defense in the South Pacific, and how witnessing all the wounded and dying brought on board from the bloody shoreline had made him feel sick to his stomach and like dying too. The war was one of the most horrible things he had ever experienced, he told me; it had changed him forever. Only the thought of his family back home kept him going, he said.

Dad paused for a second, flashing back to his childhood again, and shared a thought about growing up on a farm -- how it had given him his respect for hard work and the value of doing a day's work for a day's pay. *Earning* his money throughout his life was a real source of pride to him. He then told me about getting the same toy wagon two years in a row at Christmas. The first year it had been brand new. The second year, his parents could only repaint it for him to look like it was new because the Depression had hit and times were hard.

As I listened, it occurred to me that it is in the remembering of the stories of our lives that we live forever. "I am what survives me," the philosopher Erickson wrote. Our stores are what survive us.

My dad and I were never able to talk like that again. Over the next few months, then years, the disease that had so insidiously entered his life took that life over, and our get-togethers dwindled to exchanges of smiles and the simple "Hi, how are you?" type of greeting that Alzheimer's makes inevitable. But that late-coming and fragmented legacy conversation had helped to bring a sense of closure -- to both of us, I believe, but to me certainly. It allowed for a different kind of communication, one that connected us in a way we had never been connected before.

Five years after that conversation on the care center porch, my father died. In my eulogy at his funeral I spoke of him exactly in the way he had spoken of himself that day -- as a good and decent man who loved life, loved his family, and who never quit on either. Like the Apostle Paul, he had fought the good fight, had finished the race, and had kept the faith in all he believed in and all that he valued.

While much of what I went on to say is personal and would only be meaningful to his friends and family, I will share my closing words with you because they sum up and will help you to grasp the full importance of having the legacy conversation.

"My question today is not what to do with grief," I said. "My grief will sort itself out over time. Much like when summer turns to fall, I may not know exactly the time it is fall, but I will know when it is not summer anymore."

"No, my real question today is what to do with my Saturdays. For almost 250 of them, over a five-year span, I ate breakfast with my dad [at his care center], listening to him talk away at first, then watching him gradually fall more and more silent as his memory and the words drifted away. So, I think when this service today is over, and I have rested a bit, I will go back to that place where he spent his final years and find someone just like him, someone whose family doesn't come by as much anymore, whose friends have all forgotten or are dead, yet who has a story to tell if someone will listen.

"I think I will go and listen. I will listen because perhaps when I am old, and the sword I need for every day is, like me, bent and leaning against a wall, that perhaps the gods who run the universe will look down and say of me too, 'Maybe we should send him someone to bend his ear while they still can. After all, there's nothing like a good story.'"

11

"Parent Care Conversations with an Unwilling Parent"

"When I was younger, I could remember anything; whether it had happened or not, but my faculties are decaying now and soon I shall be so I cannot remember any but the things that never happened. It is sad to go to pieces like this but we all have to do it."

- Mark Twain

"It's paradoxical that the idea of living a long life appeals to everyone, but the idea of getting old doesn't appeal to anyone."

- Andy Rooney

"It Ain't NONE of Your Business"

One of the most popular statements of our parents' generation is that "children are to be seen and not heard..." They believe that children should not probe into the affairs of their parents and that parents will share when they are good and ready...and since they will never die.... after death will be the right time to talk about parent care matters. What you are is an adult child with a parent who you would describe as eccentric, self-centered, private, a recluse, weird, and not at all willing to talk about the important matters of parent care. What do you do? Go away and not care? Or know and act on your legal rights to protect them from themselves? If your parent says, "It ain't NONE of your Business..." at some point it may have to become your business for their safety and well-being. How do you navigate this difficult course of actions? You didn't choose your ornery parents....now what do you do with them? This chapter is about the parent care conversations that don't happen and likely will not happen.

<u>**Reality Check**</u>

Parental Myth: "My affairs are none of my child's business and they should stay out of my business..."

Fact: A parent that makes this statement does not understand the frailty of life or the fact that they will need some help someday. They may think they are invincible and will never need the caring and loving hand of another family member but the reality is that our "individual rights" are protected in this country. As one attorney told me: "Bad decisions don't count when you think they are bad." They have a right to make "bad decisions even if you as a child disagree." Sometimes we will have to stand back until the bad decisions become dangerous decisions to our parents or others and we have to intervene.

Reality Check

Parental Myth: "If my children try to take away my rights....I will cut them out of the will....I will fight them to the end..."

Fact: If this is your parent's attitude, you are to be pitied. If you are the parent and you have this attitude....you should change it while you can. This attitude sets parent and child up for a series of fights and battles that could be completely avoided. This attitude sets the child up for a series of legal fights and emotional stress. The child could say, "Hands off! I will leave the parents to their own self destruction." The alternative is a series of fights with your parents in court over the legal documentation you need to lead them against their will.

Child Neglect vs. Parent Neglect

We see almost weekly in the news a case of child neglect. A parent leaves a child in a hot car in the summer. A parent leaves the children at home while they go down the street to the bar. Some parents fill the house with smoke, drugs, or other things that endanger children. When these events happen, often the children are taken away from the parent and into the custody of the department of social services so that the child can be properly cared for.

What happens on the other end of life, when we visit our parents' home and they are not bathing properly, not feeding the dog, there is old food in the refrigerator, and they are not dressing properly? If you left a child in these conditions, you would call it child neglect. If we leave our parents in these conditions is it called "parent care" neglect? Unfortunately, when parents think they can do it and take care of themselves and you, as an adult child, see that they indeed cannot do it, you have the collision of two wills and the groundwork for confrontation is set.

<u>**When is "it Time?"**</u>

Signs that it is time for a parent not to live alone:

- They are losing weight and not eating properly.
- Their personal hygiene has declined.
- The home is messy and not as it used to be kept.
- They cannot keep up with their medications.
- Mom or Dad look tired and do not have normal sleep patterns.
- The pets are not being cared for and are losing weight.
- The "neat" house that mom used to keep is no longer "neat."
- The neighbors call you and see behaviors that you do not see.
- You get a call from the police station, that Dad is lost and doesn't know his way home (this happened to Dan).
- They are frequently losing things and can't find them.
- They put clothes on inside out or have the wrong clothes for the season.

The Parent Care Conversation with an Unwilling Parent

1. Challenges

"Mom and Dad, as we think about the prospect of you getting older...have you thought about times that we may disagree about your care and the next steps....what challenges do you see when we disagree? Do you have some thoughts on how we rectify our disagreements?"

My experience is that you may get these responses:

- "I told you that I am not going to talk about getting old so drop it."
- "I am going to make the decisions and you should stay out of it."
- "Why do you always talk down to me and think I am so stupid...I raised you."
- "I told you I have an attorney and they have everything in place."
- "I will ask your opinion when I am good and ready."
- "You have your own life to live and I am not going to burden you with my aging problems."

Reality Check

A Two Edged Sword

Parental Myth: "The determination and tenacity of the WWII generation is NOT always a good thing…"

Fact: I am a student of the WWII generation. I have more DVD's on World War II than anybody I know. I admire the tenacity and determination of "the greatest generation." They were determined that we would win the war and they worked, sacrificed, and accomplished victory by sure "will of the soul." I admire this "can do," "will do," and "must do" attitude. But the problem with this attitude is the failure to admit: "I am getting older and I may get by with a little help from our friends and family." Sometimes this generation will not admit that they "can't do something" and often to the point of adamantly refusing the help. This "I can" attitude can cause our parents to push us away rather than allowing us to assist and care for them.

Keys to Negotiations

Ed Brodow in his book: *Negotiation Boot Camp: How to Resolve Conflict, Satisfy Customers, and Make Better Deals* says this about negotiating:

The ability to negotiate successfully in today's turbulent business climate can make the difference between success and failure. With this in mind, Ed has reevaluated his list of top ten negotiation tips. Here are Ed Brodow's Ten Tips for Successful Negotiating updated for the year 2013.

1. Don't be afraid to ask for what you want. Successful negotiators are assertive and challenge everything – they know that everything is negotiable. I call this negotiation consciousness. It was Number One on my previous list and it stays at the helm in 2013. Negotiation consciousness is what makes the difference between negotiators and everybody else on the planet.

Being assertive means asking for what you want and refusing to take NO for an answer. Practice expressing your feelings without anxiety or anger. Let people know what you want in a non-threatening way. Practice 'I' statements. For example, instead of saying, "You shouldn't do that," try substituting, "I don't feel comfortable when you do that."

Note that there is a difference between being assertive and being aggressive. You are assertive when you take care of your own interests while maintaining respect for the interests of others. When you see to your own interests with a lack of regard for other people's interests, you are aggressive. Being assertive is part of negotiation consciousness.

"Challenge" means not taking things at face value. It means thinking for yourself. You must be able to make up your own mind, as opposed to believing everything you are told. On a practical level, this means you have the right to question the asking price of that new car. It also means you have an obligation to question everything you read in the newspaper or hear on CNN. You cannot negotiate unless you are willing to challenge the validity of the opposing position.

2. Shut up and listen. I am amazed by all the people I meet who can't stop talking. Negotiators are detectives. They ask probing questions and then shut up. The other negotiator will tell you everything you need to know – all you have to do is listen.

Many conflicts can be resolved easily if we learn how to listen. The catch is that listening is the forgotten art. We are so busy making sure that people hear what we have to say that we forget to listen.

You can become an effective listener by allowing the other person to do most of the talking. Follow the 70/30 Rule – listen 70 percent of the time, and talk only 30 percent of the time. Encourage the other negotiator to talk by asking lots of open-ended questions – questions that can't be answered with a simple "yes" or "no."

3. Do your homework. This is what detectives do. Gather as much pertinent information prior to your negotiation. What are their needs? What pressures do they feel? What options do they have? Doing your homework is vital to successful negotiation. You can't make accurate decisions without understanding the other side's situation. The more information you have about the people with whom you are negotiating, the stronger you will be. People who consistently leave money on the table probably fail to do their homework.

4. Always be willing to walk away. I call this Brodow's Law. In other words, never negotiate without options. If you depend too much on the positive outcome of a negotiation, you lose your ability to say NO. When you say to yourself, "I will walk if I can't conclude a deal that is satisfactory," the other side can tell that you mean business. Your resolve will force them to make concessions. Clients often ask me, "Ed, if you could give me one piece of advice about negotiating, what would it be?" My answer, without hesitation, is: "Always be willing to walk away." Please note that I am not advising you to walk away, but if you don't even consider the option of walking away, you may be inclined to cave in to the other side's demands simply to make a deal. If you are not desperate - if you recognize that you have other options - the other negotiator will sense your inner strength.

5. Don't be in a hurry. Being patient is very difficult for Americans. We want to get it over with. Anyone who has negotiated in Asia, South America, or the Middle East will tell you that people in those cultures look at time differently than we do in North America and Europe. They know that if you rush, you are more likely to make mistakes and leave money on the table. Whoever is more flexible about time has the advantage. Your patience can be devastating to the other negotiator if they are in a hurry because they start to believe that you are not under pressure to conclude the deal. So what do they do? They offer concessions as a means of providing you with an incentive to say YES.

6. Aim high and expect the best outcome. Successful negotiators are optimists. If you expect more, you'll get more. A proven strategy for achieving higher results is opening with an extreme position. Sellers should ask for more than they expect to receive, and buyers should offer less than they are prepared to pay. People who aim higher do better. Your optimism will become a self-fulfilling prophecy. Conversely, if you have low expectations, you will probably wind up with a less satisfying outcome.

7. Focus on the other side's pressure, not yours. We have a tendency to focus on our own pressure, on the reasons why we need to make a deal. It's the old story about the grass being greener in the other person's backyard. If you fall into this trap, you are working against yourself. The other side will appear more powerful. When you focus on your own limitations, you miss the big picture. Instead, successful negotiators ask, "What is the pressure on the other side in this negotiation?" You will feel more powerful when you recognize the reasons for the other side to give in. Your negotiation power derives in part from the pressures on the other person. Even if they appear nonchalant, they inevitably have worries and concerns. It's your job to be a detective and root these out. If you discover that they are under pressure, which they surely are, look for ways to exploit that pressure in order to achieve a better result for yourself.

8. Show the other person how their needs will be met. Successful negotiators always look at the situation from the other side's perspective. Everyone looks at the world differently, so you are way ahead of the game if you can figure out their perception of the deal. Instead of trying to win the negotiation, seek to understand the other negotiator and show them ways to feel satisfied. My philosophy of negotiation includes the firm belief that one hand washes the other. If you help the other side to feel satisfied, they will be more inclined to help you satisfy your needs. That does not mean you should give in to all their positions. Satisfaction means that their basic interests have been fulfilled, not that their demands have been met. Don't confuse basic interests with positions/demands: Their position/demand is what they say they want; their basic interest is what they really need to get.

9. Don't give anything away without getting something in return. Unilateral concessions are self-defeating. Whenever you give something away, get something in return. Always tie a string: "I'll do this if you do that." Otherwise you are inviting the other negotiator to ask you for additional concessions. When you give something away without requiring them to reciprocate, they will feel entitled to your concession, and won't be satisfied until you give up even more. But if they have to earn your concession, they will derive a greater sense of satisfaction than if they got it for nothing.

10. Don't take the issues or the other person's behavior personally. All too often negotiations fail because one or both of the parties get sidetracked by personal issues unrelated to the deal at hand. Successful negotiators focus on solving the problem, which is: How can we conclude an agreement that respects the needs of both parties? Obsessing over the other negotiator's personality, or over issues that are not directly pertinent to making a deal, can sabotage a negotiation. If someone is rude or difficult to deal with, try to understand their behavior and don't take it personally.

You can go pretty far with these basic ideas. If you want to dig deeper, read my book, Negotiation Boot Camp, and – better yet – invite me to speak at your organization's next meeting or convention.

2. Alternatives

"Mom and Dad, let's discuss some of the options that you think might be available when our disagreements are beyond our ability to resolve?"

- · "We don't have disagreements…just leave me alone."
- · "You want to throw me in a nursing home and I told you I'm not going."
- · "Just stay out of my life and I won't hurt your feelings".
- · "If I needed your help…I would ask for it".
- · "We could seek out a third party mediator".

· "I have fought in wars and seen people die…I can take care of myself."

Intervention Meeting

One alternative to consider is an "intervention" meeting. I sometimes call it a "coalition of love." This would be a meeting where you get the minister, neighbors, sister or brother and whoever else may be appropriate and you call a meeting. This can be shocking to the parent, but if the people who love your parents the most all show up and together say… "we think it best that you not live alone" this could be the shock they need to make a change.

---

3. Resources

"Mom and Dad, let's think of some resources that you are familiar with already that could help us work through or think through disagreements in your next steps of care?

With parents who will not talk, you may not get anywhere with the thought of resources.

The steps you may try include the following:

1. Seek to have the parent care conversations with your parents.
2. Talk with your parent's doctor to see if he will have the discussion on matters like they should no longer live alone or that it's time to quit driving.
3. Talk with your parents' minister or rabbi and see if he can talk to them about the parent care decisions.
4. See if your parents are willing to talk to a geriatric case manager or a Parent Care Specialist.
5. Finally, seek legal counsel from an elder care attorney about your rights and the parents' rights.

> ### "I will take you to Court"
>
> One of the most difficult discussions with our parents is about when is it time to stop driving. There can be a lot of interpretation about what is good and what is bad driving. I know of one father who refused to stop driving and he took his case to court to fight the children to keep his license. He spent $2,000 and still lost his license.

4. Experience

"Mom and Dad, think about the growing older experience you would ideally like to create for yourselves and tell me what that experience would look like? If we disagree...what should we do?"

Likely the parents who refuse to talk are not going to have a good experience in their final days. Some parents are self-centered and unwilling to work with the rest of the family and they are basically a negative and angry person. When friends, neighbors, and those who love them the most can't get them to cooperate, then pursuing legal options may be the only way to go. Let this be your last options, but in some cases to prevent parents from harming themselves or other actions may have to be taken.

I discussed the legal option in an interview with Elder attorney Charles Black from Columbia, South Carolina.

Parent Care Conversations with an Unwilling Parent

Legal Rights and Options in Actions

(Interview with Elder Attorney, Charles Black)

Key Questions about Uncooperative Parents

Kevin: What is an elder attorney?

Charles: I would contrast or compare an elder attorney to an estate-planning attorney. They do wills and trust. That is a component to what we do, but I am more concerned about taking care of you while you are still with us; not just focusing solely on how we're going to pass your assets at your death. We not only do wills and trust, but more importantly, durable power of attorney and healthcare power of attorney.

Kevin: So Estate Planning pertains to after death and an elder care attorney helps in the last chapter of life?

Charles: Yes, during life, trying to help manage things, to the extent that we can preserve assets and tap into other benefits to help pay for long term care insurance, how and who is going to manage the assets; and if you should become incapacitated, it prevents you from having a probate court proceeding.

Kevin: My mom and dad refused to talk about care options; I'm an adult child. What are their legal rights and my rights?

Charles: No one has the legal rights to control what someone else does until that person has been declared incapacitated. So in regards to the adult child's legal rights to force mom or dad to do what the child wants to do; there are very little legal rights to do that.

Kevin: How long does the adult child sit there and observe the signs of decline? You made a comment about a case that a bad decision doesn't necessarily mean it's a wrong decision, just because the child thinks it's a wrong decision.

Charles: It all comes down to personal freedom and self-determination and if you want to live with 37 cats, and if the city of Columbia isn't coming to shut you down, you should be able to do those things. I think where it crosses the line is when you do things that are dangerous to yourself or potentially dangerous to others. I think the important thing is to start early on. Don't wait until there is a problem. Have those conversations early because it is a scary thing for a parent to have their kid come to them to talk about assisted living or about having caregivers come in. The whole loss of independence is a gradual process and if you can start early and do a little step at a time, you have a much greater chance of getting the parent invested and participating in the plan rather than waiting for crisis management.

Kevin: I can remember in my 40s, Charles, looking at my dad and seeing the gray hair, the slight shuffle in his step. It hit me that dad is getting old. Where was I the last 15 years? I was taking kids to ball practice, to football games, working, trying to build my business and I wake up and they are old.

Charles: That's why they call it the sandwich generation. Sandwiched in between taking care of our own children, building careers and trying to take care of our parents, who are getting older. I think when that light bulb goes off that your dad is getting older, that's a good time to have the conversation and see if they have done their planning and have their basic documents in place. Do they have a will? Do they have a power of attorney? You may meet with some resistance initially but as long as you are starting early, you can keep at it; keep chipping away. Sooner or later, a lot of folks come around to the idea that they do need to make some planning decisions for themselves so someone else isn't deciding what happens to them.

Kevin: But when you can put popcorn in the microwave and have it in 2 minutes, we want to solve this problem quickly. We are the popcorn generation. We feel like we need to fix this *now* and we want mom and dad to cooperate *now*. Explain your comment about what's the difference between a bad decision and the decision an adult child should consider to intervene.

Charles: It's probably different in every case. You have to look at the circumstances and personality. You need to consider involving the doctors, other family members, or a sibling; sometimes the message comes better from one child than from another. It's a difficult situation to get your hands around and see what is the best approach. Are your parents doing things that are dangerous to themselves? Are they setting the stove on fire, falling asleep while smoking or continuing to drive when they shouldn't be driving? In the issue of driving, that's a situation where if they are seeing a doctor on a regular basis and they have a good relationship with the doctor, the doctor could step in and give your parent an evaluation and then ask your parent to give them the driver's license. Not everyone is going to be that easy, but that's the case where the doctor is stepping in and making it easier for the child by telling the parent to stop driving and hand over the keys.

Kevin: I know some folks where the father is taking kids to court because they are trying to take his license away.

Charles: The whole driving thing is huge because it is your independence. You can go shopping, go to church, go get food, come and go as you please whenever you want; taking that away from someone is a major loss of independence.

Kevin: When parents won't cooperate explain when you go to the level of declaring incompetence. What is guardianship and conservatorship? These are terms we hope to never use in parent care, but what are they?

Charles: Guardianship and conservatorship, those are the processes by which the probate court declares someone incapacitated. In South Carolina, we differentiate between guardian and conservator. The guardian takes care of the person and makes decisions on where they live and what kind of health care they are going to get. The conservator takes care of the protected person's assets. Frequently, it is the same person appointed to fill both roles. They are two separate and distinct roles and when you go into probate court, you file one petition for the appointment of guardian and one petition for the appointment of conservator. The process is pretty much the same for both; the court appoints medical examiners to examine the person and report back to the court to see if the examiner thinks the person meets the definition for incapacitated. A doctor or at least one medical doctor has to sign off on that, and at least one other medical professional. There is a guardian ad litem that's appointed for the person to represent that person's interests before the court to act as a reporter back to the court. The court is trying to gather as much information as it can about what's going on with the person. The person has the right to contest that action. They have to be served with the petitions for guardianship and conservatorship. They can file responsive pleading. They can go hire an attorney and say "heck no! I don't think I'm incapacitated". You can get into fights about that. You may not be on the favorite child list, but that has to be taken into consideration when you pull that trigger for guardianship and conservatorship because if the court decides that mom and dad may have a *little* problem cognitively or functionally, but they are not to the point of needing a guardian or conservator appointed, they probably aren't going to be real happy with you for having them dragged to probate court. This is also where you see big fights about guardianship and conservatorship, when the children fight over who's going to be the guardian or the conservator.

Kevin: If someone is in a different state, guardianship and conservatorship issues need to be researched with an attorney in that state, correct?

Charles: Yes, in some states they are just going to call it guardianship. Florida for example, just says guardianship, which means someone takes care of the person and the assets. As for South Carolina, we call guardianship, the one who cares for the person and conservatorship, the person who takes care of the assets. The laws and definitions are probably going to be pretty similar. The procedures may vary a little bit. There is a uniform probate code out there that a lot of states move toward adopting. When South Carolina adopted it, they made a lot of changes to it, and other states tinker with it also. But by and large, the process is going to be similar. There are going to be some medical examiners that will be involved to report back to the court, there will be a guardian ad litem, the opportunity for an attorney for the allegedly incapacitated person and a lot of the courts these days, particularly in South Carolina, are big on Alternative Dispute Resolution (ADR), which is mediation. So if we have a contested guardianship, where there is some argument on whether or not the person is incapacitated, or more likely, where there is some argument about who is going to act as guardian and conservator, many times the court will now refer that to an outside mediator to see if the parties can't come to some agreement.

Kevin: Does this actually happen often? Because I know we have gotten calls on the show, and they hesitate taking it this far because they know they could lose the case, they could be cut out of the will, become the black sheep; how do you navigate these waters?

Charles: I would say the majority of the guardianship or conservatorship cases typically arise because someone has not taken the action they needed to in terms of power of attorney or creating a trust or something to say how their assets are going to be managed if they become incapacitated. A good example of this is if you have a 401k or IRA or something like that, you can't put someone as a joint account holder on that. So if you become incapacitated, unless you have someone you've appointed as an attorney, to access those funds, to pay for your care, we're going to have to go into probate court on a conservatorship action, and have you declared as incapacitated. When we do these types of cases, we are doing it because the person is too far gone to be able to execute power of attorney. There is usually little question at that point whether or not they are incapacitated. There may be some issue about who is going to manage the funds, but in the grand scheme of things, it probably doesn't really matter a whole lot because the guardians and the conservators have to report back to the probate court periodically. So there is someone watching what's going on typically you either have a bond or a restricted account agreement. The vast majority of the guardianship and conservatorship cases come up in that context. We don't have the tools we need; that person is beyond being able to execute the power of attorney or create a trust, so we have no alternative but to go into court. The more contested, or more controversial guardianship and conservatorship cases where mom or dad are making bad decisions, let's go make them declared incapacitated, those are much less frequent. I think most people try as much as they can to manage these cases a little bit at a time, enlisting ministers, family members, or neighbors, to try to patch things together as much as they can until that parent is beyond where there is any question about them being incapacitated.

There aren't a lot of cases out there where there is a true fight over the capacity issue.

Kevin: When it comes to parent care, what does the power of attorney allow you to do or not to do in helping your parent?

Charles: The terms of the power of attorney depends on what you can and can't do when helping with your parent. You can have a limited power of attorney, you can have a general power of attorney that's broad and allows you to do all sorts of things. A lot of it comes down to the comfort level of the parent who is executing the power of attorney and appointing their spouse or children as agents. And the good thing about power of attorney is you can customize it and tweak it and put conditions in it; however you think you need to do it to make it palatable to whoever is executing it. But that document is going to define the scope of the agent's authority. An important aspect of the power of attorney is the idea from the parent's perspective, or the principle's perspective (the person who is executing the document; granting the authority), that just giving someone power of attorney doesn't keep you from being able to do anything for yourself. A lot of people are worried about that; they feel that if they give their children power of attorney, that it means they can't go manage their own affairs and their kids are going to step in and do it. That's not really the case. It authorizes somebody else to do things in addition to the things you can still do for yourself. The power of attorney is really out there as a safety valve if something happens where you *can't* continue to manage your own affairs; here's who I want to take over and handle things for me. Here are the things that I want them to be able to do.

Kevin: What if my siblings and I have a difference on the care needed for our parents? I've learned that all siblings in families are not all wired the same, so when you get into the task of parent care; you have one with the loyalty genes, one with the not so loyal gene. How do we handle that? Do I need to hire an attorney like you?

Charles: Particularly, from the parent's standpoint, part of the responsibility is on the parent to recognize the differences and part of the attorney's responsibility is to help the parent talk through that and the idea that you don't have to treat your children equally in terms of who you decide is going to make decisions for you. It may be that one child you feel more comfortable making healthcare decisions for you and another child making business decisions for you. You may want to split those roles up. If you're concerned that the person you're appointing isn't going to make the decisions that you want made, you need to rethink that idea and come up with someone else. Now within that whole framework, I had one case that I did recently where the parent had one son who they were confident in his ability to manage money, but they were concerned that he would pull the trigger too quickly in putting them into a facility or not putting them into a facility or not wanting to spend the money on that. They were happy with him managing the money but not so much with the healthcare decisions. So we decided to make this son the power of attorney with the business decisions and the other son the power of attorney with healthcare decisions. We put a provision in the power of attorney for the son making the business decisions that he would need to defer to the healthcare decision maker to make funds available for the care, if they deemed appropriate. They mesh the two areas together. That's where you get into the benefits of having an attorney that understands different conflicts and aspects. You can't get that if you download a form off the Internet or something at an office supply store. Being a family counselor is definitely one of the roles of elder law; every child has a different personality, different strengths and weaknesses and it's not a one size fits all. I need to stress to the parents, don't feel like you have to name all your children in some role; some of them are clearly stronger at managing money, some are stronger at making emotional decisions, healthcare decisions, and you need to play off the strengths of those children.

Kevin: Sometimes they call it tough love; if I go against my parents' wishes and push it to the limit and I end up in a probate court, and I lose. What happens?

Charles: The court isn't going to toss you in jail. Your parents will probably be upset with you and they could end up changing their estate plan and cutting you out; that can happen.

Kevin: That's a huge risk in exercising tough love.

Charles: It is, and that's why guardianship and conservatorship is a last resort and that's why we would prefer people to be proactive on the front end early on, having conversations with mom and dad and go ahead and set up the powers of attorney so we can start working through these decisions and have a framework for handling things rather than fighting in probate court. Having a court decide something is never the best way to go in any scenario.

Kevin: What about this scenario: what if I get my pastor, my sisters, parents, uncles, aunts, neighbors, and bring them all together for a meeting with mom and dad to convince them that they shouldn't be living alone. Is that a good strategy?

Charles: I think that can be at times, but you need to be careful so it doesn't look like you are ganging up on them. A lot of that has to do with the personality of the parent. If you have four kids, that message may come better from one or two of them than from the others. It's the primary caregiver child, the one that's local, that's there doing everything; they become the lightening rod and the target for the parents' frustration. The parent is getting used to what they have to say and is going to refuse whatever they say. If they are mad at you already, they are not going to listen to what you have to say, whereas you have a sibling who lives out of town and comes to town for Christmas and they hear the same message from them, it may be received better. So that goes back to the whole idea of playing off the strengths of the various players in the group. If there is a minister that they have a long-standing relationship with, that message might be better received by him than from a family member. Or maybe a geriatric care manager, we have hired a geriatric care manager to come in and help assess what's going on and come up with a care plan and have a conversation. Maybe it's a long time doctor. Every situation is different; figure out who is going to get that message to the parent and try to utilize them. A group or intervention may work but I'd be a little careful about how you go about it; you don't want the parent to get defensive immediately if they feel everyone is ganging up on them. You want it to be perceived as everyone is here because they care about what's going on with you, not that they are trying to force or bend you to their will.

221

Kevin: If my parents live in another state, do I need to find an elder law attorney in their state?

Charles: Generally, I do think you need to be looking for an elder attorney in your parents' state. The requirements for executing power of attorney are different. We execute documents differently in different states. It's important that whatever planning documents you put into place are going to be valid where you need them to be valid. Certainly, guardianship and conservatorship actions are going to vary a little bit state to state. I think you would be well served to find an elder law attorney in your parents' home state. If you are the adult child, you can look up an elder law attorney in your own state and have them find an elder attorney in your parent's state, or you can go to the National Academy of Elder Law Attorneys (NAELA www.naela.org) to find an attorney.

12

"THE FAIR AND UNEQUAL CONVERSATION"

Quote "What's equal is not
always fair, and what's
fair is not always equal."
- Unknown

Have you ever wondered which hurts the most: saying something
and wishing you had not, or saying nothing, and wishing you had?
- Unknown

Note: If you are an only child this chapter may be skipped.

When does "fair" become Unequal?

Once upon a time there was the great American "nuclear" family. You
remember the son, the daughter, the dog and the white picket fence.
In some families there were three or four children. Mom would have
dinner ready at five when dad came home and then they would watch
a little TV on the old black and white. Remember the good old days of
"Batman and Robin" and "Gilligan's Island" and "Lost in Space" and
the classic cartoons like "Bugs Bunny". Mom and Dad looked at the
family and said, "Life is good." From such a perfect family (which few
of us really had) came the belief that all the children should be treated
"fair" and "equal". Which means that when mom and dad got older we
would share the duties equally....that is only "fair." Right?

Somehow from that beginning, the outcomes of life often became "unequal" and so "fair" can become more "unequal."

How do we translate these realities in the parent care duties and expectations? How do we pay and compensate the family members who go above and beyond in the task of parent care? How should a will and beneficiary form be changed so that unequal becomes fair? That will be the focus of this chapter.

Honor, Duty, and the Weakest Link

In the task of parent care, two words come to mind....honor and duty.

You remember the great commandment: "Thou shalt honor thy father and mother.

"Honor" is defined as noun

1. honesty, fairness, or integrity in one's beliefs and actions: a man of honor.
2. high respect, as for worth, merit, or rank: to be held in honor.
3. such respect manifested: a memorial in honor of the dead.

"Duty" is defined as
noun, plural du·ties.

1. something that one is expected or required to do by moral or legal obligation.
2. the binding or obligatory <u>force</u> of something that is morally or legally right; moral or legal obligation.
3. an action or task required by a person's position or occupation; function: the duties of a clergyman.
4. the respectful and obedient conduct due a parent, superior, elder, etc.
5. an act or <u>expression</u> of respect.

I have found that when it is time to roll up your sleeves and do the task of parent care....too often the majority falls on one or a few of the children. Sometimes this is just the personalities involved, sometimes it's because children live at a distance. When the burden falls on one or two it consumes their time and energy and often they have to quit work or cut back at work in the caring for their parents. When I took math I learned about equal. You know, 100/2=50, 100/3=33.33, 100/4=25. If equal was applied to parent care, two children would share responsibility equally, three would share equally, or four would share equally. In my years of working in parent care, I have yet to find many examples where the task of parent care was even close to being equal. I have always asked, "How can that be fair?" and what steps and conversations can families have to right the inequality?

Reality Check

Parental Myth: Some parents think like this: "I love all my children equally and I want to treat them all equally and give to them equally when I am gone..."

Fact: Parental love is an amazing thing. We love our children equally and fairly, but then as we grow older and they grow older we see different qualities evolve in them. Then these children begin to show and do acts of love and kindness for us as parents and the levels of affection can be altered. Do we give and reward our children equally when their efforts in parent care become so vastly unequal?

Here is a typical family unit and how they are different in responsibility in the task of parent care:

Child One: (Son)

> Age 48
> Never calls
> Married to a lady who does not like the parents
> Lives out of state
> Usually doesn't remember the parents' birthdays
> Could not be depended on to help in parent care

Child Two: (Daughter)

> Age 54
> Does whatever she can for the parents
> Runs errands for the parents

Calls to tell the parents she loves them
Brings the grandchildren over to see the parents
Has said when needed she will do whatever is needed to care of them

Child Three: (Son)

Age 50
Is a workaholic
Cares about his business more than family
Has been divorced twice
Would help if the parents asked but they don't want to bother him

Welcome to the model of most of the families I know. They are equally the offspring of their parents, but it is apparent that in the task of parent care the responsibility will not be shared equally. So should each of the children expect an equal share when the parent care journey is over? Would it be fair?

Now given these family descriptions of children, fair and equal are certainly not the same.

Reality Check

Parental Myth: "I know that some of my children are getting the family business and some are not working in the business...how do I make things equal..."

Fact: I (Kevin) have a client who has a large business and four children. Two sons are in the business and a daughter and son that are not. When the parents pass away, they want to make things equal; however, with two siblings a part of the business and two that aren't, this makes it unfair. The business is a large part of the parent's net worth. To equalize the estate, the parents have a $5 million dollar second to die life insurance policy. Upon their death, a large amount of the policy goes to the daughter and son not in the business. Then the two sons get the business. The daughter and the other son get the cash. That makes things fair and close to equal.

The Fair and Equal Conversation

Note: The "Fair and Equal Conversation" may be a conversation only between husband and wife or between parent and one of the children providing the most parent care support. The conversation is designed to get parents to see beyond the traditional "equal" thought process and know that all children will not make equal sacrifices in the task of parent care.

When having the "Fair and Equal' conversation using the C.A.R.E system it may sound like this:

1. Challenges

"Mom and Dad, as you consider the children and their involvement in the parent care duties….what are the challenges you see with what is fair in regards to duty and what is equal in regards to duty?"

Responses:

- "I want to treat all of you equal…you are my children."
- "The will says "share and share alike."
- "Well Bob lives in California, and Mary lives in Ohio…they won't be much help…"
- "I don't want any hard feelings with the children when I am gone so I want everything split equal."
- "I do know that all of the children have not shared equally in many ways."

Who does the task of parent care usually fall upon? A good friend of mine owns a home companion business. He said that his target client who calls him regarding their parent's care is a 50 to 55 year old female who is the one that carries the brunt of the parent care load. She is the one taking the parents to doctor's appointments, stopping by to check on them, fixing them meals, and going the extra mile. This is the one who is putting in the hours, quitting work, or reducing hours for the sake of parent care. How is this caregiver to be treated equally when they have an unequal amount of the responsibility?

If you are a parent reading this, I would encourage you to get a set of unequal eyes. Take an honest look at the child or children that are doing the most in parent care and consider rewarding them for their efforts if you have the resources to do so. It will be much easier to do so while you are alive than after you are gone.

2. Alternatives

"Mom and Dad, let's discuss some of the options that you think might be available to meet the challenges that we just discussed regarding what's equal and fair with the children?"

- "You can hire Miss Mary down the street to stay with us…"
- "We could hire these home companion care companies…"
- "We could put a "senior cottage" in your back yard."
- "We could move in with you and you take care of us…"
- "We could add on to your house and build a "mother-in-law suite"
- "You can quit your job and I will pay you to take care of us while we grow old…"

The last option may not be a bad choice. It is not a right fit for everyone, but for some children this may be a "win-win" for parent and child. If given the choice between hiring a non-medical service at $18-$20 per hour or hiring your child, what would you choose?

When I discuss this with clients the light comes on and they think it is a great idea. So how do I contract my child to work for me and take care of me in the task of parent care? Write a "Caregiver Contract."

Understanding the Caregiver Contract

There is one child who has, what I call, the "loyalty" gene. They will love and care for their parents at all cost. As they watch their parents age, they are willing to give up their job, reduce their job to part time or do whatever it takes to make sure mom and/or dad are cared for. That child, by choice or default, has taken and made a financial sacrifice for the care of mom and dad. Some think that such a task should be done on the basis of love and affection. The bottom line is that in the world of parent care, if this child is not compensated for the time and service, it is unfair.

Strategy: The parents and family could consider a caregiver contract. Such a contract would then pay and compensate the child who is going above and beyond in the task of parent care. An agreed upon price and number of hours are stated and this child is paid for services rendered. When a caregiver contract is in place then things can become fair again in the task of parent care.

Sample Caregiver Contracts

WARNING. As with any form contract, or, for that matter, any legal information, it is highly unwise to make use of this sample without seeking legal advice. Users are strongly urged to seek legal advice before making any legal arrangement using this sample.

EXAMPLE: SERVICE AGREEMENT

1. The parties to this agreement are:
   _____, who will be referred to in this document as "Client", who is to receive care and assistance. Employer, acting in the name of Client in the following capacity:
   ☐ guardian ☐ attorney-in-fact ☐ _____.
   Employee, _____, who will be referred to as "Caregiver". Caregiver's address and telephone number are:

   _____

2. The purpose of this agreement is to set out the terms of employment and to establish what assistance Caregiver will provide to Client.

3. Client is a person with impaired abilities, and is a vulnerable person. Client is dependent on Caregiver and is not able to deal with Caregiver on equal terms. Caregiver will take special care not to take advantage of Client and not to unnecessarily influence Client's choices. Caregiver will not negotiate terms of employment with Client. Caregiver will immediately disclose to Employer all gifts from Client, and will return any gifts that Employer decides are excessive. Caregiver will under no circumstances assist Client to write checks unless authorized to do so in writing by Employer. Caregiver will not influence Client in any way whatsoever regarding the writing of a will or other estate planning.

4. Caregiver will assist Client to live at home and to have as much control over the home environment and life as possible, under the circumstances.

5. Caregiver will be responsible directly to Employer to direct and approve the actions of Caregiver. Services provided may include any of the following:

Personal Services: Assistance with the activities of daily living such as bathing, dressing, feeding, and other activities detailed in the Caregiver's Notebook.

Personal Care: Assistance carrying out physician's directions regarding care of Client, carrying out the Care Plan, assistance with mobility and transfers, record keeping, preventing Client from wandering or otherwise harming self.

Household Services: Meal preparation according to a plan approved by Employer, shopping, errands, house cleaning, laundry.

Record Keeping: Caregiver will keep records as set out in Caregiver's Notebook.

Caregiver will accompany Client on errands and appointments as directed by Employer.

Caregiver will know the whereabouts and the physical condition of Client at all times while on duty, and will keep Employer informed of any changes.

Caregiver will make a written record of any accidents or other sudden events that bring harm or risk of harm to Client. Caregiver will make use of emergency contact procedures to speak with a Employer representative personally about any such incidents.

Other services as agreed between caregiver and Employer.

6. **Driving**.

☐ [check if applicable] Caregiver states that s/he has a valid State Driver's License, and agrees to provide a copy of such license.

[*Choose one*]

☐ Caregiver will provide transportation for Client in Client's vehicle to appointments, errands, shopping, and for social purposes. Employer is responsible for maintaining appropriate insurance coverage.

❑ Caregiver will provide transportation for Client in Caregiver's vehicle to appointments, errands, shopping, and for social purposes. Caregiver agrees to provide proof of liability and uninsured motorist insurance with policy limits of at least: $ 100,000.00 for bodily injury, $300,000.00 per incident maximum, and $50,000.00 property damage. Caregiver promises to notify Employer immediately if insurance is terminated. If use of the caregivers auto for work purposes is routine, caregiver will notify caregivers auto insurance carrier.

7. **Work Schedule**. Caregiver agrees to work according to a schedule established by Employer in consultation with Client, and will not alter the schedule without at least 48 hours advance notice to Employer (to allow Employer to approve the alteration or make other arrangements.) Caregiver will not revise this schedule without the consent of Employer.

8. **Household Expenses**. If Caregiver is provided with funds for household expenses, Caregiver will keep detailed records on forms provided by Employer. Caregiver will only make purchases that are approved by Employer.

9. **Probation Period**. During the first three months of employment Employer may terminate this agreement at any time with or without notice and without severance pay.

10. **Termination**. This agreement may be terminated at will by either Employer or caregiver with two (2) weeks advance written notice.

Employer may terminate employment without cause with no advance notice. If this occurs, Caregiver will be entitled to two weeks' severance pay at the rate of the average compensation over the past three months.

Employer may terminate employment with no advance notice and no severance pay if Caregiver has violated the terms of this agreement, or has been negligent, or acted in a way that could have allowed harm to Client.

11. This agreement will be interpreted according to the laws of the State of _____. In any proceeding in which this agreement is construed or interpreted against its drafter, that construction or interpretation will not apply, and this agreement will be construed or interpreted to give effect to the parties' intent in accordance with the terms of this agreement.

12. Legal Representation. Caregiver acknowledges that s/he was told that s/he was free to consult with a lawyer to review this agreement prior to signing it and had ample opportunity to do so. Caregiver acknowledges that this is an arms-length transaction in which she was free to negotiate and did negotiate the terms of this agreement.

13. Attorney's Fees. In the event of any breach of this agreement, the party responsible for the breach agrees to pay reasonable attorneys' fees and costs incurred by the other party in the enforcement of this agreement or suit for recovery of damages. The prevailing party in any suit instituted arising out of this agreement will be entitled to receive reasonable attorneys' fees and costs incurred in such suit.

14. Hours, Compensation. The hours and hourly compensation of caregiver are subject to change at any time as agreed between Caregiver and Employer. The initial arrangement is as follows:

Hours/days _____
Compensation _____

Client, _____
Date: _____

Caregiver _____

Example: Caregiver Agreement

Following is an example of a Personal Care Contract

On September 3, 2003, the time the contract was entered into, _____ was in a nursing home. The personal care contract was with her daughter, _____. Under the terms of the contract, _____ paid $11,000 to her daughter two weeks before submitting her application for Medicaid benefits.

The agreement was contained in an article written by, Esq. and, Esq., attorneys practicing in the state of _____.

NOTE: Just because this agreement was upheld in one state does not mean it will be in your state. Check with an experienced lawyer before modifying the agreement to your circumstances and executing it.

Example: Personal Care Contract

This agreement is entered into by and between _____ (CARE RECIPIENT) and _____ (CARE PROVIDER). It sets forth the terms under which CARE PROVIDER will provide personal assistance to CARE RECIPIENT.

1. DUTIES OF CARE PROVIDER. CARE RECIPIENT contracts to receive and CARE PROVIDER agrees to provide the following services for the lifetime of the CARE RECIPIENT on an "as needed" basis:
   a. Attend to needs of CARE RECIPIENT, including preparation of nutritious, appropriate meals and snacks; house cleaning; laundry;
   b. Assist CARE RECIPIENT with grooming, bathing, dressing, laundry, and personal shopping, as needed;

c. Purchase, with funds made available by CARE RECIPIENT, or assist CARE RECIPIENT in purchasing clothing, toiletries, and other personal items for CARE RECIPIENT as needed, taking into account CARE RECIPIENT's ability to pay for such items;

d. Purchase, with funds made available by CARE RECIPIENT, or assist CARE RECIPIENT in purchasing hobby, entertainment or other goods for CARE RECIPIENT's use and enjoyment, as needed, taking into account CARE RECIPIENT's ability to pay for such items;

e. Monitor CARE RECIPIENT's physical and mental condition and nutritional needs on a regular basis in cooperation with health care providers;

f. Arrange for transportation to health care providers and to the physician of CARE RECIPIENT's choice. CARE PROVIDER will also arrange for assessment, services and treatment by appropriate health care providers, including but not limited to, physicians, nurses, nursing home services, physical therapists, and mental health specialists as needed for CARE RECIPIENT;

g. Assist CARE RECIPIENT in carrying out the instructions and directives of CARE RECIPIENT's health care providers;

h. Arrange for social services by social service personnel as needed by CARE RECIPIENT;

i. Even if additional services are not needed, visit at least weekly with CARE RECIPIENT and encourage social interaction;

j. Arrange for outings and walks in keeping with CARE RECIPIENT's lifestyle, if reasonable and feasible for CARE RECIPIENT;

k. Interact with and/or assist any agent of CARE RECIPIENT in interacting with health professionals, long-term care facility administrators, social service personnel, insurance companies, and government workers in order to safeguard CARE RECIPIENT's rights, benefits, or other resources as needed.

1. The privacy of CARE RECIPIENT shall be preserved and respected as to visitors, telephone conversations and personal mail. Family members shall be permitted to visit CARE RECIPIENT.

2. DURATION. The services indicated above shall be provided to CARE RECIPIENT by CARE PROVIDER for the lifetime of CARE RECIPIENT.

3. COMPENSATION. The parties stipulate that as of the execution of this Agreement, CARE RECIPIENT is 76 years of age. CARE RECIPIENT agrees to pay, and CARE PROVIDER agrees to accept, in payment for the aforesaid services to be rendered by CARE PROVIDER, the compensation set forth below, which compensation the parties stipulate and agree to be fair and reasonable and commensurate with the quality and extent of the services and their fair market value.

Professional geriatric care managers typically receive $20.00 per hour for performance of the services noted above. The parties stipulate and agree that the CARE PROVIDER shall receive $12.00 per hour.

The parties agree and stipulate that CARE PROVIDER shall furnish the services set forth over the lifetime of CARE RECIPIENT on an "as needed" basis. Therefore, the parties understand that the hours expended in performance of said services will fluctuate over said lifetime according to CARE RECIPIENT's needs. There may be periods where more than 20 hours per week may be required. Conversely, there may be intervals when the services require less time. The parties agree that over the lifetime of CARE RECIPIENT, CARE PROVIDER will expend, on average, 4 hours per week or more.

The parties agree and stipulate that CARE RECIPIENT is 76 years of age. Based on the actuarial tables published by the National Center for Health Statistics, the life expectancy of CARE RECIPIENT is 11.3 years. This Agreement is for the duration of CARE RECIPIENT's life, regardless of its length. Although CARE RECIPIENT may live beyond said life expectancy or survive for a shorter duration, the parties agree and stipulate that compensation to the CARE PROVIDER be based upon said life expectancy of 11.3 years.

The parties, therefore, agree and stipulate that compensation to the CARE PROVIDER shall be computed as follows: $12.00 per hour, multiplied by 4 hours, multiplied by 11.3 years, multiplied by 52 weeks equals $28,204.80.

Thus, the maximum reasonable fair market value compensation is $28,204.80.

The parties recognize that CARE RECIPIENT does not possess sufficient assets to pay the maximum compensation. Therefore, the parties agree that as full compensation for the services contemplated hereunder, CARE RECIPIENT shall pay to CARE PROVIDER in cash and/or other assets of equivalent value the amount of $11,000.

The parties agree that the agreed upon compensation of $11,000.00 is less than the reasonable and fair market value of the services contemplated hereunder; nonetheless, CARE PROVIDER agrees to accept such amount as full compensation.

4. NON-ASSIGNABILITY. This Agreement is for services unique to CARE RECIPIENT. CARE PROVIDER agrees to personally perform the above services. CARE PROVIDER shall have no obligation to render services or otherwise be liable to any other person or entity.

5. LIABILITY. Medical care is to be provided at the expense of CARE RECIPIENT. CARE PROVIDER shall not be liable for the cost of CARE RECIPIENT's care. CARE RECIPIENT agrees to reimburse CARE PROVIDER for any reasonable out-of-pocket expenses incurred on CARE RECIPIENT's behalf.

6. EFFECTIVE DATE. This Agreement shall take effect and be binding on the parties hereto upon payment of the agreed upon compensation set forth above for CARE PROVIDER.

7. ARBITRATION CLAUSE. The parties agree that any dispute between them regarding the services under this Agreement or any other aspect of this Agreement, will be determined by submitting it to arbitration under the laws of the State of Missouri, rather than by a lawsuit through the court process.

8. This Agreement contains the entire Agreement and understanding between the parties, surpassing all prior communications, either written or oral, concerning the subject matter of this Agreement. This agreement may be changed only by a written instrument executed by both parties hereto.

9. This Agreement shall be governed by and construed in accordance with the laws of the State of Missouri.

THIS IS A LEGALLY BINDING AGREEMENT. EACH PARTY HAS READ THE ABOVE AGREEMENT BEFORE SIGNING IT. EACH PARTY UNDERSTANDS THE AGREEMENT HE OR SHE IS MAKING, HAVING HAD THE OPPORTUNITY TO ASK TO HAVE EACH TERM THAT THE PARTY DOES NOT UNDERSTAND FULLY EXPLAINED.

(Presumably the agreement also included space for both parties to sign as well as the date of signature)

3. Resources

"Mom and Dad, let's think of some resources that you are familiar with as you consider making things both fair and equal with the task of Parent Care?"

Response:

- "We can make our house senior friendly and live here."
- "We can move in with you or add on to your house and live with you."
- "We can put a senior cottage in your back yard and move in with you."

- "We can contact non-medical home companion companies to hire people to help us."
- "We can put a camera in our house so you can monitor us night or day."
- "I could work part time for you in my retirement to make some extra money."
- "I could do a video explaining to the other children why our estate was divided unequally."
- "I could change my will and my beneficiary forms to reflect what I believe is fair with regards to my estate and personal items."
- "I will give away some things to the children in an unequal but fair way."

What is "ECHO Housing or "Senior Cottage"

Mom or Dad need a place to stay…you want them close by…but you don't want to build on….what is the solution?

Some are considering what is called "an elder cottage" or an Echo house.

It is a small, temporary housing unit that can be installed in a backyard -- most commonly used to accommodate older adults.

ECHO housing units are self-contained prefab homes (usually between 400 and 800 square feet) that allow someone to remain largely independent while still living within earshot of family. ECHO housing usually includes all the amenities of a house -- a kitchen, a bedroom, a bathroom, and a living room -- albeit on a very small scale.

A disadvantage of the idea is that many neighborhood associations will not allow these structures in the neighborhood, but for many it is a temporary solution that can be sold or moved when it is no longer needed for parent care. Do a search on "Echo" Housing or "elder cottage". www.eldercottages.com

---

"Don't Pay Me now...Pay Me Later"

Mom and dad need your help now, but can't afford to pay you now. What you may consider is helping them and keeping a log of the hours rendered. If there is anything left in the estate, then the personal representative pays you for services rendered and whatever is left is divided among the heirs. Now I believe that is fair!! The parents would have to change their will and beneficiary forms to reflect such a division of the assets.

---

4. Experience

"Mom and Dad, as you think about this issue of your care and treating your children 'fairly and equally' could you tell me what that experience would look like?"

- "I don't want the children to fight after we are gone."
- "I don't want the one child to think they were cheated or short changed."
- "I will put in writing or video why I did what I did."
- "I will explain why I was fair....but my division of assets was not equal."
- "I believe in responsibility....and I don't believe in entitlement."
- "I don't reward entitlement....I do reward responsibility."

A Picture is worth a Thousand words

If you have not seen the movie "Ultimate Gift" it is a must see. The grandfather gives his grandson a challenge and if he gets it right, he inherits the majority of his assets. The grandfather was more concerned that his grandson has good qualities in life than material things. He uses a video to communicate this after he is gone.
If you want to leave things to your heirs 'unequal' but 'fair' you may consider creating a video explaining your logic.

Also, take a look at the sequel to The Ultimate Gift movie, The Ultimate Life.

Conclusion:

I know you were an almost perfect parent! I know you raised your children the best you could. I know that you did all you could so they would turn out to be the best but the reality is that they are not equal. They are not the same. They may not share your parent care matters equally. Therefore, we may consider looking at this realistically. I will love my children but I will love most the children who gave most, did most, and were there in my darkest, loneliest and final hours. I will reward the child who holds my hand, changes my diaper, puts up with my dementia, and takes me to the doctors. I will reward the child who has patience, love and kindness. I will reward my child who puts cold towels on my head when I am breathing my last breath, swabs my dry mouth, and makes sure I have an honorable memorial service. That is the child I will reward. I will be unequal because that is what is fair. Maybe you have a child that you can reward fairly and unequally!

13

"THE FINAL PREPARATION CONVERSATION"

Ready for the Final Flight

I have several friends who are pilots and on a number of occasions I have had the opportunity to fly with them. I am amazed at the pre-flight checklist that they go through. They check the oil, the gas, the rudders, the tires, and a long list of other things. All of this is done to make sure the plane is safe for flying. When we leave this life some use the analogy of "flying away." Wouldn't it be helpful to have a checklist to make sure we are ready for the final flight? A conversation about final wishes and plans would be a wise move for many families.

The Night Momma Died (Kevin)

It was 11:30 p.m. on December 19, 2011 when my mom died. I was the only child left as my brother passed away in 2009. Mom was finally at peace, her pain and suffering was over, she had breathed her last breath. I called the funeral home and they came. Now I had to plan for the funeral. I thought, wouldn't it be nice to have a checklist to make sure I didn't forget anything? I knew some of mom's wishes, but not all of them. This chapter is for those who will have a night when "momma" or "daddy" dies and a checklist to help you on that day or night.

The Final Preparation Conversation

1. Challenges

"Mom and Dad, let's look down the road at your final wishes and your funeral or memorial service and discuss what you think are some of the biggest challenges we as children will face?"

Responses:

- "I don't like to talk about death and dying."
- "We know where we want to be buried and we have bought plots."
- "I think when we die that is the end…cremation will be fine for me."
- "I don't have enough money for a big funeral, let's do it cheap."
- "If I pre-pay my funeral, how do I know the funeral home will be in business when I die?"
- "My children live out of state and I may be staying close to them when I die."
- "We don't need an expensive casket and vault; we have taken care of this."
- "I will pay my expenses now in present dollars so you don't have to pay in future dollars."

> ### Reality Check: Not the time or Place
> ### for Negotiations (Kevin)
>
> I was sitting in the funeral home with my mom for my stepfather's funeral. My stepfather's father had bought the plot. The funeral director gave us the price of the funeral, casket, service, etc., approximately $8,900. My first thought was that this amount is too much; thinking we would take the body and go down the street and shop around. Well, that is hard to do when planning and paying for a funeral on the spot. That was not the time or place to negotiate. I felt like we had no negotiating power.
>
> But when I planned my mom's funeral in December 2011, and I went the frugal route, it still was over $10,000. The funeral director explained that the price is why the trend is moving towards cremation.

One of the biggest challenges many face is our own mortality. Many of us get busy with life and really do not think that today would or could be our final day. Therefore, it takes a real effort and level of self-awareness to overcome the denial that one day we will pass from this world. Once this "challenge" has been overcome, there are many factors to consider when planning for the final checklist.

2. Alternatives

"Mom and Dad, let's discuss some of the options you might consider when it comes to your final wishes, funeral planning and preparation."

Responses:

- "Just put me in a pine box and put me in the ground."
- "I say do a viewing and then I would elect cremation."
- "I would like to give my body to science to make the world a better place."
- "I am an organ donor, so I can help someone else."
- "I want my service at _____ and I want _____ and _____ to do the service."

- "Can you have the pastor read Psalm 23?"
- "I have already bought the plot and all is set."
- "I want my service to be a celebration."
- "I would like a military funeral and 21 gun salute."

When it comes to final planning, the first alternative to consider is do I want cremation or a casket burial? The choice between the two depends on the person and some of the personal and sometimes spiritual beliefs about the afterlife. The details of how funerals are handled can vary widely. A friend of mine owns a funeral home and we discussed the cultural and religious differences in how we lay our loved ones to rest.

Why Preplan?

Thinking about your own funeral leaves most people feeling a little uneasy, but more adults are finding that preplanning a funeral offers great emotional and even financial security for them and their families. With preplanning, families find comfort in knowing that the funeral reflects what their loved one wanted. It also gives them peace of mind to not have to make important decisions at a stressful time.

If you are considering prearranging a funeral, you should contact funeral homes in your community. A funeral director can walk you through the prearrangement process.

The National Funeral Directors Association (NFDA) developed the Bill of Rights for Funeral Preplanning as a resource for understanding what to expect from a pre-need contract.

Once you've made the prearrangements, keep a copy of the plan and any pertinent paperwork in a safe place. Also, inform a close friend or relative about the arrangements that have been made and where the information may be found.

If you choose, there are several ways to prepay for your funeral that can offer you financial benefits. However, prepaying is not required; it's an option that many individuals find helpful.

If you feel prepaying is a wise decision, then be sure to go over all available options with your funeral director. Remember, like any contract, ask any and all questions you may have regarding your pre-need plan before you sign an agreement.

NFDA Model Consumer Protection Guidelines for State Pre-need Funeral Statutes

The Model Consumer Protection Guidelines for State Pre-need Funeral Statutes were first approved by the NFDA Policy Board in October, 2000. They were designed to ensure that consumers who purchase pre-need funeral goods and services make informed decisions, deal with ethical and licensed pre-need sellers and agents, and retain the right to cancel pre-need funeral contracts or transfer pre-need funding to different funeral providers. The Pre-need Guidelines were recently amended to include 100 percent trusting, following action by the NFDA Policy Board at its October 18, 2003, meeting in Las Vegas, Nevada.

Get more details at www.nfda.org

What are the advantages and disadvantages of direct cremation?

Direct Cremation Advantages:

Direct cremation offers an affordable alternative to traditional body burial. While direct cremation can significantly reduce funeral home costs, you can reap additional financial benefits from the cemetery and headstone dealer. If you choose not to bury the cremated remains—and many people do not-you can eliminate many items that make the traditional funeral so expensive.

Here is a list of costs you can eliminate by choosing direct cremation:

- Expensive casket
- Embalming
- Funeral home staff and facilities charge
- Cosmetic and hair dressing charges
- Funeral chapel or church fees
- Viewing or visitation charges
- Transportation fees (hearse, flower cart, utility vehicle, etc.)

- Burial plot or mausoleum crypt
- Vault or grave liner
- Grave opening and closing costs
- Headstone or grave marker

But price is not the only advantage in choosing direct cremation. Many people prefer cremation because the cremains (i.e. ashes) are portable. This allows families to take remains with them when they move. Many people also feel that choosing cremation over body burial is friendlier to the environment because no land is disturbed.

Direct cremation is also simpler and more expedient. The entire affair usually takes place in just two or three days; furthermore, direct cremation requires less time commitment from the family. This can be especially important if surviving family members are ill, disabled, or live far away.

Cremation also offers a wide range of disposition options. While most families decide to keep remains at home, other options exist.

Cremation Disadvantages:

While direct cremation offers many advantages, you also need to consider its potential disadvantages before finalizing your plans.

Because many families find comfort in holding a traditional funeral service, a simpler direct cremation may not be therapeutic enough to satisfy surviving family members.

In addition, direct cremation does not allow the family to celebrate the decedent's life, nor does it give friends an opportunity to say goodbye. And because the funeral home makes less money when providing direct cremation services, funeral home employees may try harder to sell you extras.

Lastly, even though you may not have to buy a grave site or headstone, you will incur an additional expense if you decide to purchase an urn.

Requirements for a Military Service:

Some may desire to have a military service or to be buried at a military cemetery. Barbara Salazar Torreon has put together a white paperwork on frequently asked questions. It is entitled: *Military Funeral Honors and Military Cemeteries: Frequently Asked Questions*

And can be found at: http://www.fas.org/sgp/crs/misc/RS21545.pdf

National Cemetery Administration

Military Funeral Honors

"Honoring Those Who Served"

The Department of Defense (DOD) is responsible for providing military funeral honors. "Honoring Those Who Served" is the title of the DOD program for providing dignified military funeral honors to Veterans who have defended our nation.

Upon the family's request, Public Law 106-65 requires that every eligible Veteran receive a military funeral honors ceremony, to include folding and presenting the United States burial flag and the playing of Taps. The law defines a military funeral honors detail as consisting of two or more uniformed military persons, with at least one being a member of the Veteran's parent service of the armed forces. The DOD program calls for funeral home directors to request military funeral honors on behalf of the Veterans' family. However, the Department of Veterans Affairs (VA) National Cemetery Administration cemetery staff can also assist with arranging military funeral honors at VA national cemeteries. Veteran's organizations may assist in providing military funeral honors. When military funeral honors at a national cemetery are desired, they are arranged prior to the committal service by the funeral home.

The Department of Defense began the implementation plan for providing military funeral honors for eligible Veterans as enacted in Section 578 of Public Law 106-65 of the National Defense Authorization Act for FY 2000 on Jan. 1, 2000.

Questions or comments concerning the DOD military funeral honors program may be sent to the address listed below. The military funeral honors Web site is located at www.militaryfuneralhonors.osd.mil. [Link will take you off the VA web site.]

Office of the Assistant Secretary of Defense for Public Affairs
Community Relations and Public Liaison
1400 Defense Pentagon, Room 2D982
Washington, DC 20301-1400

To arrange military funeral honors, contact your local funeral home.

Costs for a Funeral
According to funeral-tips.com.

Today, the average North American traditional funeral costs between $7,000 and $10,000. This price range includes the services at the funeral home, burial in a cemetery, and the installation of a headstone. While cremation is gaining in popularity, the traditional funeral is still the most popular manner for disposing of the deceased.

Although funeral prices vary considerably between funeral homes and geographic areas of the country, here is a reasonable "ballpark" estimate of the main costs that are involved:

- fee for the funeral director's services: $1,500
- cost for a casket: $2,300
- embalming: $500
- cost for using the funeral home for the actual funeral service: $500
- cost of a grave site: $1,000
- cost to dig the grave: $600
- cost of a grave liner or outer burial container: $1,000
- cost of a headstone: $1,500

In this example, total costs would approximate $9,000....and that's just for the "main" items. There could be additional charges for things like placing the obituary in the newspaper and buying flowers.

Cost for Cremation
According to Caring.com:

The cost of cremation typically ranges from $2,000 to $4,000 if arranged through a funeral home and from $1,500 to $3,000 if arranged directly through a crematory. Although the cost of cremation differs depending on locale, it's almost always substantially less than the cost of a full body burial -- which is one of the reasons cited for cremation's growing acceptance and popularity.

However, in addition to the cost of the basic cremation service -- processing a body into the ash-and-bones mixtures called "cremains" -- a number of other charges may be added for related paperwork, goods, and services, including:

- Getting an original death certificate and copies.
- Obtaining a certificate releasing the body for cremation, usually issued by a medical examiner or coroner.
- Transporting the body from the place of death to the place of cremation.
- Disposing of the cremains by burying or scattering them.
- Removing a pacemaker.
- Handling charges paid to funeral industry personnel (if involved).
- Purchasing or renting a casket or container.

Although these incidental charges can add a few hundred to a few thousand dollars to the cost of cremation, the item that's potentially the priciest is a casket, which can range from $500 for a simple wooden version to $35,000 or more for an ornate style. Many people who choose cremation opt not to purchase a casket, but some prefer to have one during a funeral or memorial.

Considerations

As you consider planning for your final expenses, there is no one way that fits everyone. Because of the many choices and options, it is the greater part of wisdom for parents and adult children to discuss preferences and desires when it comes to final arrangements. Having The Final Preparation Conversation can certainly bring a measure of peace of mind.

3. Resources

"Mom and Dad, let's think of some resources that you are familiar with in regards to making a final checklist for your wishes and planning for your funeral and last details?"

Responses:

- "I have talked with my pastor and he knows what I want in my service."
- "My favorite bible verse is….."
- "I want _____ to speak and give the eulogy"
- "I have enough resources and money to pay for the funeral."
- "I want to go fishing and fall off the boat…."
- "I bought my plot many years ago…I call it 'the ranch' ….one day I am going to 'the ranch'."
- "I don't know if you can trust the funeral home with your money….what if they go out of business?"

Funeral Planning Scams to Avoid

Discussion of death and dying can certainly be an emotional conversation. Because emotions are high, there are those who would seek to prey on those emotions and scam others. The Better Business Bureau and the Federal Bureau of Investigation offer these tips:

- Be an informed consumer. Take time to call and shop around before making a purchase. Funeral homes are required to provide detailed price lists over the phone or in writing.

Product markups can be significant. Ask if lower priced items are included on the price list.

- Check out the funeral service. Contact the BBB for a report on the funeral home. Check whether the funeral services director or embalmer is licensed.

- The low-down on caskets. Sellers who claim to have a product or service that will preserve human remains over the long term are misleading you. Funeral providers cannot determine how long a casket will preserve a body, so keep that in mind when deciding whether to purchase the more expensive "sealed" or "protective" casket. Also, a casket is not legally required for a direct cremation.

- Research funeral home service fees when shopping for products elsewhere. The Federal Trade Commission's Web site at www. ftc.gov has information on charges that are prohibitive.

- Embalming is not always required. You are not required to have embalming if you choose direct cremation or immediate burial.

- Resist high-priced sales pitches from funeral industry vendors. They should treat you with compassion; not pressure you.

- Consult a friend or family member. It might be a good idea to take along a friend or relative when you visit the funeral home. Someone who is not as emotionally invested as you are can assist with difficult decisions.

- Require all proposed plans and purchases to be put in writing. Compare the posted prices and any oral promises with those listed in the contract. The contract should itemize all prices and specify any future costs. Check the contract for any restrictions. (Source: www.bbb.org)

- Carefully read contracts and purchasing agreements before signing. Ask if the agreements you sign can be voided, taken back or transferred to other funeral homes.

- Prepaying for a funeral has advantages, as well as risks. If you choose to prepay, make a well-informed decision, carefully research your options and know your rights. You can always make plans in advance, without prepaying. Be sure to share your specific wishes with those close to you.

Websites for Final Preparation:

> www.funeral.org
> www.caregiverslibrary.org
> www.imsorrytohear.com
> www.funeraldecisions.com/costquotes
> www.aftercareplanning.com

As you consider the resources needed for a funeral or cremation, it is best that families talk. Conversation and communication can go a long way to saving money and meeting the wishes of a loved one who has passed.

4. Experience

"Mom and Dad, think about your final service and memorial, what are some things that you would like for the family to experience on that day?"

Responses:

- "I want it to be a day of celebration."
- "I don't want people to have to take care of a single detail"
- "I want these Bible verses read at my service:_____"
- "I don't want everyone to be teary eyed"
- "I learned from my parents the wisdom of pre-planning".
- "I remember how hard it was on the family when my dad died without a plan…we had to all guess about his wishes."

One of the most amazing movies I have seen about planning your funeral is the 1998 movie "What Dreams May Come" with Robin Williams. In the movie Robin Williams is in a car accident and one scene has him attending his own funeral. It is a very touching scene and one that we can imagine as we plan the details of that day. It is not a thought that we want to think about, but one that we will need to think about if we are going to plan for that day and not burden others to do so.

Funeral Etiquette

Funerals serve several purposes. In addition to commemorating the life of the deceased, a funeral offers emotional support to the bereaved and an opportunity for friends and family to pay tribute to their loved one. The process of going through the planning and final disposition helps the family come to terms with the fact that a death has occurred. This is a necessary part of the grieving process. It is common for people to enter a period of denial when a family member or loved one has died.

Friends offering fond remembrances are often helpful during this time. Customs for expressing sympathy vary according to religious and ethnic customs. The following information is offered merely as a guideline for what is generally accepted in various circumstances during a funeral.

General guidelines for guests:

Expressing Sympathy: Simple, brief expressions of sympathy are usually best. While most people find themselves at a loss for words, the family will appreciate a sincere expression of condolence-however brief. "I'm sorry," or, "I'm so sorry to hear of your loss," are the most commonly used expressions, and they are perfectly adequate when said in a sincere, sympathetic voice. If you knew the deceased well enough, it is often helpful to say so; "I always counted Bob as a good friend," or, "Jane will be missed by everyone." Kind words are always welcomed. Follow the lead of the family member. If they want to talk about the deceased, lend an ear and a few minutes of your time. Being a good listener may be the best solace you can provide for them.

When attending calling hours, do not feel you have to stay for a lengthy period of time. Follow your instincts as to how long to stay. If the deceased was a good friend, you may feel it necessary to stay longer, to tend to your own grief at the same time as paying your respects to the family. If you have never met the family, introduce yourself and let them know how you are connected to their loved one. Colleagues and co-workers of the deceased may attend calling hours together, but try not to descend on the bereaved all together. Offer individual sympathy and a word or two of support; "I am so sorry for your loss," and/or, "Let me know if there is anything I can do to help."

If, indeed, you are able to offer assistance with childcare, or food gifts, or picking up out-of-town relatives, by all means, do so. These thoughtful gestures are invaluable. Sudden, or tragic deaths, may be so emotionally draining, your ability to assist the bereaved will be long remembered and appreciated. In the case of the elderly woman or man who has lost a spouse and may not have children close by to attend to their needs, a lending hand with transportation or running errands can make the ordeal so much easier on them.

Many times funerals become a place to share memories. Visitors are encouraged to talk about their memories of the deceased. Sometimes the family learns new things about their loved one that they didn't know before! While we all accept the somber atmosphere of a funeral setting, sharing stories and laughter can personalize the occasion and actually help ease the pain. Sorrow is an individual suffering, but joyful stories shared freely can make the grief easier to bear.

DRESS

Subdued colors are most appropriate for funerals. It is becoming more acceptable to wear brighter colors today, to celebrate the life of the deceased, but the truth is, etiquette requires modesty and somberness. Out of respect for the family, try to keep your dress simple but not too casual. Many orthodox cultures still adhere to the traditional black attire, and if you opt for that choice, you will never go wrong.

VIEWING THE BODY

If the funeral is open casket, you are welcome to view the deceased and/or pray for them. This is not required. If there are calling hours but the family is not present, you may still view the body. If you wish to have a family member escort you to the casket, don't be afraid to ask. Regardless of your religious affiliation, a few moments of silence is always appreciated.

GENERAL GUIDELINES FOR THE BEREAVED

Cause of death can be a difficult subject. While most people will have read the obituary or may ask others how the death occurred, you should be prepared to answer this question. Especially in the event of a sudden death brought on by tragic or unexplained circumstances.

Specifying the cause of death in the obituary will help allay the "What happened?" questions. How you approach the inquisitiveness of visitors to the funeral is a purely personal decision. If the deceased has passed on due to an illness you do not care to discuss, such as cancer or HIV, or suicide, prepare an honest answer to the "What happened?" question, but don't feel the need to elaborate. Visitors may merely be making conversation and hoping to give you a venue to express your grief.

It's standard practice to greet callers during calling hours. You do not have to keep track of visitors as they will approach you during their visits, but always welcome them with kindness and express your appreciation at their attendance.

In the event someone attends calling hours that you particularly do not like, be polite. In rare instances, an altercation may occur causing you to ask the funeral director to escort a visitor out. Your attitude will do much to keep disruptions from happening. Treat everyone with respect and let them know you are touched by their effort to pay their respects. A funeral is not the place to air grievances or foster rudeness.

You will likely see people you have not seen in years! As with any gathering, you are the host or hostess and must make an effort to speak to each person who attends. While it is not your responsibility to seek them out, it is your responsibility to make sure there is a guest sign-in book. This enables you to know who attended in order to write the thank-you card. Try not to spend an inordinate amount of time with only one or two people. If you have a lot to catch up on, invite them to visit you after the funeral, or make plans for a luncheon date. This will help both of you in dealing with the effects of the death.

THANK YOU NOTES

Anyone who presented, sent a gift or card to the family, deserves a thank you note. Examples would be to thank anyone who has sent in a memorial contribution, brought food to the house of the grieving family, sent flowers, or in some other tangible way acknowledged the death. Those visitors who attend the calling hours do not require a thank you card.

It is suggested that thank you notes be sent within two weeks of the death. In the past, thank you notes included a personal letter from the grieving family, but today a simple thank you card with a signature, is accepted. Many people include a personal note or a hand written thank you, but that is a personal choice.

THANKING CLERGY

A personal note is recommended for thanking your clergy person. If an honorarium or offering is sent, send it in a separate envelope. Do not include it with the thank you note.

PALLBEARERS

A separate note to each pallbearer is recommended. Personal messages of thanks will be appreciated by each individual who graciously assisted in this important task.

FLOWERS

For individuals, you may wish to include a personal word or two of thanks on the acknowledgement card. For groups or organizations, send the note to the leader of the group and remember to include all the members of the group in your note. If individual member names appear on the floral card, a separate note should be sent to each one. You do not have to include a personal message in this instance.

Flowers that were sent from a group of neighbors or employees require a separate thank you to each name included on the floral card. You may or may not include a hand written message of thanks.

FRIENDS WHO HAVE HELPED OUT

Friends who have volunteered their help in any way such as driving a car in the funeral procession, helping the family with arrangements or food, etc. deserve a separate written thank you.

As stated earlier, it is not necessary to send thank you cards to friends or visitors that stop in at the home of the grieving family or that attend the calling hours at the funeral home.

If the neighbors or friends who have volunteered their help are close to the family, you may feel better thanking them in person. In this instance, use your own judgment to determine if a written note is necessary.

The Funeral Check List

As I consider the details of planning for my final wishes what are some things for me to consider?

I prefer:

- ☐ Autopsy or Not:
- ☐ A normal burial:
- ☐ Cremation:
- ☐ Cemetery plot _____
- ☐ If one has been previously purchased, bring the deed to the plot with you, if you have it, to the funeral home when you make your plans. If you know you have a plot but don't have the deed in your possession, the funeral director can contact the cemetery overseer to arrange confirmation. Otherwise a plot will need to be purchased. The funeral director will assist you with this.
- ☐ Vault _____
- ☐ Choose a vault. Your funeral director will describe the various types available.
- ☐ Mausoleum _____
- ☐ Organ Donor or not _____
- ☐ Select the casket or container
  - o Wood _____ Metal _____ Cardboard (cremation) _____ Urn _____
- ☐ Open or closed casket
- ☐ Decide whether it will be opened or closed casket.

The location that I would like to be buried:

- ☐ Church cemetery _____
- ☐ Military cemetery: _____
- ☐ Public cemetery: _____
- ☐ Cremation and ashes to: _____

I have done pre-planning with the following funeral home:

_____

Details for the Funeral or Memorial Service

Location of the service:

- ☐ Church or Synagogue: _____
- ☐ Funeral Home Chapel: _____
- ☐ Other Location: _____

Speaker/Eulogy for Service:

- ☐ Pastor/Minister/Rabbi/Priest_____
- ☐ Friends: _____
- ☐ Family:_____
- ☐ Co-Worker: _____

Details for Service:

- ☐ Which funeral home: ____
- ☐ Order of Service
- ☐ Type of service (memorial, wake, military, Jewish ceremony, etc.)
- ☐ Who to write eulogy for newspaper and which papers to include. _____
- ☐ Who to handle music and details of service: _____
- ☐ Pall Bearers _____ _____ _____ _____
- ☐ Music/Songs: _____
- ☐ Flowers
- ☐ Photos that will be displayed
- ☐ Favorite Scripture: _____
- ☐ Pictures/Video: _____
- ☐ Clothes to wear for deceased
- ☐ Who to do hair or make-up: _____
- ☐ Cemetery Plot: _____
- ☐ Website for deceased: _____
- ☐ Internet Stream of service
- ☐ When to do visitation: Night before or day of service.
- ☐ Where the family will meet
- ☐ A grave marker and inscriptions
- ☐ Compensation for participants
- ☐ Memorial register or memorial cards

- ☐ Transportation and funeral cars
- ☐ Discuss who will be responsible for funeral expenses for billing purposes. If there is an executor for the estate of the deceased, this person usually handles this responsibility, but it is entirely up to the family to determine who should handle this responsibility
- ☐ Gather the information you will need for the completion of the death certificate at the funeral home. Parent's names including middle initials, also the social security number.

Examples of Order of Service

The following are examples of order of service to help you with planning. You will notice that the first example (Dan's) is a very informal service, more of a celebration of life than a funeral. It was performed at a large banquet hall with refreshments and more of a party setting per Dan's wishes. The next two are very formal in content and format and were held in 'houses of worship'.

Order of Service for Dan Taylor

Celebration for the Life of
Daniel James Taylor
January 9, 2010

Opening and Welcome: Kevin Skipper
    Statement:
    Quotes:

Opening Tribute to Dan Taylor:
    Video: Pictures and songs honoring Dan's life

Speeches:

Dan Taylor: The Coach: Dan Sullivan

Dan Taylor: The Attitude: Jon Locucca

Dan Taylor: The Humorist: Charlotte Roberts

Dan Taylor: Mr. Determination: Mark Bass

Dan Taylor: The Mentor: Kevin Skipper

Conclusion: Dan Taylor Remembered:
    Video: Pictures and songs of Dan's life

Order of Service for Kevin's Dad
July 19, 2007

Prelude- 9:55 a.m. Seating	Seating of the Family	Time Allotted
Opening Comments		3
Open Chorus -- "Rejoice in the Lord Always and Again I say Rejoice" Opening Hymn—"Blessed Assurance Jesus is Mine."	Congregation	4
Video Presentation: Brad Paisley: "When I get Where I am Going" Presentation done by Courtney		12
Scripture and Comment:	Stevens	5
Granddaughters Tribute: Song:		4
Scripture & Comments	Cook	5
Song "His Eye is On the Sparrow"		3
Honoring Dad	Children in Order	
	daughter	3
	daughter	3
	son	3
	son	3
	son	10
Closing Prayer	son	3
Closing Hymn "When We all Get to Heaven"	Congregation	3
We will need to conclude the service by 11:05 a.m. to get to the cemetery for the color guard schedule…		

Order of Service for Kevin's Mom December 22, 2011, 2 p.m.		
Prelude Music:	"How Great Thou Are"	
Opening Remarks:		Pastor
Song:	"Victory in Jesus"	Congregation
Scripture:		Pastor
Song:	"The Old Rugged Cross"	Congregation
"Life Lessons I Learned from Mom"		
Song:	"What a Day That Will Be"	
Message:		Pastor
Closing Song:	"Beulah Land"	
Postlude Music:	"When We All Get To Heaven"	

Losing someone we love is one of the hardest things any of us will ever go through. Taking the time to have The Final Preparation Conversation can be one of the best things for your family. We hope that this chapter will help you with the guidance and resources to effectively help you plan for your final services.

PART THREE

IMPLEMENTING PARENT CARE DECISIONS

Parents are like shuttles on a loom. They join the threads of the past with threads of the future and leave their own bright patterns as they go.

- Fred Rogers, TV's *Mister* Rogers

14

EXECUTING ESSENTIAL LEGAL DOCUMENTS AND FINANCIAL STRATEGIES

Decisions and Documents

In the wake of the 11.5 conversations you've just had, you and your parents should have made good progress in addressing the eight hundred-pound gorilla in the room that is the parent care issue, and resolving many questions. However, if you still can't get your folks to open up on this issue and provide direction for you, there is not much more you can do except wait for that phone call from the neighbor telling you that your mom has fallen and can't get up or that your dad is walking down the street in his pajamas trying to give away the family dog. At least you now have a heads-up about the psychological, emotional, and financial whirlwind that will follow. Assuming, though, that you have made good progress, you should now be at the point where your parents will need to prepare some legal documents and execute some legal strategies that will enable them to accomplish what they want with a minimum of difficulty and complexity.

> ## Reality Check
>
> **Parental Myth:** "My affairs are not complicated; I'll just put down what I want done on a legal pad."
>
> **Fact:** Parents who believe this are the dream of estate attorneys who specialize in the contesting of wills. One thing that makes America and thirteen other nations (make a game of figuring out which ones) unique on this planet is our sharing of uniform property laws governing who owns and who inherits. In other words, there are guidelines and structures (i.e., documents) for supporting those guidelines, the sole purpose of which is to definitively determine the wishes of the deceased and to carry them out to the letter. Hastily scribbled notes on a legal pad documenting an "uncomplicated" estate plan typically result in vaguely worded wishes and often conflicting promises expressed in semi-legible handwriting that lead to lawsuits between surviving family members, the breakup of families, and fat bank accounts for attorneys.

As I noted early in the book, the 11.5 conversations are the "what" of the parent care solution. These documents and strategies are the "how." Without them, you and your parents will have had some great conversations together but nowhere to go with the decisions that emerged from them. It's like planning the vacation of a lifetime but then not taking it. Let me give you an example.

Brian and Paula Wilson had just retired from their respective careers in dentistry and teaching, and had decided to do some traveling. Brian's dental practice had grown in value substantially over the years. Since his two younger partners had been working under an associate's arrangement wherein Brian owned the practice and they were salaried employees, all three were anxious to replace this arrangement. The Wilsons always visited their attorney to get their affairs in order before they traveled anywhere, so that in the event anything should happen to them, their two daughters and Brian's partners would know what to do.

The attorney drew up the appropriate sales documents, the note securing financing, and the buyout agreement for Brian and his partners to sign, as well as other estate plan documents. The income from the practice note would be a large part of the Wilsons' retirement income, and since Brian owned the building where the dental practice was located, the rental income from the partners would be another source of retirement revenue for him and his wife. In addition, they had money in separate retirement plans as well as a couple of brokerage accounts at a local branch of Bank of America. The intent was for these assets to be overseen by their children, acting together, once they were gone.

After the attorney had drawn up all the documents, the Wilsons decided they would take them home and review them carefully over the weekend before signing them, just to make sure they understood everything. The attorney agreed. These documents, which also included a new will and powers of attorney replacing old ones that had long since been misplaced, were all the Wilsons now had to disburse their assets.

Early Saturday morning, Brian Wilson went for his customary walk. When he returned, he found his wife slumped over the kitchen table, dead from what was later discovered to have been a massive stroke. Overcome with shock and grief, Brian struggled to phone 911, but the stress of the moment caused him to suffer a stroke as well, one that so severely damaged his brain that he expired later that day.

> ## Reality Check
>
> **Parental Myth:** "I can buy some estate planning software and document things myself, less expensively."
>
> **Fact:** There's a reason that home haircut kits and do-it-yourself brain surgery software have never caught on. Some things are better left to the pros. Estate planning and other legal document software are excellent tools for doing homework -- for learning what to ask and perhaps even deciding what to do about certain issues *before* going to the attorney, thus saving time and perhaps some money.

The police notified the Wilsons' children, Grace and Isabelle, both of whom lived out of town, of their parents' deaths. But due to HIPAA (Health Insurance Portability and Accountability Act of 1996) regulations, when the women got to the hospital, personnel were prevented from giving them any details about their parents' situation or allowing the bodies to be moved until they could produce sufficient documentation stipulating them as next of kin. It took the women almost thirty-six hours to come up with the required proof of who they were. Once they moved their parents' bodies to a local funeral home, they got another shock; they were told that since they were from out of town, the funeral costs (caskets, vaults, gravesites, and preparatory expenses) had to be prepaid to the tune of some $13,000!

Because the Wilsons died intestate (without at will*), their estate ended up being divided equally between their two daughters, but it required nearly a year of bureaucratic red tape and mountains of paperwork to make that happen. Grace and Isabelle inherited their parents' home, personal belongings, and investment accounts, but the latter passed to them minus the tax man's 50 percent bite of the value of the apple due to an unsigned designated beneficiary form.

And then there was the dental practice. Because the note and documents of sale had not been signed, the partners were free to take over the business and pay the daughters a nominal 10 percent of its market value. Furthermore, because the building was in need of some repairs and renovations, the partners were in a good position to bargain over rent; in lieu of turning them out and having to find a new tenant, the daughters were forced to concede them a 50 percent rent reduction to offset the cost of the repairs and improvements they needed to make and to sustain the rent reduction for as long as it took the partners to recoup their expenses.

---

* A will had been drawn up but not signed.

> ### Reality Check
>
> **Parental Myth:** "My attorney will make sure all my affairs are in order."
>
> **Fact:** With or without your help, your parents are responsible for getting their affairs in order, not their attorney. An attorney just drafts the documents, spelling out what your parents want done for them, to sign, and it is that last act of putting their signatures on the dotted line -- not the attorney's say-so -- that will ensure their affairs are truly in order.

Essential Documents and Strategies

Every day in the United States, families, businesses, homes, and fortunes disappear just like that, due to improperly drawn up and/or executed (i.e., signed) legal documents and other papers. It doesn't do any good to go through all the parent care conversations, get into the minutiae of finances and the intimate details of property distribution and legacy goals, only to let the fruit of these discussions -- the decisions your parents have made -- die on the vine.

The Wilsons had made their care and estate plan decisions; they had gone so far as having the documents drawn up. But then, due to tragic and unforeseen circumstances that left those documents unsigned, many of those decisions could not be executed as they wished, with dire consequences to their children.

The following is a list of the most important care and estate planning documents and related items your parents will need in order to make sure the decisions they've made with your help about their future care and desires will be carried out as they wish. Because all fifty states have different forms, rules, and regulations for these documents, I strongly advise you to consult a legal specialist in your state. While there are various computer programs or do-it-yourself kits that suggest that all you need to do is fill in the blanks, I strongly urge you and your parents to use such programs and kits simply as thinking tools prior to a visit with a legal or tax professional. The areas of law that concern property, care, and possessions overlap and contain potential legal, financial, and tax consequences for the uninformed that may create disastrous results for your family. The local Bar Association or commission may be helpful in directing you to qualified legal, financial, or tax planning preparation in deciding which documents and strategies would serve you best.

Let's take a look at these documents and what they do:

- **Will.** This is really a formal letter from your parents, telling their heirs (such as you) how they want their affairs to be handled after they're gone. A will may be handwritten (often called a holographic will) or more formal (typed by an attorney). It must be witnessed, by as few as two and up to three persons and sometimes notarized by a notary public as well. Your parents can change their will by creating what's known as a codicil (see Additional Key Documents below) or by writing a new will. A detailed list of their personal property and real estate, specific gifts, or bequests is typically attached to, or included as part of, the will.

- **Declaration of a guardian.** This document allows your parents to select a person (or persons) to look after them and their property or to make important decisions about their personal and business affairs in the event that they become physically or mentally incapacitated and are unable to care for, or make decisions, themselves. If they do not choose a guardian, the courts will appoint one for them should the need arise. If, say, your parents have two children -- one of whom is the responsible type (that's you) and the other (your brother) is far too devil-may-care about everything -- then choosing wisely themselves is the way to ensure that the courts don't appoint the wrong sibling by default.

- **Powers of attorney.** Powers of attorney allow someone your parents choose to act legally and make decisions on their behalf. These legal and personal powers can be broad and all-encompassing (general power of attorney), narrow and related to one or a few things (limited power of attorney), or reserved for a certain act for a set period of time (special power of attorney).

Parents should choose this person carefully and be very sure the person fully understands what he or she is being asked to do. Your parents may set up a power of attorney so they can remove the person (revocable power of attorney) if they feel it necessary or so that the person cannot be removed in the event the parent suffers a serious illness or mental incapacity (irrevocable power of attorney). All powers of attorney cease at issuer's death.

- **Trust.** Think of a trust as sort of a legal lockbox to put assets into. Your parents can create a trust for use while they are alive (living trust) or for after they die (a testamentary trust in their will). A trust can be set up to be undone if or when desired (revocable living trust) or so that it cannot be undone (irrevocable living trust.). There are usually three parties involved in the creation of a trust:

1. **Grantor.** The person who puts assets into the trust; i.e., the parents.
2. **Beneficiary.** The person or organization that ultimately gets the assets put into the trust. Beneficiaries may be spouses, children, churches, community organizations, or friends.
3. **Trustee.** The person who watches over the assets in the trust on the grantor's behalf and for the benefit of the beneficiaries. Trustees may be family members, friends, advisors, or institutions such as banks. More than one person may be named as co-trustees.

Different trusts come with a variety of income tax, estate tax, asset protection, privacy, and personal planning advantages that a good trust or estate planning attorney can spell out for you and your parents, to help them design and implement the appropriate trust strategy.

- **Health care power of attorney.** A health care power of attorney gives the person your parent appoints the power to make important decisions concerning their health care and allows that person access to all parties involved with and information related to the parent's medical, hospital, and prescription records and needs. A health care power of attorney is an absolute must in this age of privacy issues and necessary as a practical matter to permit the sharing of a person's medical history and records at critical times under the HIPAA laws. Without having the proper health care powers assigned to them, a person's children, for example, may not be given details about a parent's condition or medical history, particularly if the children are from out of town or trying to obtain that information over the phone, even in an emergency (as was the case with Grace and Isabelle in the tragic story of their folks, the Wilsons). Think of a health care power of attorney as a master key capable of unlocking all the doors to your parents' health care needs. It functions as a sort of person possessing it the ability to

---

Reality Check

Parental Myth: "My old documents are just fine."

Fact: Assuming they really do exist, there is no way those old documents are just fine. In fact, if my twenty-five years of experience as a lawyer serves me at all well here, my guess is that your parents' documents (again, assuming they exist): (1) either don't do what your parents think or want them to do, or (2) were not executed properly to do it. Congress's gyrations over estate tax during the past four years alone are enough to render many estate plan documents drawn up between the Sputnik years and Bosnia either outdated or extinct.

---

talk to anyone, consult with anyone, or collaborate with anyone to ensure that their loved one's health care requirements and wishes are met.

Additional Key Documents

The following is a list of other documents parents may want to discuss with their attorney in arranging their legal affairs. A board-certified estate planning attorney or other professional specializing in Medicare, Medicaid, or elder care planning (such as an elder care attorney) will help determine which, if any, of these additional documents may be needed.

- **Affidavit of domicile.** This is a signed statement affirming the individual is a resident of the state, jurisdiction, city, or country that he or she claims to be. It is used as proof of residence in many legal situations as well as when applying for a driver's license, veteran's benefits, or in processing a Medicaid claim.
- **Change of beneficiary letter.** This notifies the individual's life insurance company of his or her intent to change beneficiaries on the policy. The legal impact is that the change becomes irrevocable. Therefore, make sure from the attorney creating this letter that changing the beneficiary (or beneficiaries) will not have dire tax consequences. Making the estate (rather than one's spouse, for example) the new beneficiary will result in all that insurance money being taxable upon the individual's death.
- **Codicil to the will.** This is a change to an existing will, which functions as an additional instruction to the executor. A codicil can be used to alter all or part of a will. If improperly drafted, it can have the effect of disavowing the previous will entirely, whether desired or not. Typically, one adds a codicil as the result of an afterthought or a desire to insert some minor change -- for example, including someone not previously named in the will for a small amount or excluding someone else. It is usually wise to have an attorney draw up a codicil or draft a completely new will if the changes are extensive.
- **DNR (do not resuscitate).** This form is placed in the medical file of a terminally ill individual at the request of that individual, instructing medical personnel to take no measures to restore the person's breathing once it has stopped.
- **Employee death benefits letter.** A lawyer or executor of an estate sends this to an employer as notification of the employee's death, and requesting a payout of all benefits entitled to the deceased or to his or her beneficiaries. The benefits payable in response to this type of document would include the proceeds from an individual or group life insurance policy, a burial benefit, the balance of any disability benefits, or residual payments from a pension or profit sharing plan. Any accrued but unused paid

vacation as well as any deferred bonus or compensation may be made payable as an employee benefit, as well.

· **Health care power of attorney revocation.** This document takes away the authority given the holder to act on the grantor's behalf regarding health care matters.

· **Letter to successor trustee.** A grantor creates a trust and appoints a trustee to watch over its content. According to the terms of the trust agreement, however, the trustee may be terminated or choose to resign and a successor trustee appointed. If that occurs, this letter announces the appointment of the successor trustee and grants him or her full powers of the original trustee.

· **Letter to the executor.** This is prepared as part of an estate plan and is usually filed or kept with other documents such as the will, power of attorney, health care directives, and so on. It serves to amplify, reaffirm, or create a new certain instructions the executor is being asked to perform on behalf of the deceased.

· **Living will.** Many times referred to as the "respirator will," this is a directive by a severely ill person requesting that no extraordinary means be taken to sustain his or her life at the expense of the quality of that life should the illness take a dramatic turn for the worse.

· **Medical claims form.** This is filed either by an individual or on behalf of the individual if he or she is deceased, for reimbursement of any out-of-pocket medical expenses. It is usually filed with the person's employer, or in the case of self-employed individuals, with the insurer providing the coverage.

· **Medical records transfer form.** Very often life insurance companies will require a complete file on an individual's medical history before issuing a life insurance or disability insurance policy or claim. A primary physician or health care provider usually provides these forms. They are necessary when requesting that medical records or medical information on an individual be transferred to another provider or given to someone (son or daughter, for example), requesting that certain medical benefits be paid or that certain medical procedures be performed.

- **Memorial plan.** This is a letter describing how the individual wants his or her services to be conducted when the time comes. It covers choice of music and location, number of participants and eulogies, and so on. It can be a single sheet of paper with as much or as little detail as desired. For lifelong control freaks, it is a way to script and direct the final scene in the third act of their life's drama.

- **Notice of death to insurance company.** The executor uses this document to inform the life insurance company of the policyholder's death so that benefits will be released to the beneficiary. A life insurance company will usually require a certified copy of the death certificate and sometimes even a photocopy of the deceased's driver's license or birth certificate, to substantiate the executor's authorization and request. Typically, it is filed within a few weeks after the policyholder's death.

- **Notice to terminate joint account.** A request to a financial institution such as a bank, brokerage firm, or insurance company to transfer the account or financial instrument in question either into another joint tenant, tenant in common, tenant by the entirety, or individual account. The purpose is to stop one or both of the holders from keeping withdrawal and other privileges on contents of the account.

- **Request for life insurance claim form.** A written notice to the insurance company asking that all documentation relevant to the deceased's life insurance contract is forwarded to the executor, beneficiary, or legal representative so that a proceeds letter may follow.

- **Request for life insurance proceeds letter.** The executor of the estate, the deceased's beneficiary, or a legal representative files this with the insurance company to claim the proceeds from a policy taken out on the deceased's life. In most cases, a certified copy of the death certificate must accompany it.

- **Request for death certificate.** Though some jurisdictions will allow a notarized written request, typically a request for a death certificate must be made in person at the courthouse where the deceased's public records are kept. A request for a death certificate is usually made when proof is required, in processing insurance and hospital reimbursement claims and the like, that the deceased is, in fact, deceased.

- **Revocation of power of attorney.** This document rescinds a grantor's permission to act on his or her behalf, often due to a disagreement over the way the grantor's affairs are being handled. It can also be used by the holder to give up the power of attorney to someone else if he or she is no longer up to performing, or no longer wants to perform, the duties required.

- **Self-proving affidavit.** As the word *affidavit* means "to affirm" or to acknowledge as true, this document attests to the accuracy of all information stated within by the individual about him or herself and his or her situation.

- **Social Security change form.** This is used either to request a change in the date benefits start, to stop benefits, or to change the name of the individual to whom the benefits are made payable. Such a change may be needed in the event the person becomes ill, can no longer handle his or her affairs, or is declared legally incompetent.

- **Stock power.** This gives the executor of the estate (or whomever is named to act on the deceased's behalf) the authority to buy or sell stocks owned by a decedent. The document instructs the brokerage firm or agency holding the stock certificates that the deceased owner has transferred his or her power to trade the stock to someone else. It must be notarized, and post-9/11 requires authentication of the identity of the individual, executor, estate, or personal representative given this power.

- **Veteran's request for information.** Sent to the Veteran's Administration in Washington, DC, by or on behalf of a qualifying individual to claim his or her veteran's benefits.

Choosing Advisors -- the Critical Questions to Ask

The health care system in the United States is an amalgam of often-contradictory advice and crossed paths. Forget about the vagaries of Medicare and Medicaid, just sorting through the care facility options almost requires a degree in social work or geriatric case management. When you have to consider the options of at-home medical care versus at-home non-medical care with filtering your care facility questions (see chapter 7, "The Professional Care Conversation") through the different privacy acts and the HIPAA regulations governing access to your parents' personal records, the average human being is tempted to drop his or her parents off at the emergency room in the middle of the night and just drive away. In fact, I suspect that as our population ages, we will see more and more grown children resorting to extreme options to facilitate their aging parents' care.

The yellow pages of the phone book will list all the legal, financial, and health care professionals in your area who are ready and willing to help you and your parents to sort through the paperwork and other complexities of their future care and estate planning situation. But are these professionals able, as well? You won't find the answer to that in the yellow pages. You will have to do some questioning yourself.

Here are the *essential questions* to ask any potential legal, financial, or health care advisor you may be considering to help with strategizing and executing your parents' wishes. Following each question, rate your degree of satisfaction with the advisor's response by circling one of the following numbers: 5 for "extremely satisfied," 4 for "very satisfied," 3 for "somewhat satisfied," 2 for "somewhat dissatisfied," and 1 for "keep looking!" Then check the score at the end to determine the advisor's overall pass/fail grade.

An economist is an expert who will know tomorrow why the things he predicted yesterday didn't happen today. Laurence J. Peter

The Parent Care Conversation Essential Advisor Questions

1. **What is the advisor's *primary* business?** The answer to this will tell you exactly what expertise the advisor brings to the table so that you will be able to determine what additional expertise and support you may need -- and whether the advisor has access to that expertise and support. Let's face it; in this complex world nobody has *all* the answers. If the advisor is *primarily* a geriatric caseworker or an elder care attorney, you will still need the assistance of other professionals to design and execute your care plan. **5 4 3 2 1**

2. **How long has the advisor been in business?** Every professional advisor merits at least a try-out client, but you don't want to be the one. It is possible for a law student to make it all the way through law school without ever having to take a course in wills or trusts or income taxes. Just because the advisor has a credential doesn't mean he or she has the experience and competence to go with it. **5 4 3 2 1**

3. **What was the last seminar the advisor attended in his or her field?** What you are looking for here is a commitment to learning, growth, and progress in the subject the advisor professes to be his or her life's work. Every occupation offers conferences, continuing education, and opportunities for professional advancement. If the advisor is an estate planning attorney but the only seminars he or she attends are on flower arranging, and he or she can't come up with another book read since *Danny and the Steam Shovel,* be cautious! **5 4 3 2 1**

4. **Is the advisor willing to offer references?** What you're looking for here is feedback about the advisor from some of his or her clients just like you that will fall along the continuum of: "He (or she) is the most incredible, empathetic, intelligent, up-to-the-minute, aware, connected, totally interfaced advisor on the planet" to "Yes, I would buy a used car from this person." Beware the advisor who hems and haws over this question or absolutely refuses your request. When prospective clients ask me if they can talk to some of my current clients about me, my response is always that I will be happy to open that door when I am on their short list and not just someone they are "considering." I've found that my clients are more than willing to help me acquire others just like them by offering such feedback; I just don't want them bugged by people who are not serious. Here's a helpful hint: don't ask to invade the privacy of the advisor's client list unless you are very serious about hiring the person. If you do become a client, there may be a day when someone solicits you for feedback, and the last thing you will want is that someone calling you on a Sunday afternoon just to do some tire-kicking and price shopping. **5 4 3 2 1**

5. **What is the worst thing a client has ever said about the advisor?** The advisor's response to this question will tell you how much of a straight shooter he or she is -- because if the answer is "nothing," this indicates perfection, which doesn't exist. Some of my clients have said that I am "impatient," that I "talk too fast," and that I sometimes "don't pay enough attention to them." This is all very true of me, though I would add that it is true of me only with clients who stay too long, never listen, and whine constantly. But I'm willing to say it. **5 4 3 2 1**

6. **How does the advisor see the two of you working together?** This is a great question because it lets you know how the advisor approaches setting goals and achieving objectives on your behalf. Look for the response to reveal both an interest in and an understanding of your situation as well as the role the advisor can play in responding to it. If, for example, the advisor mentions your situation and the newest model Porsche in the same sentence, use caution and proceed slowly. **5 4 3 2 1**

7. **How would working with you improve the advisor professionally?** You should be able to detect from the advisor's response to this whether there is something of real interest to him or her, something stimulating about your situation that gets the advisor's professional juices flowing. And I don't mean the prospect a fatter bank account. It might be that the advisor values the relationship and the ability to help and solve problems, or that certain technical complications must be mastered to move forward in solving your particular problem, and the advisor likes the excitement of the challenge this presents. You will know if it's just a big check the advisor is looking for if he or she goes quickly to the discount conversation. You want an interested and enthused advisor, not one that just answers roll call. **5 4 3 2 1**

8. **Will you be working with the advisor, an associate, or a team?** The answer to this question will establish the expectations you have now and in the future. Many professionals, in all fields, are good at initial meetings but terrible on follow-through

without associates or a team to back them up and delegate the details to. If they have no such backup, you may be doomed. On the other hand, having backup should not excuse them from being available when necessary. Helpful hint: If the person you are talking to in the initial meeting is just the new-business development manager, ask to see an organizational chart and to talk to the people on the team who will be directly handling your case. **5 4 3 2 1**

9. **What does the advisor charge, and how?** Get it right out on the table, what you will be charged and how the advisor is to be compensated. Will charges be on an hourly basis? If so, what is the rate per hour and how many hours does the advisor estimate his or her involvement will take? Does the advisor charge a flat fee? If so, what does the fee arrangement cover? If the person is a financial advisor, is he or she being compensated on assets under management? If so, what is the percentage you will be charged? If compensation is for the sale of commissionable products such as life insurance, health insurance, long-term care insurance, or annuities, what is the commission paid, and what are similar products paying? Right now, the only people that are faced with more disclosure rules than the financial services industry are those going through intake at the county lockup -- and for similar reasons. Today, lack of transparency and full disclosure by anyone in the financial services will result in a felony count. **5 4 3 2 1**

10. **How accessible and available will the advisor be?** I always tell my clients that while I may not always be available, I am accessible. That may not be enough for some clients, who expect the advisor to always be at their beck and call. I, for one, am not willing to interrupt or miss meetings with other clients, or to be unable to spend time with my family or engage in other important activities in order to do that. However, I am always willing to be accessible to my clients -- and immediately available *under certain conditions and circumstances,* such as an IRS agent at the client's doorstep with a subpoena or an invitation to meet with a grand jury. When advisors tell you

they personally are available 24/7/365, you can bet they don't have enough resources, opportunities, or experience not to be. **5 4 3 2 1**

11. **Is there anything the advisor would like to ask *you*?** Good advisors should have a similar list of questions they will want to cover with you. In fact, if they're really good, they'll have their own version of the CARE system to help them query you about the challenges you are facing that brought you to them; the alternatives you are considering; the resources you have to pay them and to implement their advice; and, finally, the experience you would like to have as the result of hiring them if everything works out right. **5 4 3 2 1**

Rate the Advisor

Add up the grades you gave the advisor in response to the questions; then divide the total by the number of questions on the list (eleven). The average you get will fall somewhere between one and five. Apply the same "extremely satisfied" to "keep looking!" rating definitions used in the questionnaire to determine the advisor's overall grade. For example, let's say the total score you gave the advisor is thirty-five. Divide that by the number of questions asked (thirty-five divided by eleven) and you come up with an overall grade for the potential advisor of 3.2, or "somewhat satisfied" bordering on "very satisfied," which makes that advisor a better-than-average potential candidate.

Other Consideration in Choosing a Financial Advisor

Choosing an Advisor with an Expertise in Parent Care and Retirement

A man only learns in two ways, one by reading, and the other by association with smarter people.
—Will Rogers

Some of us learn from other people's mistakes, and the rest of us have to be other people.
—Zig Ziglar

When I started helping people with IRAs many years ago, people would tell me that they had an accountant, attorney, or a financial advisor, and I thought that they had all of their IRAs, retirement, and estate planning in order. I no longer live by those assumptions. I have learned that many of the advisors who carry professional titles are not equally trained in IRA and retirement planning.

In fact, I have found just the opposite; many professionals do not know the basics of IRA planning and often they give information that may not be right or may be almost right. I do not believe that we have cornered the market on IRA knowledge, but we do know that a framework for decision making is important when you are choosing the advisor to help you with your life savings. I find that if you know what to ask advisors, they will answer, but the problem is, we don't know what to ask. I want to give you the background, credentials, and questions to help you find the right advisor for you and your family. I say *family* because the mistake made with and by your advisors can cost your heirs thousands in taxes if not given the right guidance.

History of Financial Advisor

The beginning and growth of what we know as financial advisors is shorter than most people realize. Loren Dunton set up the Society of Financial Counseling Ethics in 1969. A meeting held in Chicago in 1969 has evolved into the profession of financial planning that we know today. From this beginning, various associations and groups have evolved that provide training, support, and credentials for professionals who are in the financial services business. Some of the associations for financial professionals include:

The Financial Planning Association (www.fpanet.org)
Association for Financial Professionals (www.afponline.org)
National Association of Personal Financial Advisors (www.napfa.org)
Association of Independent Financial Advisers (www.apfa.net)
National Association of Insurance and
Financial Advisors (www.naifa.org)
The National Association of Independent Public
Finance Advisors (www.naipfa.com)

When we understand that many people who use the term "financial advisor" come from various backgrounds and offer different approaches and products, you will understand why it is important to do your homework when choosing a financial advisor. By understanding where advisors have come from on their journeys, you will have a better feel for the training, biases, methods, and strategies for your IRA planning needs.

How Do Financial Advisors Get into Financial Services?

If you ask prospective financial advisors how they became financial advisors, you will hear the story of their beginnings and the roads that have brought them to where they are presently. How they began greatly influences the philosophies, methods, and products that they will use to guide you with your IRA. As you interview financial advisors, knowing as much about them as possible will help you understand their recommendations and strategies with your plan.

What are some of the ways that advisors enter the financial services business?

Insurance Channel

Some financial professionals began their careers in the insurance industry. Many top life-insurance companies have a great training program and system that provides a brand in the marketplace that helps those new in the business get started. Some in this channel call themselves "insurance-based financial advisors." I began my career in this channel with John Hancock in 1991. From this beginning, some financial professionals remain with their original methods, products, and offerings to new clients. Others progress in the industry to offer a broader base of products and services. Some, like I did, eventually leave this channel so that they can have access to a great number of financial products for their clients.

Bank Channel

In the late 1990s, many banks were able to offer investment products, and so many banks began to recruit financial advisors to be a part of their organization. The ability of banks to offer investment advisor services brought about the repeal of the Glass-Steagall Act of 1932 with the passage of the Gramm-Leach-Bliley Act of 1999.

With this newfound opportunity, many bank customers have been invited to meet with one of bank's financial advisors or with someone from the investment or trust department. This trend has continued over the years with many banks having a very large investment advisor department with thousands of financial advisors. You will also find that some banks have their own broker-dealers and platforms for managing money, while others use outside companies. Even within the bank channel, you may find that smaller banks can offer few financial products, and larger banks can offer a larger selection of financial products.

Brokerage Channel

Other financial advisors whom you interview will have come into the financial business through a brokerage company. These companies may have focused more on stock and bond sales to their clients.

Direct Channel

When you ask prospective advisors about their backgrounds, they may say that they started their careers with a discount brokerage company.

With the technology boom of the late 1990s, there were a number of companies that emerged that sold stocks, bonds, and mutual funds and commodities. They believed that the financial advisor was not needed, and through a toll-free number and with some service help at their location, they could meet the financial needs of customers in the marketplace. Some in the financial industry today may have started using investment platforms in college and, upon graduation, went to work for this type of brokerage firm. They have since made the change to where they are now in how they present their message to the consumer for retirement-planning recommendations. For retirees who feel that they can manage their own IRAs, this channel is still a great option, with many discount brokerage firms offering great service and a great technology platform to make trades.

Let me say that there are good advisors in each of these channels; I believe it is just good to know the financial view that these advisors bring to you based on the cultures that they may have developed along their financial services journeys.

Independent Advisor

Many financial advisors, as it might say if you were looking at their third-grade report cards, do not play well with others. They are the kinds who do not like the limitations of a boss; they don't want someone limiting their opportunities, and in the task of caring for their clients, they want the greatest number of choices with the greatest opportunities for their clients. Many advisors who would call themselves independent advisors came from one of the channels above. After experience, they realized that the independent channel allowed them access to the greatest number of choices and flexibility. When you are interviewing advisors and you ask them about their broker-dealer affiliations, ask them if they are independent advisors.

I am not saying that there are not sound, responsible, and professional advisors in all the channels of financial distribution above. I am saying that it is important for you to know your prospective advisor's background so that you know what his or her biases could be when giving you direction for your IRA. Do your homework, and choose your financial advisor well.

The Maze of Financial Credentials

If you go to a prospective advisor's website or you see his or her business card, you see a long list of letters and titles. You discover that you have never heard of some of them; some sound credible. If you go to the next advisor, he has letters also. Some are the same letters, and some are different. How do you know what these credentials mean and what it took to get them, and are some more meaningful than others? These are all essential questions to have answered when choosing a financial advisor.

When it comes to credentials, financial advisors' credentials can get confusing. Some financial publications estimate that the number of so-called credentials for financial advisors has grown to over two hundred. Some of these take a few days and a few dollars, and others take several years and several thousand dollars. Without some research into these credentials, you can be led to believe that a financial advisor has more qualifications and knowledge than he actually has.

Some of the advisors you meet may be CFAs (Chartered Financial Analyst) or CFPs (Certified Financial Planner) or ChFCs (Chartered Financial Consultant). The key in your search for an advisor is to ask yourself the following:

What do these letters mean?

What did it take for the financial advisor to attain this credential?

What does it take to keep these credentials?

When you ask and answer these questions, you will find that they are not all created equal. Some are very hard to acquire, and others are quite easy to attain.

A financial credential or designation is a professional title that often includes the words *certified* or *chartered*. The concern over credentials has caused the Financial Industry Regulatory Authority (FINRA) to begin to track some of these credentials.

A key thing to note according to state securities regulators about financial credentials is that the organizations that grant credentials operate virtually unchecked. Whereas medical schools have accrediting bodies recognized by the US Department of Education and most law schools have accreditation requirements from the American Bar Association, with a process monitored by the Department of Education, there is no apparatus for accrediting the groups that grant most financial designations.

Many of the groups that train advisors are legitimate and offer students meaningful preparation in financial management. They have highly experienced teachers who must pass tough screening requirements before they are allowed to prepare advisors for careers in financial planning—and have continuing education requirements to ensure that advisors stay sharp.

The lesson for investors: Before entrusting your money to an advisor, do some legwork. Start by looking into advisors' records via FINRA's BrokerCheck, available www.finra.org, and browse data from state securities regulators at www.nasaa.org and state insurance officials at www.naic.org.

Next, interview advisors as you would any other advisor. Note how they describe their credentials. Ask two questions: "What percentages of the people who apply for that credential earn it?" and "What qualifications did your instructors in that program have?" If they can't or won't answer, that's a red flag.

Alphabet Soup

Financial services professionals who advise the public have an array of credentials to choose from. Those credentials include those that are tracked in a database kept by FINRA and others that are not as well documented. Some are even defunct but may still show up in advisors' marketing materials. Below is a list of some of the FINRA-monitored credentials:

Acronym	Designation	Issuing Organization	Educational Requirements	Continuing Education/ Experience Requirements
CFP	Certified Financial Planner	Certified Financial Planner Board of Standards, Inc.	Candidate must complete a CFP-board registered program, or hold *one* of the following: CPA, ChFC, Chartered Life Underwriter (CLU), CFA, PhD in business or economics, Doctor of Business Administration, Attorney's License	30 hours every 2 years
ChFC	Chartered Financial Consultant	The American College	6 courses and 2 elective courses	30 CE credits every 2 years
CLU	Chartered Life Underwriter	The American College	5 core and 3 elective courses	30 hours every 2 years

Most Popular You May See:

Acronym	Designation	Issuing Organization	Educational Requirements	Continuing Education/ Experience Requirements
CPM	Chartered Portfolio Manager	American Academy of Financial Management (AAFM)	Eligible candidates must successfully complete at least one of the following: AAFM-approved degree (graduate or undergraduate) in finance, tax, accounting, financial services, or law or a CPA, MBA, MS, PhD, or JD from an accredited school or organization, 5 or more approved and related courses from an AACSB- or ACBSP-accredited business school or AAFM-sanctioned program, AAFM Executive Certification training course	15 hours per year
CPFC	Certified Personal Finance Counselor	Center for Financial Certification	Completion of self-study program	20 hours over a 2-year period
CPWA	Certified Private Wealth Advisor	Investment Management Consultants Association	Candidate must complete the following: 6 month prestudy educational component, 5-day in-class portion of the program at the University of Chicago Graduate School of Business	40 hours every 2 years

CRC	Certified Retirement Counselor	International Foundation for Retirement Education (InFRE)	None	15 hours per year
CRFA	Certified Retirement Financial Advisor	The Society of Certified Retirement Financial Advisors		
CRP	Certified Retirement Planner	Retirement Planners, LLC	Candidate must complete: Certified Retirement Planner (CRP) preliminary and advanced coursework, 5 retirement planning techniques seminars	15 hours per year
CRPC	Chartered Retirement Planning Counselor	College for Financial Planning		
CRPS	Chartered Retirement Plans Specialist	College for Financial Planning	Self-study course (requiring 90–100 hours)	16 hours every 2 years
CRS	Certified Retirement Specialist			
CSA	Certified Senior Advisor	Society of Certified Senior Advisors	SCSA Course: • Classroom (3.5-day live class) or • self-study	18 SCSA credits every 3 years
CSC	Certified Senior Consultant	Institute of Business & Finance		
CSEP	Certified Specialist in Estate Planning	National Institute for Excellence in Professional Education, LLC	Completion of 6 core and 2 elective courses	16 hours every 2 years

CSFP	Certified Senior Financial Planner			
CSFP	Chartered Senior Financial Planner	Association of Chartered Senior Financial Planners	3-day review course	16 hours every 2 years
CSRP	Certified Specialist in Retirement Planning	National Institute for Excellence in Professional Education, LLC	Completion of 5 core and 2 elective courses	16 hours every 2 years
CSS	Certified Senior Specialist			
CWC	Certified Wealth Consultant	The Heritage Institute (THI)	Candidates must complete all of the following requirements: Attend and complete Advanced Practice Academy, complete 1-day personal sabbatical, complete 6-book reading list, mentor a provisional CWC member, maintain mentoring relationship with another CWC, complete at least 2 Heritage Process cases, create personal catalogue of 4 stories	Attend at least one Advanced Practice Academy per year

CWM	Chartered Wealth Manager	American Academy of Financial Management (AAFM)	Eligible candidates must successfully complete at least one of the following: AAFM online Chartered Wealth Manager course, AAFM-approved master's degree in finance, tax, accounting, financial services, law, or CPA, MBA, MS, PhD, or JD from an accredited school or organization, 5 or more approved and related courses from an AACSB- or ACBSP-accredited business school or AAFM-sanctioned program, AAFM Executive Certification training course	15 hours per year
CEIAS	Certified Equity Indexed Annuity Specialist	Association of Insurance & Financial Specialists	5.5 hours of online pre-recorded sessions	None
CEP	Certified Estate Planner	National Institute of Certified Estate Planners	Classroom or self-study course (8 modules)	8 hours every 2 years
CWS	Certified Wealth Strategist	Cannon Financial Institute	Candidates must complete the following: 2 instructor-led training sessions, 4-module directed study, Capstone project	33 hours per year

CFA	Chartered Financial Analyst	CFA Institute	Self-study program (250 hours of study for each of the 3 levels)	None
CMFC	Chartered Mutual Fund Counselor	College for Financial Planning	Self-study course (9 modules requiring 72–90 hours)	16 hours every 2 years
Master Elite	Ed Slott, Master Elite IRA Advisor Group			
RFC	Registered Financial Consultant	International Association of Registered Financial Consultants (IARFC)	Completion of approved college curriculum in personal financial planning or IARFC self-study course.	40 hours per year

The Face-to-Face Interview

When you study and prepare to choose the right financial advisor, you will learn much along the way. As you prepare for the actual face-to-face interview, you want to be armed with as many questions as you feel you need to make an accurate assessment of the advisor.

Below are some key questions to take with you to the face-to-face interview:

Vital Questions for Financial Advisors:

Questions about Advisors' Credentials and Experience

1. Can you tell me how you came into the financial services industry? How long have you been in the business?
2. Can you tell me about your financial credentials? Do you have a CFP, ChFC, or other credentials?

3. What differentiates you from other advisors? Why should I choose you over another financial advisor?

4. What is your philosophy of customer service? What is your philosophy of returning calls, e-mails, and follow-up with your clients?

5. Could I get your FINRA CRD# so that I can look up your securities track record at www.finra.org?

6. Do you have an area of specialty with your advisor practice, and do you have unique processes for your clients?

7. Are you paid by commissions or by fees? Can you explain how that works?

Questions to Ask Your Advisor That Are Often Overlooked

Concerning IRA Distribution Planning:

1. What resources or publications do you use to keep up to date with changing IRA distribution rules?

2. What is the latest IRA ruling or tax law change you are aware of?

3. Who should I name as my IRA beneficiary? Can you explain the tax reason why I should have a contingent beneficiary?

4. How do you keep track of IRA beneficiary forms?

5. Can you show me the IRS life expectancy tables you use to calculate required IRA distributions for both IRA owners and beneficiaries?

6. What will happen to my IRA after my death? What is a DBA (designated beneficiary account), and does your firm offer such accounts? Can you explain to me the three methods that my children can use to pay taxes on my IRA?

7. Whom do you call when you have questions about IRA distributions?

8. What is a stretch IRA?

9. I have company stock in my retirement plan; is there a way to get it out to pay the least amount of taxes?

10. Can you explain to me what a TOD (transfer on death) account is and if I should set my account up this way?

11. Have you ever heard of the IRD (income in respect of a decedent)? What planning strategies should I address to deal with this tax?

12. Can you explain to me the IRD deduction that could lower my taxes on this inherited IRA account?
13. Can you explain to me the relationship between my legal documents and my IRA, 401(k), and retirement plans?
14. What are the reasons I should consider a living trust? Can an IRA be put into a living trust?
15. I am thinking of sending my large IRA to a trust; can you explain if this is a good idea or bad idea? How will the beneficiaries of the trust be taxed?
16. Can you explain how the title of my assets affects my estate planning documents?

Vital Questions for Your Investment Advisor

1. Do you consider yourself a financial planner, broker, money manager, or insurance expert, or do you use some other term?
2. Are you an asset gatherer or a money manager?
3. What are your credentials and financial qualifications for managing money? What credentials do you have?
4. Do you have the CFA (chartered financial analyst) designation?
5. How much time each day do you spend with clients, and how much time are you looking at and managing portfolios?
6. What is your theory of money management, and to whom do you turn for financial mentorship?
7. How do you determine a client's risk before you invest? How do you define *risk*?
8. When there is a correction in the market, what do you do for your clients?
9. Do you have automatic systems in place to make adjustments in client investment portfolios?
10. Do you use a buy/hold, strategic asset allocation, or market timing strategy?
11. What system do you use to screen your investments to put them in a portfolio or to eliminate them from your portfolio? Can you explain your sell strategy?
12. If you were recommending to me a book I should read for financial investing philosophy and perspective, what would it be?

Vital Questions to Ask Your IRA Custodian or the Institution that Currently Holds Your IRA

1. Does your custodian IRA document allow for my heir(s) to use a stretch IRA?
2. Does your custodian IRA document allow for my heirs to establish a designated beneficiary account (DBA)?
3. If I die before my spouse is fifty-nine and one-half years of age, and I am older than fifty-nine and one-half years of age, it could be better to leave the money in a spousal beneficiary account so that my spouse can take distributions on the deceased age with penalty. Does your IRA custodian agreement allow this type of account?
4. Does your custodian IRA document allow for a beneficiary to name a beneficiary?
5. Does your custodian IRA document allow my heirs to move the IRA money to another institution after my death, or does it have to remain at your institution?
6. What does the default position of your IRA custodian agreement say? For example: If nobody is named as beneficiary and the form is blank or a beneficiary predecease, the account holder and the beneficiary is never updated, who is presumed to be the beneficiary? Does it go to the estate or to another person?
7. Can you please send to me in writing who you have in your records for my beneficiary and contingent beneficiary?
8. What is your custodian requirement on a minor IRA, and how is a minor handled when he or she is beneficiary of my IRA?

Conclusion

I come from the belief that there are some great, well-trained, smart, and professional advisors in the industry. Many of them have the highest ethics and standards for the well-being of their clients. Most want, with all of their hearts, to help their clients reach their financial goals. Most of them take the high road; they work hard and do what is in the best interest of their clients. It is the few who can cause the trouble in any profession and take the shortcuts and don't want to study. I hope you will take the information and questions in this chapter and find the right financial advisor to help you and your family to have a bright and successful financial future.

Investment Strategies for Parent Care

"An investment in knowledge pays the best interest."
—Benjamin Franklin

*"You only have to do a very few things right in your life
so long as you don't do too many things wrong."*
—Warren Buffett

When investors visit an investment advisor, they begin with the thought that most advisors do everything the same way. For many, that is a true statement.

What sets one investment advisor apart from another? Why would I choose one investment advisor over another?

If you ask an investment advisor, "What is your investment philosophy?" you will find that their guiding philosophy falls into one of three philosophies:

- Buy and Hold Asset Allocation Strategy
- Strategic Asset Allocation Strategy
- Dynamic or Tactical Asset Allocation Strategy

Understanding these different philosophies of how money will be handled and allocated is critical to the investment advisor decision.

<u>Buy and Hold Asset Allocation</u>

The Buy and Hold Asset Allocation Strategy selects a certain number of stocks, mutual funds, bonds and cash and arranges them in a collection and then provides little supervision or management of the portfolio. The approach is often "set it and forget it". Buy and Hold Asset Allocation is a long-term investment strategy based on the view that in the long run, financial markets give a good rate of return despite periods of volatility or decline. This viewpoint also contends that short-term market timing, (i.e. the concept that one can enter the market on the lows and sell on the highs), does not work for small, or unsophisticated, investors so it is better to simply <u>buy and hold</u>.

301

Buy and Hold

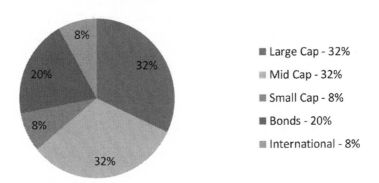

The catalyst for change with Buy and Hold Asset Allocation is either the displeased client calling the advisor and saying something is wrong and needs to be changed or the advisor that calls making a recommendation for change and the client does not always know why.

At Discipline Financial Management, we have the understanding that Asset Allocation by itself does not always work. We believe that diversification takes more active management to avoid and minimize loss. We also believe that many money managers and advisors do not have a sell strategy to move cash for defensive purposes.

The Buy and Hold Asset Allocation Strategy is considered dead today by many advisors and investors; and if not dead, at least in a coma.

Strategic Asset Allocation

The Strategic Asset Allocation Strategy adds a slightly more active approach to the management of money than the Buy and Hold Asset Allocation Strategy.

In this strategy, the client is placed in various asset classes such as stocks, bonds, and cash with each of these categories in more specific positions. The portfolio may have large, mid, and small cap stocks or mutual funds.

The portfolio may have international positions. The advisor might also have value and growth style asset classes as a part of the mix. In the bond asset, they may be divided into long, mid, and short durations. Strategic Asset Allocation involves periodically rebalancing the portfolio in order to maintain a long-term goal for asset allocation.

With Strategic Asset Allocation, the model may look like this:

Strategic Asset Allocation

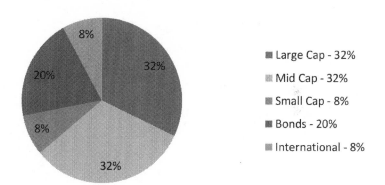

Strategic/Tactial Asset Allocation

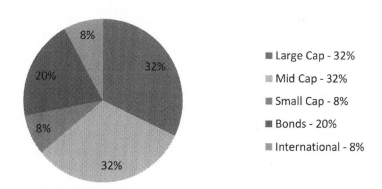

On a periodic basis, the manager or advisor may change the percentages of money that are in the various asset classes based on the belief of what asset class may perform better in the future.

A change in allocation may move the portfolio from the above to this:

Strategic/Tactical Allocation

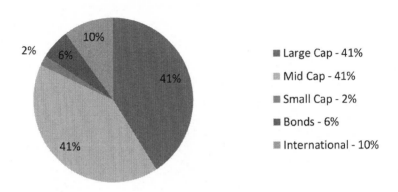

- Large Cap - 41%
- Mid Cap - 41%
- Small Cap - 2%
- Bonds - 6%
- International - 10%

While the method of managing money is an improvement, the strategy lacks a sell strategy and keeps the investor almost fully invested in a down market. With no sell strategy, this strategy leaves investors to ride the market up and then ride the market down.

Dynamic/Tactical Asset Allocation

At Discipline Financial Management, we use the Dynamic/Tactical Asset Allocation Strategy. It is the most active of the money management strategies. At the root of this strategy is the belief that there are times to participate in the market and there are times to be out of the market. This strategy believes that at times some asset classes will perform better than other assets classes and that those should be owned in a higher percentage of the portfolio.

Dynamic/Tactical Asset Allocation is a moderately active portfolio management strategy, which includes adjustments of investments with respect to short-term goals. Although the basic idea is to diversify investments and limit risks, investment preferences are given to different asset classes with respect to short-term yield predictions.

The Dynamic/Tactical Asset Allocation Strategy starts just like a Strategic Asset Allocation Strategy with diversification of portfolio with respect to long-term goals in mind. The investor/portfolio manager then readjusts the investments with different asset classes. If equities are predicted to perform well in the near future, he/she allocates more capital for it; and if bonds are predicted to perform well, then more investments in bonds, and so on. Once the preferred result is obtained, the investor returns to the original allocation ratio desired for long-term goals.

Success with Dynamic/Tactical Asset Allocation requires good money management, and ability to interpret and predict short-term trends. Investors consider Price to Earnings and Price to Book ratio of equities, fundamental indicators, various momentum and sentiment signals, and economic predictions in making decisions. The investor/portfolio manager must be keen enough to go back to original ratio, once the short-term profit opportunity is diminished. Dynamic/Tactical Asset Allocation Strategy, in theory, can offer better results than Strategic Asset Allocation Strategy; but it also has more risks associated with it.

The basis of the Dynamic/Tactical Asset Allocation was not discovered or invented by Discipline Financial Management. This strategy is rooted in what is called The Elliot Wave (www.elliotwave.com).

The Elliott Wave Principle is a detailed description of how financial markets behave. The description reveals that mass psychology swings from pessimism to optimism and back in a natural sequence, creating specific wave patterns in price movements. Each pattern has implications regarding the position of the market within its overall progression, past, present and future.

Elliott Wave Analysis is a form of technical analysis and of behavioral economics that attempts to forecast trends by identifying extremes in investor psychology, tops and bottoms in markets, and other collective activities. It is named after Ralph Nelson Elliott (1871–1948), an accountant who developed the concept in the 1930s. He proposed that market prices unfold in specific patterns, which practitioners today call Elliott waves. Elliott published his views of market behavior in the book The Wave Principle (1938), in a series of articles in Financial World magazine in 1939, and most fully in his final major work, Nature's Laws – The Secret of the Universe (1946). Elliott argued that because humans are themselves rhythmical, their activities and decisions could be predicted in rhythms, too.

The wave principle posits that collective investor psychology (or crowd psychology) moves from optimism to pessimism and back in a natural sequence creating specific Elliott wave patterns in price movements. These swings create patterns, as evidenced in the price movements of a market at every degree of trend.

Practically all developments which result from (human) socio-economic processes follow a law that causes them to repeat themselves in similar and constantly recurring series of waves of definite number and pattern. R. N. Elliott's model, in Nature's Law: The Secret of the Universe says that market prices alternate between five waves and three waves at all degrees within a trend. As these waves develop, the larger price patterns unfold in a self-similar fractal geometry. Within the dominant trend, waves 1, 3, and 5 are "motive" waves, and each motive wave itself subdivides in five waves. Waves 2 and 4 are "corrective" waves, and subdivide in three waves. In a bear market the dominant trend is downward, so the pattern is reversed—five waves down and three up. Motive waves always move with the trend, while corrective waves move opposite it.

The Parent Care Solution Document Directory Checklist Tool

The following information should be easily located and accessible to the holder of your power of attorney. Complete account numbers, phone numbers, and addresses should be noted whenever possible.

Document	Done	Date	Location
CPA			
Lawyer			
Auto title			
Home title			
Deeds			
Bank account			
Brokerage accounts			
Credit card accounts			
Employer information			
Insurance agent			
Insurance policies			
Medicare, Medicaid, health insurance cards			
Pastor, minister, priest, rabbi			
Mortgage papers			
Passport			
Physicians			
Dentists			
Ophthalmologist			
Social Security			
Investment advisor			

Financial planner			
Banker			
General power of attorney			
Healthcare power of attorney			

Record Keeping

There's an old story about the governmental agency that, when faced with a lack of any more storage room for keeping records, made the decision to destroy every file older than five years to free up more space and to make copies of them! Record keeping at home follows a similar pattern. We become pack rats. How do we know what to keep and what to shred? The following Important Documents Timeline Tool lists the key records and the time frames for holding on to them.

Two biggies are bank records and tax returns. One is usually needed to resolve a dispute with the other. The short lesson here: if you think you may need it, you probably will. Tax returns -- yes. Twenty years of Utah Power and Light bills -- no. Note: this tool applies to paper documents only. In the digital age, virtually everything is retrievable at almost any time.

The Parent Care Solution Important Documents Timeline Tool

Document	How long?	Why?
Tax return	six years	IRS can audit within three years if it suspects a filing error. Same applies if you file an amended return. IRS has six years for 25 percent understatement of income.

Canceled checks	six years	Just because
Brokerage statements	six years	Same as IRS; for IRS backup
Mutual funds statements		
Bank statements		
Real estate	six years	IRS backup
Paycheck stubs	six years	IRS backup Also save final pay stub of year for cumulative withholding information
Credit cards	six years	IRS backup, especially if business purchases have been made.
Retirement plan data	six years	Quarterly statements until end of year. The annual statement.

Meet the Jamisons

OK, so what might a future care and estate plan look like if, unlike the Wilsons, your parents had actually followed through on their decisions with signed, sealed, and ready-to-execute documents and strategies? To find out, let's meet the Jamisons.

Bill and Susan Jamison are in their seventies and have just completed The Parent Care Conversations. During these conversations, they discovered a great deal about themselves and their relationship with their four children. For example, they were delighted to discover that, contrary to their belief that they were just a burden to the children, their kids actually welcomed the opportunity to help them. And, the children discovered that the same fiscal prudence that had enabled their parents to provide all four of them with a college education had also enabled their parents to put more than enough away in investments and real estate to ensure their income would continue for the rest of their lives. Life insurance made sure that if one of them died prematurely there would be enough money for the surviving spouse, and the life insurance would shift the cost of care during the most expensive years onto the insurance company. Although this long-term care policy had seemed expensive when the Jamisons purchased it, the premiums were a fraction of what the policy would pay for care if the need arose.

With their house paid for as well as their automobiles, the Jamisons were ready to implement some of the decisions they had made.

The first thing they did was sign the wills their attorney had prepared. Because the size of their estate was not huge, these were not complicated documents. They executed what are called "I love you" wills leaving everything to the surviving spouse. At the time of the second spouse's death (or in the event of simultaneous deaths), the remaining assets were to be divided equally among the four children. If there were a disagreement among the children, the Jamisons' attorney would be the final arbiter whose power was absolute.

The Jamisons transferred the title to their home to a trust they created for the children, reserving a "life estate" in their home, which gave them the right to live there as long as they wanted and were able. Under the terms of the trust agreement, the children were free to tap into the home's equity if necessary for their parents' care. The children decided to use a portion of the equity to purchase additional life insurance on their parents and, at the same time, purchased credit insurance on the mortgage. This way, when the parents died, any equity line balance would be paid in full and the children would inherit the house free and clear. The Jamisons had also taken full advantage of The Parent Care Cost-Recovery System (see chapter 4, "The Money Conversation," for full details) to help the children recover any out-of-pocket money for their parents' care, as well.

After each other, the Jamisons nominated the two oldest children to be holders of their general powers of attorney, followed by the younger siblings as necessary. If no children were available, the local bank was to be the trustee for the Jamisons' affairs. They followed the same strategy for their health care powers of attorney. But here, if the children were unavailable to make the decisions, a three-party committee of the Jamisons' lawyer, accountant, and family physician were to make these decisions. The Jamisons also executed living wills in conjunction with the health care power of attorney, giving these individuals the right to decline or cease the use of life-support services or extraordinary medical care to prolong the Jamisons' lives in the event of a terminal illness.

Their accountant suggested a family investment company for the Jamisons' liquid assets. Under this arrangement, their investment holdings were transferred to a limited liability company (LLC) where Bill and Susan were members, but their children were the *managing* members having all rights of distribution. This strategy -- which they initiated for legitimate personal and business reasons and not to defraud the Medicaid system -- protected the Jamisons' current assets and the inheritance for the children from the Medicaid rules allowing the system to look back for a period of ten years to offset monies expended for the recipient's care by the state's Medicaid program.

The additional life insurance policies were transferred to the Jamisons' irrevocable life insurance trust with the children as beneficiaries. The children were empowered to make the premium payments using either income from the family investment company assets or the equity line on the house. At the parent's deaths, the insurance proceeds from the policy would go into the trust and then could be distributed to the surviving children or grandchildren.

The Jamisons' automobiles were also placed in the LLC, an action that enabled the children to buy, sell, or otherwise dispose of the vehicles as needs arose. Policy limits on both automobiles were increased to the maximum liability levels. The LLC also purchased an umbrella liability policy to protect assets in the event the Jamisons suffered a traffic accident and the judgment exceeded the amounts covered by their auto policies.

There were some personal items Bill and Susan Jamison wanted the children to have: Bill's pocket watch, his Scout knife, Susan's wedding rings, and her fiftieth wedding anniversary diamond necklace, which were all bequeathed in a separate document attached to the will.

Finally, Bill, Susan, and the children together decided to create a family crypt at a local mausoleum and to prepay for services. They also created a family legacy video to be passed on, consisting of snapshots of Bill, Susan, and the children as the family grew over the years. Also, the in-depth talks about their lives the Jamisons had with their children during the legacy conversation were recorded for posterity. Each child would receive a copy of the video at the death of the parents, in order to preserve their memory.

The Jamisons' story is a far cry from that of the Wilsons, which began this chapter, isn't it? If the Wilsons had carried out even a percentage of the strategies the Jamisons did with regard to their future care and estate plans, many of the dire events that befell the Wilsons' children upon the premature and tragic deaths of their parents could have been positively turned around.

Is it necessary for every family to do everything the Jamisons did? Probably not. But everything the Jamisons did is available to every family, and, therefore, should be considered as part of any parent care and estate plan solution.

As the baby boomers age and continue to reinvent the whole notion of retirement and aging, there will likely be even more innovations like those the Jamisons used and even greater capabilities for carrying out the wishes of our aging parents and preserving family relationships and finances. Stay tuned to the parent care conversation Web site (www. parentcaresolution.com) for updates and news you can use on this key issue.

DOs and DON'Ts

DO make sure that everyone who should be involved in the documenting phase is involved.

DO plan enough ahead to allow for making any changes and corrections before you actually need the document.

DO store important documents where key people can easily find them.

DO tell those key people where the important documents are.

DO create a checklist of all documents signed and the dates.

DON'T put this off.

DON'T rest until every document is signed and ready to be executed.

DON'T make any changes to your documents without telling your attorney.

15

STAYING ON TOP OF THINGS

A Work in Progress

Any future care plan, no matter how well thought out and designed, is inevitably a work in progress due to the unpredictability of life. We never know what punches life will throw at us, which makes it all the more important that we anticipate those punches as much as possible and are able to roll with them. Otherwise, what happened to the Stedman family could happen to yours.

Walter Stedman was a self-made man living in Rosemont, a suburb of Chicago. His wife, Eleanor, died four years ago from lung cancer. Walter had been managing for himself since, in the home he and his late wife had occupied throughout their almost fifty years of marriage. During Eleanor's illness it became apparent to both of them that they should discuss their future plans with their children, who lived in Indianapolis, Indiana, about a four-hour drive away. Walter and Eleanor had designed a parent care strategy. With the help of their advisors, their financial affairs were in order, their estate plan was organized, their family home was protected, and their health care directives were all signed and executed. Thus, while Eleanor's death came as no less of a shock to the family, it was made less chaotic by the plans the Stedmans had put in place. For example, they had planned for Walter to be able to stay in his home for as long as he chose and then to move to a nearby retirement village.

> ### Reality Check
>
> **Parental Myth:** "My body needs a checkup now and then, but my care plan doesn't. It's all set."
>
> **Fact:** A lot can happen between the time your parents make decisions about their future and the time that future arrives and those decisions kick in. Any parent care solution worth its salt is a living structure; it must be flexible enough to accommodate whatever changes will arise in your parents' needs and wishes as time goes by and their situation evolves.

After his wife's death, Walter began seeing Elizabeth, a widow, whom he met at a seniors' social. He eventually asked her to move in with him, and she did. During the years they had together, before Walter's own health began to deteriorate, Elizabeth assumed more and more of the day-to-day housekeeping responsibilities, functioning more like a wife than just a companion. Walter authorized her signature on his personal checking, savings, and investment accounts. While this did not legally name her as holder of those accounts, her signature authority effectively created the same situation. As the relationship developed between them, they began to commingle their monies on a more frequent basis. He would put money into her checking account, she would write checks on his for joint items, and they would jointly share the cost of things such as vacations and gifts or going out with friends. He even gave her a Rolex watch to wear that had belonged to his late wife.

A year before Walter Stedman died, he went to an attorney (not the same one he and his late wife had used) to re-form the deed and title to the house to make Elizabeth co-owner with him. He was worried that if he died or became ill and had to move to a professional care facility, she would have nowhere to live. Six months later, he sat down one evening with Elizabeth and wrote out a new will by hand, revoking an earlier will drawn up by his original attorney. This time, he left everything to Elizabeth except for a few items earmarked for his children. He spelled out everything so there would be no confusion as to who got what.

Only after his death did his children discover his actions and come to realize the depth of feeling their father had for Elizabeth. They immediately challenged the legitimacy of the handwritten will as well as Elizabeth's entitlements to their father's retirement, checking, and brokerage accounts, demanding that all monies she had taken be returned in whole to those accounts. Elizabeth refused to do this, or to leave the house, so the children filed suit against her, asking that the title to the house and everything else be restored to them as their father's rightful heirs, including their mother's Rolex watch and other jewelry.

A trial was held and the judge upheld the transfer of title to the family home to Elizabeth, stating there was no evidence that Walter had made the transfer under duress or undue influence, a fact that was confirmed by the new attorney Walter had used. In the matter of the Rolex (and other jewelry of his late wife's that Walter had given to Elizabeth), the judge ruled that she could keep what Walter had given her but was not permitted to receive any other jewelry left in the estate that had belonged to the late Eleanor Stedman. Finally, the judge ruled that while the addition of Elizabeth's signature authority on Walter's various accounts did not constitute "absolute title," the fact that she had the authority to write checks on those accounts did give her "constructive title," and he thus awarded all liquid assets and investment assets in the accounts to her. As a result, the two Stedman children were left with very little of their parents' estate. This was certainly not what their mother had wanted; in fact, it was what the original documents drawn up by their parents had sought to avoid.

It is likely that this turn of events is not what their father had wanted to happen either, but he had virtually ensured it would happen nonetheless by keeping the true nature of his relationship with Elizabeth a virtual secret from his children and not revising and updating his estate documents in line with the original strategy he and his late wife had designed. In fact, he didn't even tell his new attorney there was such a plan! He went boldly, and foolishly, off on his own without considering the fact that Elizabeth had children of her own. By making her heir, he had inadvertently shut out his own kids.

Staying On Track

The moral of the Stedman story is that once a care plan has been successfully designed and the relevant documents drawn up, it is only the beginning. It is still necessary to review and update strategies and documents as needed to accommodate changes that have occurred since the original care plan was designed and to anticipate any changes that may occur in the future. Furthermore, all interested parties (spouses, children, advisors) should be kept fully in the loop!

Here's how to keep what happened to the Stedman family from happening to yours.

Review Decisions Periodically

You will recall from earlier chapters my emphasis on the importance of confidence in transforming fear into focused thinking, communication, and action. That's what the parent care conversations do -- they help your parents develop the confidence to make decisions and move forward. Holding onto that confidence is just as important because change, no matter how slight -- but especially sudden or unanticipated change -- can totally destroy your parents' confidence about the direction they are heading, unless they have an appropriate way of dealing with potential change.

At least once a year, your parents should review (with your help and/ or that of the conversation facilitator) any material changes that have occurred in their lives during that time that might cause them to rethink any plans or decisions they have made regarding their future care. For example, as a result of the house conversation, your parents may have decided they intend to stay in their home as long as possible, but suddenly your dad's ability to move about the house has been significantly affected due to a stroke or the onset of a chronic illness. In light of this dramatic change, it may be time to revisit the house conversation and come up with a plan B.

Typically, over the course of a year the most fluctuating changes in a person's circumstances or situation, including the elderly, occur in the financial realm. Because the money conversation is the most involved of the six parent care conversations, I have created a separate review structure for parents to use in addressing any changes that have occurred in their financial situation and to rethink decisions they've made in that area so they can react quickly and effectively to them. A more general structure follows for use as a template in reviewing the five other areas of the parent care conversations, from housing and professional care decisions to property issues. Both review structures follow a similar, easy-to-use Q&A format.

The goal of an annual parent care conversation review is to get parents to:

- Examine their original thinking on the major strategic areas they need to focus on
- Reflect on changes that have occurred (or may occur) within those strategic areas
- Incorporate any changes in their own thinking or situation that have made, or would make, them reconsider aspects of their original plan

My Future Care Decisions -- Money Conversation Review

Your parents should respond precisely to each question within each category and take action with their advisor in updating plan documents and details accordingly.

1. **Cash Flow Planning**
   a. What amount of cash is in reserve and readily accessible for income or emergency needs?
   b. Has there been an increase in cash flow needs over the past year? How much and under what circumstances?
   c. What are the major outlays that may occur in the next twelve months that weren't part of my original plan?
   d. What am I earning on my cash reserves? Are there other places to invest?

2. **Income Tax Planning**
   a. Are my estimated taxes current with last year's?
   b. Should I increase or decrease my estimated tax payments or withholdings?

c. Can any taxable distributions be offset with care expenses?

d. Are there any possible medical equipment deductions that can be taken?

3. Insurance Planning

a. Are all my life, health, disability, major medical, and long-term care coverage up-to-date, at maximum affordable levels, and competitively priced?

b. Is there coverage I should increase, decrease, or let lapse?

c. Have all my deductibles been met for the year?

4. Investment Planning

a. If now taking distributions, what is the ratio of my withdrawals to earnings, and am I starting to draw down on principal?

b. Am I balancing my taxable versus nontaxable investments?

c. What is my return relative to my goals and objectives?

d. Is my portfolio balanced and operating efficiently for my goals and objectives?

5. Retirement Planning

a. If retired, how do my income and expenses relate to each other?

b. If considering retirement, how will my portfolio make or prohibit that opportunity?

c. Am I doing more of the things in retirement that I want to and less of what I don't want to?

6. Estate Planning

a. Are all my documents signed and capable of doing what I want them to?

b. What changes do I need to make because of new laws?

c. What changes do I want to make regardless of the laws?

My Future Care Decisions -- General Review

Parents should use this template for reviewing each of the other five areas of the parent care conversations (big picture, property, house, professional care, and legacy) annually in light of any changes that may have occurred in those areas during the course of a year:

1. What are the changes that have occurred in this area since we did our original thinking and planning?
2. What changes do we want to make regardless of any changes that may or may not have occurred?
3. What new challenges have arisen in this particular area that we must now face? What challenges do we no longer have to face?
4. What new alternatives or options have presented themselves in dealing with these challenges? What alternatives or options previously available to us no longer are?
5. What new resources are available to us for maximizing our options in this area? What resources are no longer available to us in our current situation?
6. What about the experience we would like to have in this area would we now prefer to be different? What about the experience we would like to have in this area might now have to change?

Rebound Quickly, Strategically, and with Focus

In some of its components, a parent care plan is a lot like an emergency kit. You buy it hoping that when the time comes to use it, it will be for a cut or a scrape and not major surgery. Mostly, though, there will not be much to do except implement the decisions called for by the plan when the moment comes. As with a good emergency kit, the fundamentals are all there. This will make it easier to rebound in those situations where, for example, a sudden change in your parents' health dictates a fast response.

Once your parents move from their home to a professional care facility, such as a retirement community or assisted-living complex, the reality is that their health is what motivated the move, so additional changes in their health will become more and more, a situation that you will have to react to quickly. With certain diseases of the elderly, such as Parkinson's or Alzheimer's, there are peaks and valleys and plateaus as the diseases run their course. There will be periods of time when it seems that you are responding to changes on almost a weekly, even a daily basis, and other periods when it seems like nothing noticeable changes at all.

More often than not, the changes that occur will require consultation with health care professionals attending to your parents' care. During my father's time in assisted living, for example, it seemed to me that I was constantly dealing with decisions about medicine changes, doctor visits, treatment regimens, or physical therapy and exercise. Each decision required a new level of attention and focus. The documents you and your parents will have put in place, such as the general and health care powers of attorney, will make it far less difficult for you to acquire the information you need to reach that new level of attention and focus, so you can respond knowledgably, strategically, and swiftly.

Anticipate and Adapt

There is an axiom of war that all battle plans change once the first shot is fired. While a parent care plan is light years beyond the alternative of digging one's head in the sand and just reacting to events as they occur, even the most carefully designed parent care plan cannot address *everything* that is likely to happen as your parents enter the twilight period of their lives. There will be times when the impact of external forces will make you feel as though you are winging it. Adaptability is key here. These are some of the external forces you can safely assume will throw a monkey wrench into any well-designed plan, so that you can anticipate and adapt quickly to them:

- **Governmental regulations.** Unless you've just arrived on the planet, you have to be aware of the massive tremors that are starting to shake the structures of Medicare and Medicaid, not to mention Social Security. The truth about these programs is that while they are well-intentioned, with a noble purpose, they have grown into huge entitlement programs that consume increasingly larger and larger portions of the federal budget. Even if certain pressures on those programs were not there, what you have is a sort of national health insurance program that has been funded by the contributions of those still working. The problem as our population ages is that we will have more people demanding services from those programs than we have people working to fund them. This won't happen all at once, but over the next twenty years look for some major changes in the way money and care will be meted out by these two systems.

This goes for Social Security as well. Social Security began as a safety net program designed to keep our citizens from falling into abject poverty as they got older by giving them a minimal level of subsistence to live on in their retirement years. But it has now become a default retirement plan for millions of Americans. While it is unlikely that Social Security will ever be dissolved completely, it is very likely that the current structure of the program will not be the same for you (depending upon your age) and definitely not for your children as it was for the World War II generation. Whether by indexing, or age-based selection, Social Security as we know it will not sustain future generations nor will the belief that it can fiscally survive, certainly in its present form, much beyond the last wave of retiring baby boomers. I tell my parent care clients this: the government is getting out of the retirement business, and that means you should be getting into it by taking responsibility right now, wherever you are, whatever your age and state of health, for the sound fiscal prognosis of your future care and well-being.

- **Rising health care costs.** Dan Taylor wrote this in the first edition: The American Medical Association and the National Trial Lawyers Association each blames the other for rising health care costs. Doctors blame trial lawyers for multimillion-dollar medical negligence verdicts. Trial lawyers blame doctors for sloppy medical practices that allegedly injure, kill, and mutilate thousands of people annually. And all the while, hospitals blame both sides, and the drug companies, for increased operating costs. Well, guess what? They're all correct, at least partially. To some degree they are all responsible for rising costs. Health care *is* expensive to administer and deliver in our society, with or without negligence and lawsuits. It's expensive because we have come to expect, almost as our right, access to the highest quality medical care, delivered to us on a just-in-time basis by the most highly skilled practitioners available in state-of-the-art medical care facilities. What about that suggests even the prospect of a discount or decrease in health care costs coming soon? Rising health care costs are one of the most predictable of all changes that will impact any parent care plan. It is estimated that roughly 20 percent of the health care costs in a person's life are incurred in the last three months of life. The average annual cost of a nursing home stay is in excess of $73,000 per year and rising at the rate of 8-12 percent per annum. To stay on top of this aspect of the care plan you and your parents have designed, increased health care costs as your parents' age must be expected and planned for *now*, with the assets and resources you have available *now*. This is why the money conversation (see chapter 4) is so important and why an annual review of the financial decisions that come out of that conversation is so critical.

Dan could not have possibly understood the impact and the potential of how much more expensive it would get. At the time of this revised edition, ObamaCare was being debated and fought over in congress. Many projections on this plan only confirm what Dan suspected. Health care costs are going up in the future. As he said… "If you think healthcare is expensive now…wait until it is free."

- **Low or unpredictable portfolio returns.** What the 1990s gave us in superior investment performance, the first years of the twenty-first century have all but taken away the economic recession of 2007 to 2009 took away. If you had a buy and hold strategy in the equity markets over the past 15 years, you have not made many net gains. For most of our parents' working lives, and our own, investors have been projecting the average growth rate in equities as between 6 percent and 8 percent on the conservative side, 8-12 percent on the moderately conservative side, and 12-15 percent on the aggressive side. Based on these assumptions, the thinking has been that we could safely withdraw 5 percent from the value of our portfolios to live on if the principal at least remained stable (it surely wouldn't drop.) Not true. In fact, one of the changes you will have to anticipate in today's market environment is an average 3-5 percent growth rate, conservatively speaking, with a 2-3 percent withdrawal rate. Those percentages are a far cry from the projections most financial advisors in the early to late 1990s said were possible. Our suggestion to today's children of aging parents: do not assume an overly aggressive rate of return from your parents' portfolios to make up for rising medical costs.

That funding will have to come from elsewhere -- insurance, perhaps, or from your own pocket.

· **Little or no inherited assets.** The real danger is not that it may cost you your inheritance to pay for your parents' future care, but that it may cost you your retirement and/or your children's inheritance as well, because your parents ran out of assets. Some years ago, there were numerous studies showing that nearly $11 trillion will be passed down by the World War II generation to their offspring, the baby boomers. It was supposed to be the largest transfer of wealth in our country's history. Well, I've got news: it's not coming. Here's why. When those studies were done, the fact that the boomers' parents are living longer than anyone imagined was not taken into account. As they live longer and incur more expensive illnesses to treat, the World War II generation is annuitizing the inheritance it had intended to pass to its offspring and grandkids. Thus, if you are a boomer or younger, you will be looking to manage the stress that comes from trying to accomplish three equally demanding fiscal tasks: (1) supplementing your parents' care costs, (2) sending your own children through college, and (3) attempting to save for your own retirement and future care needs. Be prepared.

· **Care facility housing shortage.** At this writing in October 2013, there are approximately 17,000 nursing homes in America where 1.8 million of our seniors live. That's the good news. The bad news is that we need *one million* new beds a year, and as a country we haven't even begun to plan for how those units will be financed and constructed. Thus, as noted in the professional care conversation (see chapter 7), our parents (but even more so ourselves and our children) will be more and more compelled to consider (or reconsider) the financial and other aspects of alternative combinations of care, such as at-home medical care, at-home nonmedical care, at-home physical, respiratory, and even occupational therapy. And those are just the housing needs for end-of-life issues, not the transitional type of housing most seniors, especially of the baby boom generation, will initially need. The key to dealing with this is to anticipate it, not only by reviewing and updating your parents' care plan accordingly, but your own future care plan as well.

· **The impact of the microchip.** Computerization will continue to have a huge impact on dozens of fields associated with the parent care issue, from medicine, security, and communications to financial management. In the coming years, expect technology to play a much greater role than it does even now in how health care is both delivered and monitored in this country. Already, there are technologies that allow you to monitor your parents' care from your laptop with video and audio. Health-monitoring devices are available that transmit real-time health data across wireless networks from implanted devices or flashcards that hold a lifetime of medical records. There are already security companies using the power of the Internet and fiber-optic cable to allow parents to live independently longer, with heightened levels of protection and monitoring so that the slightest variation in a parent's normal pattern of behavior triggers a support team to go into action. As such developments become more widespread and commonplace, they will play an increasingly vital role in the design, updating, and rapid-response capability of any parent care plan.

Keep in Mind!

The purpose of creating a parent care plan is to lower anxiety and increase confidence about the future for your aging parents and yourself. The continual review and updating of any plan is essential to sustaining that confidence in the future and not falling into crisis mode. Reduction in public levels of care support, more responsibility being placed on children to care for their parents, and increased reliance on technology all require that your parent care plan be updated to take into account the effects of these trends and your parents' naturally evolving circumstances on the original plan. Updating a parent care plan after its original design should be viewed much like seeing your doctor on an even more regular basis after you hit age fifty. It just makes sense.

What does a Completed Parent Care Plan Look Like?

Once you have met with your financial advisor or Parent Care Specialist and completed your Parent Care Plan you will have in hand the following:

1. You will have read this book and had or thought through the Parent Care Conversations.

2. You will have a clear understanding and strategy of how the final days of your life will be lived out.

3. You will know who among your family and friends will be of great assistance on your parent care journey.

4. You will have a notebook with all the details of your financial life and plan:

    ○ Assets and Liability
    ○ Income and Budget
    ○ Income and Budget plan for surviving spouse
    ○ Updated Will, living will, durable power of attorney, trust
    ○ Update Beneficiary forms
    ○ Funeral Planning and Checklist funeral paid for.
    ○ You will have the right amount and kinds of insurance.
    ○ Title review of your assets
    ○ Check-list with your surviving spouse on steps to take and who to contact.

5. Your family will be informed of your wishes as you move into the chapter of parent care.

6. Your family will have a trusted advisor and advocate and team to help them when the time comes.

7. You will have a clear picture of what the future will cost and how your resources will be used to meet those needs.

8. You will have the peace of mind that you did the right thing in developing a well thought out parent care plan.

An Act of Will

Caregiving is a duty, an honor, a burden, and frequently exhausting and irritating. It is, to borrow a line from Charles Dickens, "the best of times and the worst of times." It provides feelings of limitless joy and bottomless despair. It is walking to the car thinking how well your mom or dad looked one day, and walking away in tears on another, wishing, "If only this could end."

Caregiving is not for the fainthearted. It is not for the weak-minded. It is not for quitters -- definitely not for quitters. Once you have agreed to do it, you must keep doing it no matter what. You must do it when your parent is aware of your presence and knows who you are, and you must do it when your parent hasn't a clue who you are and isn't even aware you are there.

You must do it when the weather is in your favor: bright sun, clear sky, and a soft breeze. And you must do it when the elements are snow, sleet, and freezing rain. You must do it when that voice in your head keeps saying it's OK to skip today because you would rather be doing something else -- *anything else.* But you must persevere because, while many may start the caregiving project with you -- brothers, sisters, friends -- only a few will finish with you. So, caregiving is often not just about doing *your* job but the jobs of others as well. And you must do it when you feel appreciation for your efforts from all concerned, and when you feel totally taken for granted. At the beginning and at the end, caregiving may be an act of love, but in the long middle, it is purely an act of will.

Caregiving is an act of generosity, and it is in that act of generosity that the dangers lurk, for in addition to money, generosity can deplete your stores of energy, love, dedication, and time. And when these resources dwindle, what will rush in to replace them are often resentment, bitterness, anger, and exhaustion. What I hope you will understand from this admonition is that I have been there. I have been and remain a fully participating member of the caregiving cast. That's why I created the parent care conversation strategy, to help transform the caregiving experience from that of an almost totally nightmarish situation if left to the last minute to a more positive experience -- or at least as positive as possible -- if addressed early on and strategically.

When I began conceiving this book, my father was entering his fourth year in the special care ward of Brighton Gardens, in Charlotte, North Carolina. I remember him as not being able to button his shirt, wash his hair, or remember whether he had lunch or not. I would watch him struggle to line up his words with his thoughts so his sentences flowed from his mouth with the logic and in the order he wanted them to (but they seldom did). Watching this took its toll on me, though that toll was nothing compared to what he was going through. No matter how well designed a parent care plan may be, it cannot prepare you for, or prevent you from experiencing, things like that. It is a road map for care planning and caregiving, but not, unfortunately, an antidote for cancer, arthritis, Lou Gehrig's, Parkinson's, or Alzheimer's disease. It cannot place on hold the inevitabilities of getting older.

But what I can do is this. As I watched my father surrender to the disease that finally killed him, I was suddenly struck, not by how far he'd gone down but by how far I'd come up. The parent care experience had been thrust up upon me; it had moved me from being an audience member in that drama called "My Aging Dad" to a supporting role on stage. The effect on my perspective was transformational. Among other things, I had gone from having no time for conversation with my dad about his future care and my role in that care to having loads of time for conversations with him, in which he could no longer participate due to Alzheimer's. My wish for you and your parents is that the parent care conversations will open the door to the same transforming experience, but one that will enable you and your aging parents to say the things to each other and do the things for each other that you've always put off. To do them *now* -- and not wait for the memorial service, when it's too late.

Dan Taylor's Acknowledgments

Acknowledgments in books like this are much like acceptance speeches at the Academy Awards: unless you were in the movie they are more often than not meaningless.

Nothing could be further from the truth in this particular "movie." In fact, none of this book could have been written without input, inspiration, and enthusiasm from the following:

Dan Sullivan and Babs Smith, partners and founders of The Strategic Coach Program, a lifetime focusing program for entrepreneurs, that not only focused my life, but transformed it.

John McCarty, my writing collaborator whose proposal crafting expertise made Joy's work easier and my relationship with Penguin possible and whose structure allowed me to write effortlessly.

Lee Pennington and Mark Bass of Lubbock, Texas -- World-Class Financial Planners, World-Class Human Beings, and friends of mine when at times all my friends were them.

Marilyn, Julia, and Shannon Waller, who continue to provide an incredible example of family and who believe in me like a family should.

The dogs: Kate, Roxanne, and Zack, whose morning walks keep me sane and whose company daily reminds me that loyalty, love, and caring are not just limited to humans.

Finally, Christine Sheffield and her daughter Ashley who have been my family for many years now and who invested unselfishly nearly five years of Saturdays, Sundays, and midweek days to make sure I could care for my father in the way that I was able to.

Chris Sheffield's Acknowledgments

First of all, I want to thank the many friends and family members who loved me and helped me live through the worst experience of my life, losing Dan. I don't know what I would have done without you and am grateful and blessed that you are in my life.

I want to thank my mother who was the connecting link in our family who always laughed and made every occasion a very special day.

To my father, who taught me how to love someone more than life itself, how to be loyal through the worst of circumstances and how to take a vow and keep it to the very end.

I want to thank my daughter Ashley who taught me responsibility, unconditional love and who stayed by my side and kept me sane throughout my pain and healing.

I want to thank Suzanne and Ed Ghaleb who not only helped heal my physical self but also helped heal my heart and soul.

I want to thank the entire Slack Family for opening their arms and inviting me into their home at a time when mine was falling apart.

Lastly, I want to thank Dan for teaching me courage, perseverance and strength and for blessing me with this legacy of love.

Kevin Skipper's Acknowledgments

Vladimir Lenin said: "Destroy the family, you destroy the country." In America we have seen the erosion of some of the core values that I grew up being taught. I was taught by my pastor, my Sunday school teacher and several role models that:

1. It is one man married to one woman for life.
2. Children are to respect their elders and value the contribution they have made to life and society.
3. When our parents need our help, we are to do everything in our power to help them. That is how we honor our father and mother.

Writing a book like this does not come from the time it took to write. It comes from the values of family, commitment and loyalty that were taught to me by those who have impacted my core beliefs.

I acknowledge those who have impacted my life:

My wife, Audrey, of 36 years, who shares the view of marriage as forever and that family and our children are so important. She is such an awesome wife, mother, friend, and business partner. And, at the time of this writing, she is faithful in her task of parent care.

I am grateful to the church leaders in my young life that gave me so much love and encouragement:

My pastor Randall Jones
Sunday School Teacher: William Drew
RA Leaders: Hollis Squires
Youth Pastor: Ray Holland/Dennis Williams
I am grateful to my financial mentors who helped me along the way:
These include:
Freeman Todd
Steve Worthy
Dan Sullivan

I am grateful to my Parent Care Mentor: Dan Taylor. Dan was my coach in the Strategic Coach program. We immediately bonded. We shared ideas, and then the other new ideas. It was like energy feeding energy. We began the radio show, The Parent Care Show, and started several book projects. Dan had the biggest heart to love people, pets, and life. Then suddenly that day when he told me, "I have a brain tumor...and may not make it..." He fought the good fight and he didn't make it. As I write these words, I miss my friend and mentor Dan Taylor. I hope that we can continue his contribution to the world through this book. I am grateful I had the opportunity to know Dan.

35572205R00222

Made in the USA
Middletown, DE
07 October 2016